Chekhov Bibliography

Chekhov Bibliography

Works in English by and about Anton Chekhov; American, British and Canadian Performances

by

Charles W. Meister

McFarland & Company, Inc., Publishers
Jefferson, North Carolina, and London

Library of Congress Cataloging in Publication Data

Meister, Charles W., 1917–
Chekhov bibliography.

Includes index.
1. Chekhov, Anton Pavlovich, 1860–1904 – Bibliography.
2. Chekhov, Anton Pavlovich, 1860–1904 – Stage history – United States. 3. Chekhov, Anton Pavlovich, 1860–1904 – Stage history – Great Britain. 4. Chekhov, Anton Pavlovich, 1860–1904 – Stage history – Canada. I. Title.
Z8165.4.M4 1985 [PG3458] 016.8917'23 84-43221

ISBN 0-89950-154-0 (alk. paper)

Printed in the United States of America

McFarland & Company, Inc., Publishers
Box 611, Jefferson, North Carolina 28640

Table of Contents

The Importance of Chekhov Today

Ronald Hingley, translator of *The Oxford Chekhov*, felt that there had been too much adulation of Anton Chekhov as a saintly person. He thus rewrote an early biography, *Chekhov: A Biographical and Critical Study*, and it appeared as *A New Life of Anton Chekhov* in 1976. Hingley's goal was to reveal Chekhov's human failings and imperfections, as well as his better qualities.

Hingley found that his subject was indeed human. Chekhov, it was determined, often tolerated repression and czarist autocracy. He was less than candid in speaking on behalf of civil rights. He sometimes visited brothels, and he had a somewhat condescending attitude towards women. His writing, particularly in his plays, was occasionally less direct than it should have been.

What remained after these subtractions, however, was a great deal. Chekhov, Hingley found, was "gentle, sensitive, kind, helpful, truly charitable and philanthropic, free of affectation and remarkably tough-minded behind his courteous manner" (p. 318). Hingley concurred with many in finding him to be "a supreme master of the short story who also happened to be a great dramatist." Chekhov's influence upon the drama and short fiction in this century has been truly profound.

Few persons have a greater relevance for today's world than does this mild-mannered Russian doctor and writer. No practitioner of the art of the short story would dare to be ignorant of Chekhov's technique. Playwrights from Bernard Shaw to Tennessee Williams, and from the Absurdists to Sam Shepard, unite in praising the plays that at first sounded plotless and boring.

Chekhov provides a cultural bridge between Russia and America. Early Soviet distaste for his works has given way to deep understanding and appreciation. American readers, theatergoers, and critics have likewise matured in finally discerning that the pattern hid deep in Chekhov's exquisite carpet is a persistent plea for mankind's fundamental dignity and humanity.

Both cultures now applaud the advice that Chekhov gave to his brother Nikolai, an artist: Educated people respect others' personalities. They do not offend their loving parents. They are honest, and do not steal. They nurture their talents, and are not puffed up with a sense of their own importance. They cultivate good taste. They honor women, and seek to ennoble the sexual instinct. Above all, they work hard to ensure the coming of a better day for all humanity.

It is hoped that this bibliography will enable many new readers to become familiar with one of the great writers and humanitarians of modern times, and perhaps assist experienced readers in locating material that will give fresh insight and greater depth to the reading and enjoyment of Chekhov's writings.

Preface

This bibliography is limited to English-language works by and about Anton Chekhov. Works in Russian or other languages are not listed unless they are discussed or reviewed in English-language works.

There is no geographical limitation upon the inclusion of the material. Thus, works from the British Commonwealth, the Soviet Union, or the Orient are included if written in English. In several cases English-language articles are used even when the remainder of the periodical or book is in some other language. Translation into English of foreign-language articles and books merits inclusion here.

The chief newspapers consulted for this work were the *New York Times* and the *Times* (London). Many other newspapers are cited. Little use, however, has been made of pamphlets, and there is virtually no citation from reference books such as encyclopedias.

Most of the dissertations listed are doctoral dissertations from American universities. In addition, there is some mention of bachelor's and master's theses, and of British doctoral dissertations.

Some cassettes, films, and recordings are mentioned, to give an idea of the kinds of multi-media material that are available. Interested readers should consult film catalogs and video and audio cassette listings for further entries. Most of the multi-media materials cited here are available from American companies.

Part I lists the Chekhov writings that have appeared in English. Frequently content summaries and reviews are given. The name of the translator is provided whenever possible.

Part II has the English-language writings about Chekhov and his works. Additional bibliographies can be found in the doctoral dissertations. A distinction is made between books primarily about Chekhov and those containing merely passing reference to him or his works. Plays made from Chekhov tales are listed here, and if they have been produced they also appear in Part III.

Part III lists primarily the New York and London stage productions of Chekhov's works, with reviews. Representative performances of his works by American, British, and Canadian regional theaters are also given. Mention is made of some of the films and radio and television programs of his works in the United Kingdom and the United States.

Part IV is devoted to productions of works about Chekhov. Most of this material is biographical or critical.

The index lists two things: Chekhov's works, and the names of persons who do not appear in the alphabetical listings in the book. The names of play reviewers are not indexed, since in most cases they have been omitted in the interest of brevity.

A word about the transliteration of the name from the Russian as "Chekhov". The trouble spots in transliterating Chekhov's name come in three places, all involving consonants. The initial "ch" sound is that used in "church", but Constance Garnett and other translators prefixed a "t" to it to prevent confusion with its French counterpart, the "ch" in "machine". The middle consonant group, now usually shown as "kh", is the sound heard in the Scottish or German "ch", a voiceless fricative not used in English. The final consonant, though unvoiced, is more conveniently represented as "v" than "f", since it renders the Russian "B". Thus, "Chekhov" has been the predominant spelling, and is the one used in this book, except when reproducing original spellings.

Persons consulting bibliographies, card catalogs, or indexes should not be surprised, however, to find such entries as Chehoff, Tchehoff, Tchekov, and even Tscheschow.

This book began as the bibliography for a doctoral dissertation at the University of Chicago in 1948. For nearly forty years my "other vocation" has been to collect information on Chekhov. My constant helper and colleague has been my wife Eleanor, to whom I cannot adequately acknowledge my appreciation for her assistance and support.

Compiling a bibliography builds one's humility. Great gaps occur constantly, causing one to race continually from gap to gap, fearful of being flooded by rivers of neglected data. Even in this age of electronic information gathering, there are great gems (such as George Calderon's introduction to his *Two Plays by Tchekof* in 1912) which can all too easily be overlooked. Hopefully Dr. Chekhov would gaze benignly through his pince-nez glasses at this effort on his behalf, and smile courteously.

How to Use This Bibliography

The Table of Contents indicates where the reader can find general entries on plays, short stories, and other writings by Chekhov, as well as periodical articles and books dealing with his life and works.

The Index will help the reader locate material on specific plays and short stories. Numbers in the Index refer to entry numbers, not page numbers. Entries are numbered consecutively from 1 to 2505.

Periodical articles and books are listed alphabetically by author's name. A brief summary is provided of most periodical articles, especially for those that are untitled. Books on Chekhov generally have brief synopses. Books containing lesser material on Chekhov normally have brief summaries of the Chekhov references.

Abbreviations are essential in a bibliography, lest the work be unduly long. Let us translate a hypothetical entry:

429 McLeod, James W., tr. "Volodya," Virginia Q R 27 (17 Mar 1943) 13-4.

429 = entry number

Note on alphabetization: all Mc's and Mac's are listed under Mac

tr. = translator (of Chekhov's story "Volodya")

Q = Quarterly R = Review (J = Journal)

volume 27; March 17, 1943; pages 13-14

Other abbreviations frequently used are:

n.d. = no date of publication
no. = number (of a periodical); sometimes replaces the volume number
n.s. = new series (of a periodical)
O.B. = Off Broadway
O.O.B. = Off Off Broadway
Pr = Press
Univ = University
# = entry number
------. = same author (or if no author is given, the same work) as the previous entry

Translation of a play production with reviews:

The Three Sisters

14 Oct 1939 (9) Surry Theatre Players
Longacre Theatre Samuel Rosen, Dir.
Bernard G. Guerney, Tr.

Commonweal 31 (27 Oct) 14; New Republic 100 (1 Nov) 368-9; N.Y.Times, 16 Oct, p. 23; Theatre Arts 23 (Dec) 851-64; Variety 136 (18 Oct) 50.

Chekhov's play The Three Sisters opened on October 14, 1939, and ran for 9 performances. The Surry Theatre Players, directed by Samuel Rosen, staged the play at the Longacre Theatre in New York City.

Unless the city is cited, it can be assumed that American productions refer to New York City and British productions to London.

The year of the review is given only when it is not the same as the year of the production.

Part I

Works by Anton Chekhov in English

Collections: Plays and Stories Together

1 Anton Chekhov: Works. N.Y.: Black, 1929. 49 stories plus plays: The Anniversary, The Bear, The Cherry Orchard, The Forced Tragedian, The High Road, The Proposal, The Sea Gull, The Three Sisters, The Wedding.

2 The Best Known Works of Anton Chekhov.Reprint of #1. N.Y.: Blue Ribbon Books, 1936.

3 The Best Known Works of Anton Chekhov.Reprint of #1. Freeport, N.Y.: Books for Libraries Pr, 1972.

4 The Oxford Chekhov. Ronald Hingley, ed. & tr. London: Oxford Univ Pr, 1964-80. 9 vols. Vols 1-3, Plays. Vols 4-9, Short Stories. The Russian title and date of publication for each work are given on each title page. An appendix describes each work's composition; for plays, the early stage history is also given. For entries on individual volumes, see below under "Play Collections" and "Story Collections". Review:
Times Literary Supplement, 23 Jan 1981, pp. 93-4.

5 Plays and Stories: Anton Tchekhov. S.S. Koteliansky, ed. & tr. London: Dent, 1937. Chekhov's autobiography, chronological table, 14 stories, and plays: The Cherry Orchard, On the Harmfulness of Tobacco, The Sea Gull, Tatyana Riepin, The Wood Demon.

6 ------. Reprint of #5. N.Y.: Dutton, 1938.

7 The Portable Chekhov. Avrahm Yarmolinsky, ed. & tr. N.Y.: Viking, 1947. 16 letters, 28 stories, and plays:The Boor, The Cherry Orchard. Bibliog. Chronology. Reviews: Booklist 44 (15 Nov 1947) 111; Kirkus R 15 (1 Sep 1947) 478; Library J 72 (15 Nov 1947) 1610; Nation (N.Y.) 166 (22 May 1948) 581-3; New Republic 117 (15 Dec 1947) 28; New York Herald-Trib Book R, 16 Nov 1947, p. 36; New Yorker 23 (25 Oct 1947) 135; Saturday R of Lit 30 (13 Dec 1947) 25.

8 ------. Reprint of #7. N.Y.: Penguin, 1977.

9 Selected Works in Two Volumes. Moscow:Progress Publishers, 1973. Vol I - Stories; Ivy Litvinov, tr. Vol II - Plays; Kathleen Cook, tr. Vol II has intro by Konstantin Stanislavsky, afterword by G. Tovstonogov, and plays: The Anniversary, The Bear, The Cherry Orchard, The Sea Gull, The Three Sisters.

10 Tchekhov: Literary and Theatrical Reminiscences. S.S. Koteliansky, ed. & tr. London: Routlèdge, 1927. Biographical material, 6 stories, and plays: On the Harmfulness of Tobacco, Tatyana Riepin. See #1403 for full entry.

Journey to Sakhalin

11 The Island: A Journey to Sakhalin. Robert Payne, ed. Luba Terpak & Michael Terpak, trs. N.Y.: Washington Square Pr, 1967. Reviews:
Book World, 26 May 1968, p.6; Choice 5 (Dec 1968) 1314; Delos 3 (1969) 192-7; Harpers 236 (Jan 1968) 69; S. E. Hyman, The Critic's Credentials (N.Y.: Atheneum, 1978), pp. 235-40; Library J 92 (1 Apr 1967) 1491; New Republic 157 (21 Oct 1967) 26; N.Y.Times Book R, 5 Nov 1967, pp. 2,50,52; New Yorker 43 (10 Feb 1968) 113; Pacific Affairs 44 (Spring 1968) 146; Saturday R (N.Y.) 50 (7 Oct 1967) 35.
12 Reprint of #11. Westport, CT: Greenwood, 1977.

Letters

(Books -- listed alphabetically by editor or translator)

13 Cournos, John, ed. & tr. A Treasury of Russian Life and Humor. N.Y.: Coward-McCann, 1943. (7 letters, pp.79-83).
14 Friedland, Louis S., ed. & tr. Letters on the Short Story, the Drama and Other Literary Topics, by Anton Chekhov. N.Y.:Minton Balch, 1924. Letters are grouped according to Chekhov's comments on his own works, the works of other Russian writers, and selected literary topics. Reviews:
Bookman (N.Y.) 60 (Dec 1924) 506; Boston Transcript, 8 Nov 1924, p. 4; Nation (N.Y.) 119 (10 Dec 1924) 652-4; N.Y.Times Book R, 2 Nov 1924, p. 2; N.Y.World, 19 Oct 1924, p. 8e; Saturday R of Lit 1 (4 Apr 1925) 646, 654.
15 Reprint of #14. London: Bles, 1924.
16 Reprint of #14. N.Y.: Blom, 1964. Preface by E.J.Simmons.
17 Reprint of #14. N.Y.: Dover, 1966.
18 Garnett, Constance, tr. Letters of Anton Tchehov to His Family and Friends. London: Chatto & Windus, 1920. This collection of 263 letters was the first in English. Biographical sketch. Notes. Reviews:
Athenaeum, 5 Mar 1920, p. 299; Bookman (London) 57 (Mar 1920) 206; London Mercury 2 (May 1920) 94-5; Nation (London) 26 (28 Feb 1920) 742-4; New Statesman 14 (21 Feb 1920) 586; Spectator 125 (31 Jul 1920) 150; Times Literary Supplement, 13 Feb 1920, p. 103a.

19 Reprint of #18. N.Y.: Macmillan, 1920. Reviews:
American R of Reviews 61 (May 1920) 559; Booklist 16 (May 1920) 279; Bookman (N.Y.) 51 (May 1920) 327; Bookman (N.Y.) 54 (Oct 1921) 155; Cleveland Open Shelf, Oct 1920, p. 84; Dial 68 (May 1920) 626; Forum 70 (Dec 1923) 2239-40; Freeman 1 (7 Apr 1920) 93-5; New Republic 22 (14 Apr 1920) 226; N.Y.Times Book R, 18 Apr 1920, p. 192; N.Y.Times Book R, 1 Aug 1920, p. 13; Pacific R 1 (Mar 1921) 605-7; Springfield Republican, 12 Jul 1920, p. 6.

20 Garnett, Constance, tr. Letters of Anton Pavlovitch Tchehov to Olga Leonardovna Knipper. London: Chatto & Windus, 1926. Reviews:
Adelphi 3 (Apr 1926) 777; London Mercury 14 (Sep 1926) 542; Nation & Athenaeum 38 (13 Mar 1926) 814; Saturday R (London) 141 (30 Jan 1926) 125; Spectator 136 (6 Mar 1926) 428; Times Literary Supplement,18 Mar 1926,p.206.

21 Reprint of #20. N.Y.: Doran, 1926. Reviews:
Booklist 22 (Mar 1926) 250; Bookman (N.Y.) 62 (Jan 1926) 608; Nation (N.Y.) 122 (Jun 1926) 614; N.Y.Evening Post Lit R, 30 Jan 1926, p. 4; N.Y.Times Book R, 17 Jan 1926, p.2; Saturday R of Lit 4 (24 Sep 1927) 133-4; Theatre Arts Monthly 10 (Apr 1926) 277; Yale R n.s. 16 (Oct 1926) 187-9.

22 New edition of #20 with index. N.Y.: Blom, 1966.

23 Gorky, Maxim. Reminiscences. N.Y.: Dover, 1946. (The Gorky-Chekhov correspondence, pp. 87-118).

24 Guerney, Bernard G., ed. & tr. The Portable Russian Reader. N.Y.: Viking, 1947. (2 letters, pp. 628-31).

25 Hellman, Lillian, ed. The Selected Letters of Anton Chekhov. Sidonie Lederer, tr. N.Y.: Farrar & Straus, 1955. Most of these 204 letters come from the 4200 letters in vols 8-13 of the Soviet edition of Chekhov's works published from 1944 to 1951. Hellman provides a general intro, as well as intros to the 3 chronological periods. Chekhov's main correspondents are identified. Index. Notes. Reviews:
American Slavic & East European R 14 (Dec 1955) 571-2; Booklist 51 (15 Jun 1955) 426; Commonweal 62 (24 Jun 1955) 310; Delos 3 (1969) 192-7; Kirkus R 23 (1 Feb 1955) 112; Manchester Guardian, 22 Jul 1955, p. 4; Nation (N.Y.) 181 (30 Jul 1955) 102; New Republic 133 (18 Jul 1955) 18; N.Y.Herald-Trib Book R, 1 May 1955, p. 2; N.Y.Times Book R, 24 Apr 1955, p. 4; San Francisco Chronicle, 21 Aug 1955, p. 18; Saturday R (N.Y.) 38 (9 July 1955) 33;Slavic & East European J 10 (Winter 1966) 477-8; Time 65 (9 May 1955) 114; Times (London), 14 Jul 1955, p. 11d; Times Literary Supplement, 2 Sep 1955, p. 506.

26 Karlinsky,Simon & Michael H. Heim, trs. Anton Chekhov's Life and Thought: Selected Letters and Commentary. Edited with an intro by Simon Karlinsky. Berkeley: Univ of Calif Pr, 1973. Notes. Reviews:
Canadian Slavonic Papers 19 (Sep 1977) 387-8; Choice 10 (Nov 1973) 1393; Christian Sci Monitor, 8 Aug 1973,p.9; Economist 248 (15 Sep 1973) 150; J of European Studies 8 (Sep 1978) 214-6; Library J 98 (15 Oct 1973) 3002; Modern Fiction Studies 23 (Summer 1978) 326-8; Nation (N.Y.) 217 (17 Sep 1973) 247-8; N.Y.R of Books 20 (28 Jun 1973) 3; N.Y.Times Book R, 21 Oct 1973, p. 7; New Yorker 49 (23 Jul 1973) 78; Newsweek 81 (25 Jun 1973) 87; Slavic & East European J 20 (Winter 1976) 477-8; Times Literary Supplement, 21 Sep 1973, p. 1086a.

27 ------. The Letters of Anton Chekhov. Revised paperback version of #26. Reviews:
Drama no. 111 (Winter 1973) 83; Modern Fiction Studies 20 (Winter 1974) 593-4; Slavic R 33 (Sep 1974) 607-9.

28 Koteliansky, S.S. & Philip Tomlinson, eds. & trs. The Life and Letters of Anton Tchekhov. London: Cassell, 1925. "Anton Tchekhov and His Subjects" & "Tchekhov and the Theatre" by Michael P. Tchekhov; "Tchekhov's Last Hours" by Olga Knipper-Tchekhova; "A Biographical Note" by A. Zamyatin; approx 300 letters by Chekhov; a bibliog. of Chekhov's works. Index. Reviews:
Bookman (London) 68 (Apr 1925) 36; London Mercury 12 (Jul 1925) 324; Nation & Athenaeum 36 (21 Feb 1925)717; Saturday R (London) 139 (14 Mar 1925) 274; Spectator 134 (14 Feb 1925) 241 & 134 (21 Mar 1925) 460; Times Literary Supplement, 12 Mar 1925, p. 169c.

29 Reprint of #28. N.Y.: Doran, 1925. Reviews:
Bookman (N.Y.) 62 (Jan 1926) 607; New Republic 44 (4 Nov 1925) 286; N.Y.Tribune, 15 Nov 1925, p. 3; Saturday R of Lit 4 (24 Sep 1927) 133; Theatre Arts Monthly 10 (Apr 1926) 277-8; Yale R n.s. 16 (Oct 1926) 187-9.

30 The Personal Papers of Anton Chekhov. (95 letters) See #58.

31 Yarmolinsky, Avrahm, ed. Letters of Anton Chekhov. Bernard G. Guerney, Lynn Solotaroff, & Avrahm Yarmolinsky, trs. N.Y.: Viking, 1973. 412 letters in chronological order from the Soviet edition of 1944-51. Foreword discusses Chekhov as a letter writer. Index. Reviews:
America 129 (27 Oct 1973) 310; Christian Sci Monitor, 8 Aug 1973, p. 10; Library J 98 (15 Oct 1973) 3002; Nation (N.Y.) 217 (17 Sep 1973) 247-8; N.Y.R. of Books 20 (28 Jun 1973) 3; N.Y.Times Book R, 21 Oct 1973, p. 7; New Yorker 49 (3 Sep 1973) 62-6; Newsweek 81 (25 Jun 1973) 87.

32 Reprint of #31. London: Cape, 1974. Reviews:

Economist 250 (9 Feb 1974) 98; New Statesman 87 (12 Apr 1974)520; Times Literary Supplement, 29 Mar 1974,p.346.
33 Yarmolinsky, Avrahm, ed. & tr. The Portable Chekhov. N.Y.: Viking, 1947. (16 letters, pp. 596-631).

(Magazine Articles--alphabetically by author or translator)

34 Bakshy, Alexander, tr. "Love Letters of Anton Chekhov," American Mercury 36 (Sep 1935) 1-9.
35 ------."New Letters by Anton Chekhov," Saturday R of Lit, 27 Jul 1940, pp. 11-3.
36 Binder, N. de, ed. "Thirty-two Letters of A. P. Chekhov," Oxford Slavonic Papers 9 (1960) 109-28.
37 Birkmyre, Robert. "New Letters of Anton Tchekov," Fortnightly R n.s. 105 (1 Mar 1919) 434-45 (review of Chekhov's letters in Russian).
38 "Chekhov in His Letters," Freeman 1 (7 Apr 1920) 93-5.
39 "Chekhov's Code," Golden Book 20 (Sep 1934) 325.
40 Cournos, John. Dial 85 (Sep 1928) 261-4 (review of Chekhov's letters in Russian).
41 Friedland, Louis S.,tr. "Tchehoff Letters about Plays and Players," Theatre Arts Monthly 8 (Feb 1924) 91-7.
42 ------. "A Tchehoff Scenario," Theatre Arts Monthly 8 (Apr 1924) 233-7.
43 Garnett, Constance, tr. "Three Letters to Olga Knipper," Bermondsey Book 2 (Mar 1925) 23-31.
44 Hamilton, Hamish. "Letters from Chekhov," Times Literary Supplement, 2 Sep 1955, p. 506.
45 Kornfeld, L.D. N.Y.Times Book R, 27 May 1928, p. 11 (review of Chekhov's letters in Russian).
46 Koteliansky, S.S., tr. "Letters of Tchehov to Gorky," Adelphi 1 (Nov 1923) 504-10.
47 ------. "Tchehov and His Wife," Adelphi 2 (1924) 224-35.
48 ------. "The Wood Demon: A Letter to A.S. Souvorin," Adelphi 1 (Jun 1923) 42-8.
49 ------. & Katherine Mansfield, trs. "A Letter of Anton Tchehov," Adelphi 2 (1924) 38-45.
50 ------. "Letters of Anton Tchehov," Athenaeum (1919): 4 Apr, pp.148-9; 18 Apr, pp.215-6; 25 Apr, p.249; 2 May, p. 282; 23 May, p. 378; 6 Jun, pp. 441-2; 27 Jun,p.538; 11 Jul, p. 602; 25 Jul, p. 667; 8 Aug, pp. 731-2; 5 Sep, p. 858; 24 Oct, pp. 1078-9.
51 Lederer, Sidonie, tr. Lillian Hellman, ed. "Chekhov's Letters about Writers and Writing," Partisan R 21 (Jul 1954) 371-86.
52 Littell, Robert. New Republic 42 (25 Mar 1925) 131 (reviews Chekhov's letters).
53 ------. New Republic 51 (22 Jun 1927) 124-5 (reviews Chekhov's letters).

54 Nazaroff, Alexander. N.Y.Times Book R, 18 Jan 1931, p. 2 (review of Chekhov's letters in Russian).
55 Weinstein, David, tr. "What Tchekov Thought of It," English R 8 (1911) 256-66.

Memoirs and Writings

56 "Chekhov's Aphorisms and Epigrams," Russian R 4 (1918) 108. David A. Modell, tr.
57 "Chekhov's Proverbial Wisdom," in Carolyn Wells, ed., The World's Best Humor (N.Y.: Boni, 1933) p. 639.
58 The Personal Papers of Anton Chekhov. Intro by Matthew Josephson. N.Y.: Lear, 1948. Chekhov's Diary (1896-1903) & Chekhov's Notebook (1892-1904), tr. by S.S.Koteliansky & Leonard Woolf; 95 Chekhov letters on the theatre and writing, tr.by Constance Garnett; a short story, "A Moscow Hamlet." Reviews:
Nation (N.Y.) 166 (19 Jun 1948) 697; N.Y.Herald-Tribune Book R, 25 Apr 1948, p. 21; N.Y.Times Book R, 30 May 1948, p. 13; New Yorker 24 (22 May 1948) 119; San Francisco Chronicle, 13 Jun 1948, p. 19; Time 51 (19 Apr 1948) 108.
59 "Tchehov's Diary," Athenaeum 152 (2 Apr 1920) 460-1. S.S. Koteliansky & Katherine Mansfield, trs.
60 "Tchekhov's Diary," Freeman 3 (6 Apr 1921) 79-80. S.S. Koteliansky & Leonard Woolf, trs.
61 Tchekhov's Diaries (1896-1903). London: Routledge, 1927. S.S. Koteliansky, tr.
62 "Tchekhov's Notebook," Freeman 3 (1921): 13 Apr, pp. 104-5; 20 Apr, pp. 127-8; 27 Apr, pp.152-3; 4 May, pp.175-6; 11 May, pp.199-200; 18 May, pp.225-6; 25 May, pp.247-8; 1 Jun, pp. 272-3; 8 Jun, pp. 296-7; 15 Jun, pp.320-1; 22 Jun, pp. 344-5; 29 Jun, pp. 368-9; 6 Jul, pp. 392-3; 13 Jul, pp. 415-6; 20 Jul, pp. 440-1. S. S. Koteliansky & Leonard Woolf, trs.
63 "Tchekhov's Notebook," London Mercury 3 (Jan 1921)285-95. S. S. Koteliansky & Leonard Woolf, trs.
64 Tchekhov's Notebook, together with Reminiscences of Tchekhov by Maxim Gorky. S. S. Koteliansky & Leonard Woolf, trs. Richmond: Hogarth Pr, 1921. Reviews:
Nation & Athenaeum 29 (4 Jun 1921) 365-6; New Statesman 17 (16 Apr 1921) 52; Times Literary Supplement, 22 Apr 1921, p. 257a.
65 Reprint of #64. N.Y.: Huebsch, 1921. Reviews:
Boston Transcript, 11 Jan 1922, p.4; Current Opinion 71 (Oct 1921) 505-7; Double Dealer 3 (Apr 1922) 224; Freeman 4 (1 Mar 1922) 592-4; Living Age 309 (4 Jun 1921) 608-9; Nation (N.Y.) 114 (5 Apr 1922) 400; New Republic 30 (1 Mar 1922) 23-4; N.Y.Times Book R, 1 Jan 1922,p.2.

66 Reprint of #64. Derby, PA: Folcroft Library, 1973.

Novel

67 The Shooting Party. A.E. Chamot, tr. London: Paul, 1926. Reviews: Nation & Athenaeum 40 (29 Jan 1927) 602; Spectator 137 (27 Nov 1926) 976; Times Literary Supplement, 16 Dec 1926, p. 932c.

68 Reprint of #67. Phila: McKay, 1927. Reviews: Booklist 23 (June 1927) 386; Living Age 332 (15 Feb 1927) 371.

Play Collections (alphabetical by translator)

69 Bechhofer, Carl E., tr. Five Russian Plays, with One from the Ukrainian. London: Paul, Trench & Trubner, 1916. The Jubilee; The Wedding. Review: Nation (London) 20 (11 Nov 1916) 232.

70 Bentley, Eric & Theodore Hoffman, trs. The Brute and Other Farces. N.Y.: Grove Pr, 1958. The Brute; The Celebration; The Harmfulness of Tobacco; Marriage Proposal; Summer in the Country; Swan Song; A Wedding.

71 Bristow,Eugene K.,ed. & tr. Anton Chekhov's Plays. N.Y.: Norton, 1977. Norton Critical Edition. The Cherry Orchard; Impure Tragedians and Leprous Playwrights; On the Injurious Effects Of Tobacco (1886 and 1902 versions); The Seagull; The Three Sisters; Uncle Vanya. Articles by Eric Bentley, Robert Brustein, Francis Fergusson, John Gassner, Ronald Hingley, David Magarshack, Siegfried Melchinger, Vsevolod Meyerhold, Nicholas Moravcevich, Vladimir Nabokov, Charles B. Timmer, Georgy Tovstonogov, and Thomas G. Winner. Bibliog. Notes. Review: Slavic and East European J 23 (Summer 1979) 275-6.

72 Calderon, George, tr. Two Plays by Tchekhof. London: Richards, 1912. The Cherry Orchard; The Sea Gull. Intro by Calderon was the first important criticism in English of Chekhov's plays, using such terms as atmosphere, centrifugal plot, and disconnected dialogue to account for Chekhov's effects. Reviews: Athenaeum 1 (24 Feb 1912) 234; Saturday R (London), 113 (13 Apr 1912) 453; Times Literary Supplement, 1 Feb 1912, p. 45a.

73 Reprint of #72. N.Y.: Kennerley, 1912. Reviews: Bellman 12 (11 May 1912) 595; Dial 52 (16 Jun 1912)470; Harper's Weekly 58 (27 Dec 1913) 22-23; Independent 73 (5 Dec 1912) 1318-19; Nation (N.Y.) 95 (18 Jul 1912)65; N.Y.Times Book R, 5 May 1912, p. 17; Yale R n.s.3 (Apr 1914) 600.

74 Reprint of #72. London: Cape, 1924. Reviews: London Mercury 12 (Sep 1925) 551; New Statesman 23 (14 Jun 1924) 289-90.

75 Reprint of #72. London: Duckworth, 1927. Review: Times Literary Supplement, 21 Jul 1927, p. 507b.
76 Chekhov: Plays. N.Y.: Doric Books, 1950. The Anniversary; The Cherry Orchard; On the High Road; The Sea Gull; The Three Sisters; The Wedding.
77 The Cherry Orchard and Other Plays. N.Y.: Grosset & Dunlap, 1936. The Anniversary; The Bear; The Cherry Orchard; The Sea Gull. Woodcuts by Howard Simon.
78 Corrigan, Robert W., tr. Six Plays of Chekhov. N.Y.: Holt Rinehart & Winston, 1962. Intro by Corrigan. Foreword by Harold Clurman. The Cherry Orchard; Ivanov;The Sea Gull; The Three Sisters; Uncle Vanya; The Wood Demon.
79 ------. Paperback of #78. N.Y.: Drama Books, 1979.
80 Dunnigan, Ann, tr. Chekhov: The Major Plays. N.Y.:Signet, 1964. Intro by Robert Brustein. The Cherry Orchard;Ivanov; The Sea Gull; The Three Sisters; Uncle Vanya. Reviews: Choice 1 (1964) 428; Slavic & East European J 10 (Winter 1966) 475-7.
81 Eisemann, Fred & Olive F. Murphy, trs. The Sea Gull and The Tragedian in Spite of Himself. Boston: International Pocket Library, 1965. The Sea Gull tr. by Eisemann; The Tragedian in Spite of Himself tr. by Murphy.
82 Fell, Marian, tr. Plays by Anton Tchekoff. N.Y.:Scribner, 1912. Ivanov; The Sea Gull; Swan Song; Uncle Vanya. Reviews: American R of Reviews 47 (May 1913) 632;Athenaeum 7 Dec 1912, p. 699; Chautauquan 71 (21 Jun 1913) 57-9; English R 13 (Feb 1913) 502; Harper's Weekly 58 (27 Dec 1913) 22-3; Independent 73 (5 Dec 1912) 1318-9; Nation (London) 12 (4 Jan 1913) 601-2; Nation (N.Y.) 95 (18 Jul 1912) 65 & 95 (21 Nov 1912) 492; N.Y.Times Book R, 6 Oct 1912, p. 17; Springfield Republican, 24 Oct 1912, p. 5; Yale R n.s. 3 (Apr 1914) 599-600.
83 ------, & Julius West, trs. Five Famous Plays by Anton Chekhov. London: Duckworth, 1939. The Bear, The Cherry Orchard, The Three Sisters tr. by West. The Sea Gull & Uncle Vanya tr. by Fell.
84 ------. Reprint of #83. N.Y.: Scribner, 1939.
85 ------. Six Famous Plays by Anton Chekhov. London: Duckworth,1949. Same as #83, plus The Proposal, tr. by West.
86 Fen, Elisaveta, tr. Anton Chekhov: The Sea Gull and Other Plays. London: Penguin, 1953. The Bear; A Jubilee; The Proposal; The Sea Gull; Uncle Vanya. Chekhov biography.
87 ------. Anton Chekhov: Three Plays. London: Penguin,1951. The Cherry Orchard; Ivanov; The Three Sisters.
88 ------. Eight Plays by Anton Chekhov. Franklin Center,PA: Franklin Library, 1976. Reprint of #89.
89 ------. Plays: Anton Chekhov. London: Penguin, 1959. Consists of #86 plus #87.
90 ------. Plays by Anton Chekhov. Franklin Center,PA:Franklin Library, 1979. The Cherry Orchard; Ivanov; The Sea Gull; The Three Sisters; Uncle Vanya.

91 Four Great Plays. N.Y.: Bantam, 1958. The Cherry Orchard; The Sea Gull; The Three Sisters; Uncle Vanya.

92 Garnett, Constance, tr. Chekhov Plays. London: Heron Books, 1969. The Cherry Orchard; Ivanov; The Sea Gull; The Three Sisters; Uncle Vanya. Intro & critical essay by Arnold B. McMillin. Illustrations by Mette Ivers.

93 ------. The Cherry Orchard and Other Plays. London:Chatto & Windus, 1923. The Bear; The Cherry Orchard; The Proposal; The Sea Gull; Uncle Vanya.

94 ------. Reprint of #93. N.Y.: Seltzer, 1924.

95 ------. The Cherry Orchard and The Three Sisters. Intro by John Gielgud. N.Y.: Limited Editions Club, 1966.

96 ------. Nine Plays of Chekhov. N.Y.: Grosset & Dunlap, 1946. Same plays as #98.

97 ------. The Plays of Anton Chekhov. N.Y.:Modern Library, 1929. Preface by Eva Le Gallienne. The Anniversary; The Cherry Orchard; On the High Road; The Sea Gull; Three Sisters; Uncle Vanya; The Wedding.

98 ------. The Plays of Anton Chekhov. N.Y.: Three Sirens Pr, 1935. Woodcuts by Howard Simon. Same plays as #97, plus The Bear and On the Harmfulness of Tobacco.

99 ------. The Plays of Anton Chekhov. Cleveland: World, 1942. Same plays as #98.

100 ------. The Plays of Anton Chekhov. N.Y.: Caxton House, 1946. Same plays as #98.

101 ------. The Plays of Anton Chekhov. N.Y.: Hartsdale House, 1947. Same plays as #98.

102 ------. The Plays of Anton Chekhov. N.Y.: Perma Giants, 1950. Same plays as #98.

103 ------. Three Sisters and Other Plays. London: Chatto & Windus, 1923. The Anniversary; Ivanov;On the High Road; Swan Song; Three Sisters; An Unwilling Martyr; The Wedding. Review: Times Literary Supplement, 6 Dec 1923, p. 841b.

104 Hingley, Ronald, ed. & tr. Chekhov: Five Major Plays. London: Oxford Univ Pr, 1977. The Cherry Orchard; Ivanov; The Sea Gull; Three Sisters; Uncle Vanya. Intro by Hingley shows Chekhov's development as a dramatist.

105 ------. Reprint of #104. N.Y.: Bantam, 1982.

106 ------. Ivanov; The Sea Gull; and Three Sisters. London: Oxford Univ Pr, 1968. Review: Times (London), 3 Feb 1968, p. 21h.

107 ------. Platonov; Ivanov; The Sea Gull. Vol II of The Oxford Chekhov. London: Oxford Univ Pr, 1967. See #4 for general entry.

108 ------. Short Plays. Vol I of The Oxford Chekhov. London: Oxford Univ Pr, 1968. The Anniversary; The Bear; Night before the Trial; On the High Road; The Proposal; Smoking Is Bad for You; Swan Song; Tatyana Riepin; A Tragic Role; The Wedding. See #4 for general entry. Review: Slavic & East European J 14 (Fall 1970) 379-81.

109 ------. Uncle Vanya and The Cherry Orchard. London: Oxford Univ Pr, 1965.

110 ------. Uncle Vanya; Three Sisters; The Cherry Orchard; The Wood Demon. Vol III of The Oxford Chekhov. London: Oxford Univ Pr, 1964. See #4 for general entry.

111 Koteliansky, S.S., tr. Three Plays. Harmondsworth: Penguin,1940. The Cherry Orchard; The Sea Gull; The Wood Demon.

112 Magarshack, David, tr. Anton Chekhov: Four Plays. London: Allen & Unwin, 1969. The Cherry Orchard; The Sea Gull; The Three Sisters; Uncle Vanya.

113 --------. Paperback reprint of #112. N.Y.: Hill & Wang, 1969.

114 Plays. N.Y.: Doric Books, 1950. The Anniversary; The Cherry Orchard; On the Road; The Sea Gull; The Three Sisters; The Wedding.

115 Senelick, Laurence, ed. & tr. The Cherry Orchard and The Sea Gull. Arlington Heights, IL: AHM Publishing Corp, 1977. Intro by Senelick. Bibliog. Chronology. Guide to pronunciation. Notes.

116 Szogyi, Alex, tr. Four Plays. N.Y.: Washington Square Pr, 1968. The Cherry Orchard; The Sea Gull; The Three Sisters; Uncle Vanya. Intro by Szogyi. Notes.

117 ------. Ten Early Plays. N.Y.: Bantam, 1965. The Anniversary; The Bear; Ivanov; On the Harmfulness of Tobacco; On the High Road; The Proposal; The Reluctant Tragedian: Life in the Country; Swan Song; The Wedding; The Wood Demon. Intro by Szogyi. Chronology of Chekhov's life and principal works.

118 West, Julius, tr. Four Short Plays by Anton Tchekoff. London: Duckworth, 1915. The Anniversary; The Bear; The Proposal; The Wedding.

119 ------. Plays by Anton Tchekoff: Second Series. London: Duckworth, 1916. The Anniversary; The Bear; The Cherry Orchard; On the High Road; The Proposal; The Three Sisters; A Tragedian in Spite of Himself; The Wedding. Reviews: Spectator 116 (19 Feb 1916) 264; Times Literary Supplement, 29 Jun 1916, p. 304.

120 ------. Reprint of #119. N.Y.: Scribner, 1916. Reviews: American R of Reviews 53 (Mar 1916) 377; Booklist 13 (Dec 1916) 114; Boston Transcript, 16 Feb 1916, p. 25; Dial 62 (8 Feb 1917) 100; Independent 86 (10 Apr 1916) 75; Nation (N.Y.) 102 (13 Apr 1916) 419; New Republic 7 (8 Jul 1916) 256; N.Y. Branch Library News 3 (Mar 1916) 43; Pratt, Apr 1916, p. 33.

121 ------, & Marian Fell, trs. See #83, #84, & #85.

122 Young, Stark, tr. Best Plays of Chekhov. N.Y.: Modern Library, 1956. The Cherry Orchard; The Sea Gull; The Three Sisters; Uncle Vanya. Intro by Young.

Individual Plays (alphabetical by translator)

The Anniversary (also known as The Celebration; The Jubilee)

123 The Anniversary. Cook, Kathleen, tr. See #9.
124 ------. Garnett, Constance, tr. See #97; #103.
125 ------. Hingley, Ronald, tr. See #108.
126 ------. Szogyi, Alex, tr. See #117.
127 ------. West, Julius, tr. See #118; #119.
128 ------. See also #1; #76; #77; #114.
129 The Celebration. Eric Bentley & Theodore Hoffman, trs. See #70.
130 The Jubilee. Bechhofer, Carl E., tr. In New Age n.s. 17 (30 Dec 1915) 207-10. See also #69.
131 ------. Fen, Elisaveta, tr. See #86.
132 ------. Murphy, Olive F., tr. In Poet Lore 31 (Winter 1920) 616-28.

The Bear (also known as The Boor; The Brute)

133 The Bear. Cook, Kathleen, tr. See #9.
134 ------. Egerton, Earle, tr. For Milwaukee Repertory Theatre production on 22 Mar 1979.
135 ------. Fen, Elisaveta, tr. See #86.
136 ------. Garnett, Constance, tr. See #93; #98.
137 ------. Hingley, Ronald, tr. See #108.
138 ------. House, Roy T., tr. N.Y.: Moods Publ. Co., 1909.
139 ------. Sykes, Arthur S., tr. N.Y.: 1911.
140 ------. Szogyi, Alex, tr. See #117.
141 ------. West, Julius, tr. See #83; #118; #119.
142 The Boor. Barker, Gary, tr. For Louisville Actors Theater production on 9 Oct 1973.
143 ------. Baukhage, Hilmar, tr. N.Y.: French, 1915.
144 ------. Clark, Barrett H., tr. N.Y.: French, 1915.
145 ------. Yarmolinsky, Avrahm, tr. See #7.
146 The Brute. Eric Bentley & Theodore Hoffman,trs. See #70.

The Cherry Orchard

147 Alfreds, Mike & Lydia Sokolov, trs. For Oxford Playhouse Company production (London) on 9 Aug 1982.
148 Ashley, Leonard R.,tr. In Leonard R.Ashley, ed., Mirrors for Man: Twenty-Six Plays of the World Drama (Cambr,MA: Winthrop, 1974).
149 Ball, William & Dennis Powers, trs. For American Conservatory Theater (San Francisco) production on 19 Mar 1974.
150 Bonazza, Blaze O., tr. In Blaze O. Bonazza & Emil Ray, eds., Studies in Drama (N.Y.: Harper & Row, 1963).

(The Cherry Orchard, cont.)

151 Bristow, Eugene K., tr. See #71.
152 Butler, Hubert, tr. London: Deane, 1934. Intro by Tyrone Guthrie.
153 Calderon, George, tr. See #72.
154 Cook, Kathleen, tr. See #9.
155 Corrigan, Robert W., tr. See #78.
156 Covan, Jennie, tr. N.Y.: Brentano, 1922.
157 Daniels, Camilla Chapin & George R. Noyes, trs.In George R. Noyes, ed., Masterpieces of the Russian Drama (N.Y.: Appleton, 1933) pp. 691-737.
158 Dunnigan, Ann, tr. See #80.
159 Fen, Elisaveta, tr. See #87; #90.
160 Garnett, Constance, tr. See #92; #93; #95; #97.
161 Gielgud, John, tr. London: Heinemann, 1963. Intro by Michel Saint-Denis.
162 Gill, Peter, tr. For production at Riverside Studios, Hammersmith (London) on 12 Jan 1978.
163 Goldstone, Herbert, ed. Chekhov's The Cherry Orchard. Boston: Allyn & Bacon, 1965. Allyn & Bacon Casebook Series. See #1386.
164 Griffiths, Trevor. English version from a translation by Helen Rappaport. London: Pluto Press, 1978.
165 Guthrie, Tyrone & Leonid Kipnis. Minneapolis: Univ of Minnesota Pr, 1965.
166 Heim, Michael H., tr. For Cincinnati Playhouse production on 19 Feb 1980.
167 Hingley, Ronald, tr. London: Oxford Univ Pr, 1965.
168 ------. See #109; #110.
169 Itallie, Jean-Claude van, tr. N.Y.: Random House, 1977.
170 James, Kenneth, tr. London: 1943.
171 Koteliansky, S.S., tr. See #5; #111.
172 Magarshack, David, tr. See #112.
173 Mandell, Max S., tr. Called The Cherry Garden. New Haven: Whaples, 1908.
174 Monarch Plays. N.Y.: Simon & Schuster, 1978.
175 Navrozov, L., ed. Moscow: Foreign Lang. Publ. House, 1956.
176 Poliakoff, Vera & Marie Seton, trs. London: 1938.
177 Rappaport, Helen, tr. See #164.
178 Robbins, J.J., ed. Typescript of an acting version.1950.
179 Salamander Press. Carmel, CA: 1983.
180 Senelick, Laurence, tr. Arlington Heights, IL: Davidson, 1977.
181 ------. See #115.
182 Sergievsky, Nicholas S., tr. N.Y.: International Univ Pr, 1946.
183 Skariatina, Irina, tr. In E.H. Weatherly et al, eds., The Heritage of European Literature (Boston: Ginn, 1948) vol II, pp. 602-26.

(The Cherry Orchard, cont.)

184 Szogyi, Alex, tr. See #116.
185 West, Julius, tr. See #83; #119.
186 Yarmolinsky, Avrahm, tr. Henry Popkin, ed. N.Y.: Avon, 1965. Critical articles by W.H. Bruford, Francis Fergusson, Ronald Hingley, Vladimir Nemirovich-Danchenko, Konstantin Stanislavsky, & Kenneth Tynan. Biography of Chekhov. Bibliog. See also #7.
187 Young, Stark, tr. N.Y.: French, 1947. See also #122.
188 Zenkowsky, Jennifer, tr. N.Y.: Farrar, Straus & Giroux, 1984.
189 See also #1; #76; #77; #91; #114.

A Forced Declaration

190 Gottlieb, Vera, tr. See #1394.

Impure Tragedians and Leprous Playwrights

191 Bristow, Eugene K., tr. See #71.
192 Gottlieb, Vera, tr. See #1394.

Ivanov

193 Brooks, Jeremy & Kitty Hunter Blair,trs. For Yale Repertory Theatre production on 19 Nov 1976.
194 Corrigan, Robert W., tr. See #78.
195 Dunnigan, Ann, tr. See #80.
196 Fell, Marian, tr. N.Y.: Brentano, 1923. See also #82.
197 Fen, Elisaveta, tr. See #87; #90.
198 Garnett, Constance, tr. See #92; #103.
199 Gielgud, John, tr. English version based upon a translation by Ariadne Nicolaeff. London: Heinemann, 1966.
200 Hingley, Ronald, tr. London: Oxford Univ Pr, 1968.
201 ------. See #104; #106; #107.
202 Magarshack, David, tr. N.Y.: 1966.
203 Nicolaeff, Ariadne, tr. See #199.
204 Szogyi, Alex, tr. See #117.
205 Winer, Elihu, tr. In Barry Ulanov, ed., Makers of the Modern Theatre (N.Y.: McGraw-Hill, 1961).

Night Before the Trial

206 Hingley, Ronald, tr. See #108.

On the Harmfulness of Tobacco
(also known as Smoking Is Bad for You; The Tobacco Evil)

207 Bentley, Eric, tr. In Carolina Q 9 (Fall 1956) 25-9.
208 ------. & Theodore Hoffman, trs. See #70.

(On the Harmfulness of Tobacco, cont.)

209 Bragg, Bernard. Adapted for the National Theater of the Deaf (N.Y.C.) production on 5 Mar 1969.
210 Bristow, Eugene K., tr. See #71.
211 Fischer, Charles, tr. For Yon Enterprises (N.Y.C.) production on 5 Mar 1968.
212 Forman, Henry J., tr. Called The Tobacco Evil. In Theatre Arts 7 (Jan 1923) 77-82.
213 Garnett, Constance, tr. See #98.
214 Hall, Philip Baker & D.H. Hall & Patrick Tovatt, trs. Acting version for Arizona Civic Theater (Tucson) production on 2 Feb 1978.
215 Hingley, Ronald, tr. Called Smoking Is Bad for You. See #108.
216 Koteliansky, S.S., tr. See #5; #10.
217 Szogyi, Alex, tr. See #117.

On the High Road

218 Batz, Michael, tr. For Yorick Players (London) production on 25 Jan 1982.
219 Garnett, Constance, tr. See #97; #103.
220 Hingley, Ronald, tr. See #108.
221 Modell, David A., tr. In Drama 22 (May 1916) 294-322.
222 ------. In I.D. Surguchev, The Fiddles of Autumn (N.Y.: International Pr, 1952) pp. 111-50.
223 Szogyi, Alex, tr. See #117.
224 West, Julius, tr. See #119.
225 See also #1; #76; #114.

Platonov (for variant titles see below)

226 Ashmore, Basil, tr. Called A Play Without a Title. London: Nevill, 1952.
227 ------. Called Don Juan (in the Russian Manner). London: British Book Centre, 1953. Review: Saturday R (N.Y.), 30 May 1953, pp. 35-6.
228 Cournos, John, tr. Called A Play Without a Title. London: Dent, 1930. Reviews: Nation & Athenaeum 47 (10 May 1930) 192; Spectator 144 (12 Apr 1930) 627-9; Times Literary Supplement, 6 Mar 1930, p. 185.
229 ------. Called That Worthless Fellow Platonov. N.Y.:Dutton, 1930. Reviews: Cleveland Open Shelf, May 1930, p. 73; New Republic 62 (2 Apr 1930) 198;N.Y.Herald Book R, 9 Mar 1930, p. 13; N.Y.Times Book R, 2 Feb 1930, p. 1; N.Y.World, 18 May 1930, p. 9; Pittsburgh Monthly Bulletin 35 (Jun 1930) 49; Poetry R 31 (1930) 196-200; Saturday R of Lit 6 (7 Jun 1930) 1104; Time 15 (20 Jan 1930) 64; Yale R n.s.19 (Jun 1930) 860-1.

(Platonov, cont.)

230 Frayn, Michael. Called Wild Honey, Frayn's adaptation of Platonov was produced by the National Theatre Company (London) in Aug 1984.
231 Hingley, Ronald, tr. London: Oxford Univ Pr, 1968.
232 ------. See #107.
233 Magarshack, David, tr. London: Faber & Faber, 1964. Review: Times Literary Supplement, 8 Apr 1965, p. 272.
234 ------. N.Y.: Hill & Wang, 1964. Review: Library J 89 (1 Dec 1964) 4822.
235 Makaroff, Dmitri, tr. London: Methuen, 1961.
236 Szogyi, Alex, tr. Called A Country Scandal. N.Y.:Coward-McCann, 1960.
237 See also #107.

The Proposal
(also known as A Marriage Proposal & Popping the Question)

238 Baukhage, Hilmar & Barrett H. Clark, trs. Called A Marriage Proposal. N.Y.: French, 1914.
239 Bentley, Eric & Theodore Hoffman, trs. See #70.
240 Chambers, W.H. Called A Marriage Proposal. In Alfred Bates, The Drama (London: Smart & Stanley, 1903) vol 18, pp. 175-92.
241 Fen, Elisaveta, tr. See #86.
242 Garnett, Constance, tr. See #93.
243 Golden Book 13 (Feb 1931) 70-5.
244 Hingley, Ronald, tr. See #108.5.
245 International: A R of Two Worlds (N.Y.) 8 (May 1914) 150-5.
246 Neugroschel, Joachim, tr. In Richard H. Goldstone & Abraham H. Lass,eds.,The Mentor Book of Short Plays(N.Y.: New Amer Library, 1969).
247 Nolan, Paul T., adapter. In Plays 29 (May 1970) 83-92.
248 Prishvin, Irina & X.J. Kennedy, trs. In X.J. Kennedy, ed.,Literature: An Introduction to Fiction, Poetry, and Drama 2nd ed. (Boston: Little,Brown, 1979).
249 Selver, Paul, tr. Called Popping the Question. In New Age n.s. 14 (16 Apr 1914) 756-60.
250 Szogyi, Alex, tr. See #117.
251 West, Julius, tr. See # 85; #118; #119.

The Sea Gull

252 Alfreds, Mike & Lydia Sokolov, trs. For Shared Experience production in Almeida, Islington, on 13 Oct 1981.
253 Anderson, Brenda & A. Colin Wright, trs. For production at Queen's Univ in Fall 1977.
254 Bristow, Eugene K., tr. See #71.

(<u>The Sea Gull</u>, cont.)

255 Calderon, George, tr. See #72.
256 Cook, Kathleen, tr. See #9.
257 Corrigan, Robert W., tr. See #78.
258 Cottrell, Richard, tr. For Old Vic Theatre production in Bristol on 30 Aug 1978.
259 Davis, J.P., tr. For Arts Theatre (London) production in Apr 1953.
260 Dunnigan, Ann, tr. See #80.
261 Eisemann, Fred, tr. In <u>Poet Lore</u> 24 (1913) 1-41.
262 ------. Boston: Badger, 1913.
263 ------. See #81.
264 Fell, Marian, tr. See #82; #83.
265 Fen, Elisaveta, tr. See #86; #90.
266 French, David, tr. Toronto: Playwrights Co-op, 1977.
267 Garnett, Constance, tr. See #92; #93; #97.
268 Gnesin, Maurice, tr. Chicago: 1930.
269 Goodman, Randolph, tr. In Randolph Goodman, ed., <u>From Script to Stage: Eight Modern Plays</u> (San Francisco: Rinehart, 1971.
270 Hasnain, Arif, tr. For the Manitoba Theater Center (Winnipeg) production on 15 Feb 1980.
271 Hingley, Ronald, tr. London: Oxford Univ Pr, 1965.
272 ------. See #104; #106; #107.
273 Iliffe, David, tr. London: French, 1953.
274 Itallie, Jean-Claude van, tr. N.Y.: Harper & Row, 1977. Commentaries by William M. Hoffman & Daniel Seltzer. Textual notes by Paul Schmidt.
275 Jellicoe, Ann & Ariadne Nicolaeff, trs. For the Arizona Theatre Company (Tucson) production on 4 Mar 1980.
276 Kilroy, Thomas, tr. For the English Stage Company (London) production on 8 Apr 1981.
277 Koteliansky, S.S., tr. See #5; #111.
278 Lachman, Anya & Mack Scism, trs. For the Oklahoma City Mummers Theater production in the 1968 season.
279 Lau, Patrick & Vilma Hollingbery, trs. For production at Gardner Centre, Brighton, on 5 Feb 1980.
280 Le Gallienne, Eva, tr. For the National Repertory Theatre (N.Y.C.) production on 5 Apr 1964.
281 Leontovich, Eugenie, tr. For Universalist Church production (N.Y.C.) on 21 Feb 1977.
282 MacDonald, Robert D., tr. For production at Citizens Theatre, Glasgow, on 10 Nov 1978.
283 Magarshack, David, tr. London: Dobson, 1952. Edited with an intro by S. D. Balukhaty. Production score by Konstantin Stanislavsky.
284 Meck, Galina von & Lindsay Anderson, trs. For Lyric Theatre (London) production on 28 Oct 1975.

(The Sea Gull, cont.)

285 Reeve, Franklin D., tr. In Franklin D. Reeve, ed., An Anthology of Russian Plays, vol 2. N.Y.: Vintage Books, 1963.
286 Select English Plays. Shanghai: Commercial Pr, 1936.
287 Senelick, Laurence, tr. See # 115.
288 Sznycer, Bernard W., tr. London: Poets' & Painters' Pr, 1974.
289 Szogyi, Alex, tr. See #116.
290 West, Julius, tr. London: Henderson, 1915.
291 Woolgar, Mark, tr. For Triumph Theatre (London) production in Sep 1976.
292 Young, Stark, tr. N.Y.: Scribner, 1939. Reviews: N.Y. Times Book R, 26 Feb 1939, p. 9; Southern R 5 (Winter 1940) 559-67.
293 See also #1; #76; #77; #91; #114.

Swan Song

294 Bentley, Eric & Theodore Hoffman, trs. See #70.
295 Carnovsky, Morris, adapter. New Haven: 1972.
296 Fell, Marian, tr. See #82.
297 Garnett, Constance, tr. See #103.
298 Gassner, John, adapter. In John Gassner & Morris Sweetkind, eds., An Anthology Introducing the Drama (N.Y.: Holt, Rinehart & Winston, 1963).
299 Hingley, Ronald, tr. See #108.
300 Hoffman, Theodore, tr. For the California Actors' Theater (Los Gatos, CA) production on 9 Nov 1978.
301 Szogyi, Alex, tr. See #117.

Tatyana Riepin

302 Hingley, Ronald, tr. See #108.
303 Koteliansky, S.S., tr. In London Mercury 12 (Sep 1925) 579-97.
304 ------. London: Routledge, 1927.
305 ------. See #5; #10.
306 Racin, John, tr. For Judson Poets' Theater (N.Y.C.) production on 31 Mar 1978.

The Three Sisters

307 Bond, Edward & Richard Cottrell, trs. For English Stage Company (London) production in 1967.
308 Bristow, Eugene K., tr. See #71.
309 Budberg, Moura, tr. London: Davis-Poynter, 1971.

(The Three Sisters, cont.)

310 Carnicke, Sharon M., tr. For Lion Theater Co. (N.Y.C.) production on 1 Feb 1979.
311 Cook, Kathleen, tr. See #9.
312 Corrigan, Robert W., tr. See #78.
313 Covan, Jennie, tr. N.Y.: Brentano, 1922.
314 Davis, J. P., tr. For John Fernald Company (Rochester, MI) production in the 1966 season.
315 Dunnigan, Ann, tr. See #80.
316 Fell, Marian, tr. See #83.
317 Fen, Elisaveta, tr. See #87; #90.
318 Garnett, Constance, tr. See #92; #95; #97; #103.
319 ------, & Theodore Komisarjevsky, trs. London: 1926.
320 Guerney, Bernard G., tr. In Bernard G. Guerney, ed., A Treasury of Russian Literature (N.Y.: Vanguard, 1934) pp. 802-62.
321 Guthrie, Tyrone, tr. For The Acting Company (Juillard Drama School) production on 4 Nov 1975.
322 ------, & Leonid Kipnis, trs. For Tavistock Repertory Company production at Canonbury,England, on 4 Nov 1966.
323 Hingley, Ronald, tr. London: Oxford Univ Pr, 1965.
324 ------. See #104; #106; #110.
325 Itallie, Jean-Claude van, tr. N.Y.: Dramatists Play Service, 1979.
326 Jarrell, Randall, tr. N.Y.: Macmillan, 1969.
327 McAndrew, Andrew R., tr. In John Gassner, ed., Twentieth Century Russian Drama (N.Y.: Bantam, 1963).
328 Magarshack, David, tr. See #112.
329 Nicolaeff, Ariadne, tr. For Oxford Playhouse Company (London) production in Apr 1964.
330 Popkin, Henry, tr. N.Y.: 1965.
331 Russian Reading Made Easy. London: Hugo's Institute for Teaching Foreign Languages, 1916. Three Sisters in Russian, with literal English translation and explanatory notes.
332 Six Great Modern Plays. Laurel Editions Editors. N.Y.: Dell, 1964.
333 Szogyi, Alex, tr. See #116.
334 West, Julius, tr. See #119. Review: New Republic 7 (8 Jul 1916) 256-8.
335 Young, Stark, tr. N.Y.: French, 1941.
336 ______. See #122.
337 See also: #1; #76; #91; #114.

A Tragedian in Spite of Himself
(For variant titles see below)

338 Bentley, Eric, tr. Called Summer in the Country. In Tulane Drama R 2 (Feb 1958) 52-6.

(A Tragedian in Spite of Himself, cont.)

339 ------, & Theodore Hoffman, trs. Called Summer in the Country. See #70.
340 Garnett, Constance, tr. Called An Unwilling Martyr. See #103.
341 Hingley, Ronald, tr. Called A Tragic Role. See #108.
342 Murphy, Olive F., tr. In Poet Lore 33 (Autumn 1922) 268-73.
343 ------. See #81.
344 Szogyi, Alex, tr. Called The Reluctant Tragedian. See #117.
345 West, Julius, tr. See #119.
346 See also #1.

Uncle Vanya

347 Bristow, Eugene K., tr. See #71.
348 Caylor, Rose, tr. N.Y.:Covici-Friede, 1930. Reviews: Nation (N.Y.) 130 (7 May 1930) 554; N.Y.Evening Post, 31 May 1930, p. 8m; N.Y.Herald-Trib Books, 6 Jul 1930, p. 11; N.Y.World, 19 May 1930, p. 9; Outlook 155 (18 Jun 1930) 270.
349 Chwat, Jaques, ed. N.Y.: Avon, 1974.
350 Corrigan, Robert W., tr. See #78.
351 Cottrell, Richard, tr. For Milwaukee Repertory Theater production on 25 Feb 1983.
352 Covan, Jennie, tr. N.Y.: Brentano, 1922.
353 Dunnigan, Ann, tr. See #80.
354 Fell, Marian, tr. See #82; #83.
355 Fen, Elisaveta, tr. See #86; #90.
356 Garnett, Constance, tr. See #92; #93; #97.
357 ------, & Theodore Komisarjevsky, trs. London: 1926.
358 Gems, Pam, tr. London: Methuen, 1979.
359 Guthrie, Tyrone & Leonid Kipnis. Minneapolis: Univ of Minn Pr, 1969. "A Director's Intro" by Guthrie. Review: Slavic & East European J 14 (Fall 1970) 379-81.
360 Hampton, Christopher & Nina Froud, trs. In Plays of the Year, Chosen by J.C.Trewin vol 39 (London: Elek, 1971).
361 Hampton, Christopher & Anthony Page, trs. London: Royal Court Theatre, 1970.
362 Heim, Michael H., tr. For Pittsburgh Public Theater production in Oct 1976.
363 Hingley, Ronald, tr. London: Oxford Univ Pr, 1965.
364 ------. See #104; #109; #110.
365 Johnson, Douglas, tr. For Berkeley (Calif) Repertory Theater production on 28 Mar 1975.
366 Magarshack, David, tr. In The Storm and Other Russian Plays (N.Y.: Hill & Wang, 1960) pp. 231-81.
367 ------. See #112.

(Uncle Vanya, cont.)

368 Monnoyer, Frederick, tr. For Royal Alexandra Theater Co. (Washington, D.C.) production on 14 Dec 1978.
369 Murrell, John, tr. Toronto: Theatrebooks, 1978.
370 Nicolaeff, Ariadne, tr. For Royal Exchange Theatre Company (Manchester) production on 17 Feb 1977.
371 Poggi, Jack, tr. For Actors Alliance (N.Y.C.) production on 15 Apr 1977.
372 Saphro, Frances Arno, tr. In Poet Lore 33 (Autumn 1922) 317-61.
373 Szogyi, Alex, tr. See #116.
374 Todd, Albert & Mike Nichols, trs. For Circle in the Square (N.Y.C.) production on 4 June 1973.
375 Townsend, Rochelle S., tr. London: 1914.
376 Young, Stark, tr. N.Y.: French, 1956.
377 ------. See #122.
378 See also #91.

The Wedding

379 Bechhofer, Carl E., tr. In New Age n.s. 16 (29 Apr 1915) 697-700; also, New Age n.s. 17 (30 Dec 1915) 207-10.
380 ------. See #69.
381 Bentley, Eric, tr. For Tower Theatre (London) production in May 1959.
382 ------, & Theodore Hoffman, trs. See #70.
383 Carnovsky, Morris, adapter. New Haven: 1972.
384 Garnett, Constance, tr. See #97; #103.
385 Hingley, Ronald, tr. London: Oxford Univ Pr, 1965.
386 ------. See #108.
387 Szogyi, Alex, tr. See #117.
388 West, Julius, tr. See #118; #119.
389 See also #1; #76; #114.

The Wood Demon

390 Corrigan, Robert W., tr. See #78.
391 Fishman, Morris, tr. For Birmingham Crescent Theatre production in Edinburgh in Aug 1961.
392 Friedland, Louis S., tr. A Chekhov Scenario (The Demon of the Woods). In Theatre Arts Monthly 8 (1924) 233-7.
393 ------. #392 also in #14.
394 Hingley, Ronald, tr. London: Oxford Univ Pr, 1965.
395 ------. See #110.
396 Koteliansky, S.S., tr. In Calendar of Modern Letters 2 (Dec 1925, Jan 1926) 217-43, 289-316.
397 ------. London: Chatto & Windus, 1926. Reviews: Nation & Athenaeum 40 (4 Dec 1926)340; New Statesman 29 (21 May 1927) 190; Observer (London), 15 May 1927, p. 6; Times Literary Supplement, 11 Nov 1926, p.790. See #5; #111.
398 Szogyi, Alex, tr. See #117.

Story Collections (alphabetical by translator)

399 Chamot, A.E.,tr. The Grasshopper and Other Stories. London: Paul, 1926. 12 stories. Reviews: Fortnightly R n. s. 121 (1 Apr 1927) 575; Times Literary Supplement, 21 Oct 1926, p. 724c.

400 ------. Reprint of #399. Philadelphia: McKay, 1926.

401 ------. Reprint of #399. Freeport, NY: Books for Libraries Pr, 1972.

402 ------. Short Stories. London: Commodore Pr, 1946. 10 stories.

403 Chertok, I.C. & Jean Gardner, trs. Late-Blooming Flowers and Other Stories by Anton Chekhov. N.Y.: McGraw-Hill, 1964. 8 stories. Reviews: Best Sellers 23 (15 Feb 1964) 401; Library J 89 (1 Mar 1964) 1112; N.Y.Times Book R, 1 Mar 1964, p.4; Saturday R (N.Y.) 47 (7 Mar 1964) 37.

404 Coulson, Jessie, tr. Selected Stories of Chekhov. Intro by Coulson. London: Oxford Univ Pr, 1963. Review: Times (London), 7 Nov 1963, p. 15e.

405 Dunnigan, Ann, tr. Anton Chekhov: Selected Stories.N.Y.: Signet, 1960. 20 stories. First English translation of 10 stories. Foreword by Ernest J. Simmons.

406 ------. Ward Six and Other Stories. N.Y.: Signet, 1965. Afterword by Rufus W. Mathewson. Review: Slavic & East European J, 10 (Fall 1966) 343-4.

407 Fell, Marian, tr. Russian Silhouettes. N.Y.: Scribner, 1915. 29 stories. Reviews: Book Buyer 40 (Oct 1915)129; Boston Transcript, 18 Dec 1915, p. 7; Current Opinion 61 (Oct 1916) 263-4; Dial 61 (15 Aug 1916) 103-4; Independent 85 (10 Jan 1916) 60; Little R 1 (Sep 1914) 44-9; Nation (N.Y.) 101 (11 Nov 1915) 572; N.Y.Times Book R, 26 Dec 1915, p. 20.

408 Reprint of #407. London: Duckworth, 1915. Review: Athenaeum 2 (4 Dec 1915) 416.

409 Reprint of #407. Salem, NH: Arno, 1972.

410 ------. Stories of Russian Life. N.Y.: Scribner, 1914. 24 stories. Reviews: American R of Reviews 50(Aug 1914) 248; Book Buyer 39 (Jun 1914) 102-3; Bookman (N.Y.) 40 (14 Oct 1914) 171; Boston Transcript, 17 Jun 1914, p. 22; Literary Digest 49 (3 Oct 1914) 638; Nation (N.Y.) 99 (16 Jul 1914) 75; N.Y.Times Book R, 7 Jun 1914, p. 19; Outlook 107 (27 Jun 1914) 502.

411 Reprint of #410. London: Duckworth, 1914. Reviews:Athenaeum 2 (26 Dec 1914) 664; New Age n.s. 16 (4 Feb 1915) 376; Spectator 114 (2 Jan 1915) 10. See also #485.

412 Fen, Elisaveta, tr. Anton Chekhov: Short Stories. London: Folio Society, 1974. 13 stories. Intro by Fen. Aquatints by Nigel Lambourne.

413 Fitz-Lyon, April & Kyril Zinovieff, trs. The Woman in the Case and Other Stories. London: Spearman & Calder, 1953. 24 stories. Intro by Andrew G. Colin. Reviews: Atlantic 193 (Jun 1954) 78; Chicago Sunday Tribune, 11 Apr 1954, p. 8;New Statesman & Nation 47 (30 Jan 1954) 139; Time 63 (5 Apr 1954) 112; Times Literary Supplement, 8 Jan 1954, p. 21.

414 Garnett, Constance, tr. The Bishop and Other Stories. London: Chatto & Windus, 1919. 7 stories. Reviews: Athenaeum, 22 Aug 1919, p.777; Times Literary Supplement, 14 Aug 1919, p. 435.

415 Reprint of #414. N.Y.: Macmillan, 1919. Reviews: ALA Bulletin 16 (Dec 1919) 98; Dial 67 (1 Nov 1919) 388; Nation (N.Y.) 110 (6 Mar 1920) 306; N.Y.Call, 30 Nov 1919, p. 10; N.Y.Evening Post, 25 Oct 1919, p. 2; N.Y. Times Book R, 7 Mar 1920, p.1; Springfield Republican, 6 Jan 1920, p. 8.

416 ------. Chekhov: Great Stories. Ed. with an intro by David H. Greene. N.Y.: Dell, 1959. 8 stories.

417 ------. The Chorus Girl and Other Stories. London:Chatto & Windus, 1920. 12 stories. Review: London Mercury 1 (Feb 1920) 476.

418 Reprint of #417. N.Y.: Macmillan, 1920. Reviews: Booklist 16 (May 1920) 283; Cleveland Open Shelf, Aug 1920, p. 70; Dial 69 (Oct 1920) 432; Nation (N.Y.) 111 (10 Jul 1920) 48; New Republic 22 (21 Apr 1920) 254; N.Y.Call, 9 May 1920, p. 10; N.Y.Times Book R, 27 Jun 1920, p. 22.

419 ------. The Cook's Wedding and Other Stories. London: Chatto & Windus, 1922. 25 stories.

420 Reprint of #419. N.Y.: Macmillan, 1922. Reviews: Booklist 18 (Jun 1922) 334; Boston Transcript, 29 Apr 1922, p. 6; Freeman 5 (21 Jun 1922) 358-9; Literary R, 15 Jul 1922, p. 810; Nation (N.Y.) 114 (24 May 1922) 625; New Republic 30 (22 Mar 1922) 114; Pittsburgh Monthly Bulletin 27 (Jun 1922) 260; Springfield Republican, 4 Jun 1922, p. 7a.

421 ------. The Darling and Other Stories. London: Chatto & Windus, 1916. 10 stories. Reviews: Athenaeum, Dec 1916, p. 595; New Statesman 8 (18 Nov 1916) 159-60; Saturday R (London) 122 (2 Dec 1916) 532; Times Literary Supplement, 9 Nov 1916, p. 537a.

422 Reprint of #421. N.Y.: Macmillan, 1916. Reviews: American R of Reviews 55 (Jan 1917) 103; Dial 61 (30 Nov 1916) 470; N.Y.Call, 24 Dec 1916, p. 15; N.Y.Times Book R, 29 Apr 1917, p. 171; Russian R (N.Y) 3 (Jan 1917) 57-8; Springfield Republican, 12 Jan 1917, p. 6.

423 Reprint of #421. N.Y.: Ecco, 1984.

424 ------. The Duel and Other Stories. London: Chatto & Windus, 1916. 8 stories. Reviews: Athenaeum, Dec 1916, p. 595; Times Literary Supplement, 9 Nov 1916, p. 537a.

425 ------. Reprint of #424. N.Y.: Macmillan, 1916. Reviews: American R of Reviews 55 (Jan 1917) 103; N.Y. Times Book R, 29 Apr 1917, p. 171; North American R 205 (Jan 1917) 152; Russian R (N.Y.) 3 (Jan 1917) 57-8; Springfield Republican, 12 Jan 1917, p. 6.

426 ------. Reprint of #424. N.Y.: Ecco, 1984.

427 ------. The Horse Stealers and Other Stories. London: Chatto & Windus, 1921. 22 stories.

428 ------. Reprint of #427. N.Y.: Macmillan, 1921. Reviews: Literary R, 26 Nov 1921, p. 200; Nation (N.Y.) 113 (24 Aug 1921) 210; N.Y. Times Book R, 14 Aug 1921, p. 24.

429 ------. The Lady with the Dog and Other Stories. London: Chatto & Windus, 1917. 9 stories. Reviews: Athenaeum, Aug 1917, p. 416; Times Literary Supplement, 29 Jun 1917, p. 306.

430 ------. Reprint of #429. N.Y.: Macmillan, 1917. Reviews: Boston Transcript, 18 Jun 1917, p. 6; Cleveland Open Shelf, Sep 1917, p. 103; Dial 64 (3 Jan 1918) 27; Nation (N.Y.) 105 (19 Jul 1917) 70; New Republic 13 (17 Nov 1917) 12; N.Y.Branch Library News 4 (Sep 1917) 131; N.Y.Times Book R, 22 Jul 1917, p. 274; Yale R n. s. 7 (Oct 1917) 189.

431 ------. Love and Other Stories. London: Chatto & Windus, 1922. 23 stories.

432 ------. Reprint of #431. N.Y.: Macmillan, 1923. Reviews: Bookman (N.Y.) 57 (Mar 1923) 93-5; Cleveland Open Shelf, Jun 1923, p. 43; Dial 75 (Jul 1923) 96; Freeman 7 (11 Jul 1923) 430; Nation (N.Y.) 116 (23 May 1923) 601; N.Y.Times Book R, 4 Mar 1923, p. 11; Outlook 133 (28 Mar 1923) 588; Springfield Republican, 22 Jul 1923, p. 7a.

433 ------. The Party and Other Stories. London: Chatto & Windus, 1917. 11 stories. Review: Athenaeum, Nov 1917, p. 597.

434 ------. Reprint of #433. N.Y.: Macmillan, 1917. Reviews: American R of Reviews 56 (Nov 1917) 557; Catholic World 106 (Feb 1918) 689; Dial 64 (3 Jan 1918) 27; Independent 93 (26 Jan 1918) 150; New Republic 13 (17 Nov 1917) 12; N.Y.Times Book R, 3 Dec 1917, p. 570; Outlook 117 (3 Oct 1917) 134.

435 ------. The Schoolmaster and Other Stories. London: Chatto & Windus, 1921. 29 stories. Reviews: Times Literary Supplement, 22 Apr 1921, p. 257 & 22 Sep 1921, p. 609.

436 ------. Reprint of #435. N.Y.: Macmillan, 1921.

437 ------. *The Schoolmistress and Other Stories*. London: Chatto & Windus, 1920. 21 stories. Reviews: *Athenaeum*, 7 Jan 1921, p. 11; *Times Literary Supplement*, 19 Nov 1920, p. 756c.

438 Reprint of #437. N.Y.: Macmillan, 1921. Reviews: *Booklist* 17 (Feb 1921) 191; *Dial* 71 (Aug 1921) 242; *Freeman* 3 (6 Apr 1921) 90; *Literary R*, 5 Feb 1921, p. 3.

439 ------. *Select Tales of Tchehov*. London:Chatto & Windus, 1927. 25 stories. Reviews: *Bermondsey Book* 5 (Mar-May 1928) 98-100; *Nation & Athenaeum* 42 (24 Dec 1927) 487; *New Adelphi* 1 (Mar 1928) 266-9; *Observer* (London), 8 Jan 1928, p. 7; *Spectator* 139 (10 Dec 1927) 1063.

440 New ed. of #439. London:Chatto & Windus,1949.29 stories.

441 Reprint of #440. N.Y.: Macmillan, 1951.

442 ------. *The Short Stories of Anton Chekhov*. Avon, CT: Cardavon Pr, 1973. 21 stories. Intro by Helen Muchnic.

443 ------. *Short Stories of Tchehov*. N.Y.: Macmillan, 1928. 32 stories. Index of Constance Garnett's translations of Chekhov's stories. Intro by Evelyn May Albright arranges the stories by subject matter.

444 ------. *Tales from Tchehov*. London: Penguin, 1938.

445 ------. *The Wife and Other Stories*. London: Chatto & Windus, 1918. 9 stories. Reviews: *Athenaeum*, Jun 1918, p. 285; *Nation* (London) 23 (25 May 1918) 193-4; *Times Literary Supplement*, 17 May 1918, p. 231a.

446 Reprint of #445. N.Y.: Macmillan, 1918. Reviews: *American R of Reviews* 58 (Aug 1918) 219; *Booklist* 15 (Nov 1918) 71; *Boston Transcript*, 31 Jul 1918, p. 6; *Everyman* 12 (1 Jun 1918) 182; *Nation* (N.Y.) 107 (24 Aug 1918) 208; *N.Y.Times Book R*, 16 Feb 1919, p. 69; *Yale R*, n.s. 8 (Oct 1918) 196.

447 ------. *The Witch and Other Stories*. London: Chatto & Windus, 1918. 15 stories. Reviews: *Athenaeum*, Jun 1918, p. 285; *Nation* (London) 23 (25 May 1918) 193-4; *Times Literary Supplement*, 17 May 1918, p. 231a.

448 Reprint of #447. N.Y.: Macmillan, 1918. Reviews: *Booklist* 15 (Nov 1918) 71; *Boston Transcript*, 31 Jul 1918, p. 6; *Everyman* 12 (1 Jun 1918) 182; *Nation* (N.Y.) 107 (16 Nov 1918) 589; *N.Y.Times Book R*,16 Feb 1919, p.69.

449 ------. See also #485; #498.

450 Goldberg, Isaac & Henry T. Schnittkind, trs. *Nine Humorous Tales by Anton Chekhov*. Boston: Stratford, 1918. Reviews: *Athenaeum*, Jun 1918, p. 285; *Book News Monthly* 36 (Jun 1918) 372; *Boston Transcript*, 24 Apr 1918, p. 8; *New Republic* 15 (22 Jun 1918) 241; *Springfield Republican*, 28 Apr 1918, p. 17; *Times Literary Supplement*, 16 May 1918, p. 231a.

451 Revised 2nd ed. of #450. Freeport, NY: Books for Libraries Pr, 1970.

452 Gottlieb, Nora, tr. Chekhov: Early Stories. London: Bodley Head, 1960. Review: Times (London), 1 Sep 1960, p. 13c.

453 ------. Reprint of #452. N.Y.: Doubleday, 1960.

454 Hinchliffe, Arnold, tr. The Sinner from Toledo and Other Stories. Rutherford, NJ: Fairleigh Dickinson Univ Pr, 1972. All these stories were written by 1895. 7 of the stories are here translated for the first time.

455 Hingley, Ronald, tr. & ed. Chekhov: Seven Short Stories. London: Oxford Univ Pr, 1974. Intro by Hingley.

456 ------. Chekhov: Stories, 1889-91. Vol 4 of The Oxford Chekhov (see #4). London: Oxford Univ Pr, 1980. 8 stories. Bibliog. Intro. Notes. Review: Slavic & East European J 25 (Summer 1981) 92-3.

457 ------. Chekhov: Stories, 1889-91. Vol 5 of The Oxford Chekhov (see #4). London: Oxford Univ Pr, 1970. 6 stories. Bibliog. Intro. Notes.

458 ------. Chekhov: Stories, 1892-93. Vol 6 of The Oxford Chekhov (see #4). London: Oxford Univ Pr, 1971. 12 stories. Bibliog. Intro. Notes.

459 ------. Chekhov: Stories, 1893-95. Vol 7 of The Oxford Chekhov (see #4). London: Oxford Univ Pr, 1978. 9 stories. Bibliog. Intro. Notes.

460 ------. Chekhov: Stories, 1895-97. Vol 8 of The Oxford Chekhov (see #4). London: Oxford Univ Pr, 1965. 15 stories. Bibliog. Intro. Notes. Review: Saturday R of Lit, 19 Feb 1966, p. 49.

461 ------. Chekhov: Stories, 1898-1904. Vol 9 of The Oxford Chekhov (see #4). London: Oxford Univ Pr, 1975. 17 stories. Bibliog. Intro. Notes. Review: Russian Language J 30 (1976) 173.

462 ------. Eleven Stories by Anton Chekhov. London: Oxford Univ Pr, 1976. Intro by Hingley. Review: New Statesman, 13 Feb 1976, pp. 192-3.

463 Jones, Frances H., tr. St. Peter's Day and Other Tales. N.Y.: Capricorn Books, 1959. 22 stories. Chekhov wrote these stories for comic magazines while he was in medical school. Intro gives dates of publication & a glossary of meanings of names. Reviews: N.Y.Herald-Tribune Book R, 20 Mar 1960, p. 10; N.Y.Times Book R, 6 Dec 1959, p. 66; New Yorker 36 (20 Feb 1960) 174; Saturday R (N.Y.) 43 (23 Jan 1960) 30; Springfield Republican, 6 Dec 1959, p. 3d.

464 Kaye, Adeline Lister, tr. The Steppe and Other Stories. London: Heinemann, 1915. 9 stories. Reviews: Athenaeum 1 (5 Jun 1915) 505; New Statesman 5 (24 Jul 1915) 373.

465 ------. Reprint of #464. N.Y.: Stokes, 1915. Reviews: Independent 85 (10 Jan 1916) 60; N.Y.Times Book R, 14 Nov 1915, p. 20.

466 The Kiss and The Duel and Other Stories. N.Y.: Avon,n.d.

467 Koteliansky, S.S.,ed. & tr. Anton Chekhov Short Stories. Polybooks Todd Publishing Company, 1943.

468 ------. See #5; #10; #1403.

469 ------, & Gilbert Cannan, trs. The House with the Mezzanine and Other Stories. N.Y.: Scribner, 1917. 7 stories. Reviews: Dial 64 (3 Jan 1918) 27; New Republic 13 (17 Nov 1917) supplement 12; N.Y.Call, 12 Jan 1918, p. 14; N.Y.Times Book R, 9 Sep 1917, p. 22; Springfield Republican, 6 Sep 1917, p. 6.

470 ------. Re-issue of #469, called My Life and Other Stories. London: Daniel, 1920. Reviews: Spectator 125 (31 Jul 1920) 150; Times Literary Supplement, 16 Jul 1920, p. 455b.

471 ------. Reprint of #470. Freeport, NY: Books for Libraries Pr, 1971.

472 ------, & J. M. Murry, trs. The Bet and Other Stories. Dublin: Maunsel, 1915. 13 stories. Reviews: Athenaeum 2 (25 Dec 1915) 480; Nation (London) 18 (27 Nov 1915) 334; New Statesman 6 (27 Nov 1915) 186-7; Spectator 115 (20 Nov 1915) 714; Times Literary Supplement, 25 Nov 1915, p. 428c.

473 ------. Reprint of #472. N.Y.: Luce, 1915. Reviews: Dial 61 (15 Aug 1916) 103-4; N.Y.Times Book R, 3 Sep 1916, p. 342.

474 Linscott, Robert H., ed. The Stories of Anton Tchekov. N.Y.: Modern Library, 1932. 22 stories. Intro by Linscott.

475 Litvinov, Ivy, tr. A.P. Chekhov: Short Novels and Stories. Moscow: Foreign Languages Publishing House, 1954. See also #485.

476 Long, R.E.C., tr. The Black Monk and Other Stories. London: Duckworth, 1903. 12 stories. Reviews: Athenaeum, 13 Feb 1904, p. 205; R of Reviews, 28 (Nov 1903) 515.

477 ------. Reprint of #476. N.Y.: Stokes, 1915. Review: N.Y.Times Book R, 14 Nov 1915, p. 443.

478 ------. Reprint of #476. Freeport, NY: Books for Libraries Pr, 1970.

479 ------. The Kiss and Other Stories. London: Duckworth, 1908. 15 stories. Reviews: Athenaeum, 20 Feb 1909, p. 224; New Age n.s. 4 (18 Mar 1909) 423.

480 ------. Reprint of #479. N.Y.: Scribner, 1912. Reviews: Catholic World 96 (Feb 1913) 683; N.Y.Sun, 7 Dec 1912, p. 7; N.Y.Times Book R, 12 Jan 1913, p. 18; Outlook 102 (21 Dec 1912) 865.

481 ------. Reprint of #479. N.Y.: Stokes, 1915. Review: N.Y.Times Book R, 14 Nov 1915, p. 20.

482 ------. Reprint of #479. Freeport, NY: Books for Libraries Pr, 1972.

483 Magarshack, David, tr. The Lady with the Lapdog and Other Stories. London: Penguin, 1959. 11 stories.

484 Makanowitzky, Barbara, tr. Anton Chekhov: Seven Short Novels. N.Y.:Norton, 1971. Contains "The Duel"; "In the Ravine"; "My Life"; "Peasants"; "Three Years"; "Ward No. 6"; "A Woman's Kingdom." Bibliog. Chronology. General intro & prefaces to each story by Gleb Struve. Notes.

485 Matlaw, Ralph E., ed. & tr. Anton Chekhov's Short Stories. Tr. by Marian Fell, Constance Garnett, Ivy Litvinov, & Ralph E. Matlaw. N.Y.: Norton, 1979. Includes bibliog, biographical sketch by Maxim Gorky, selections from Chekhov's letters, and critical articles by A. B. Derman, Karl Kramer, D. S. Mirsky, Nils Ake Nilsson, Renato Poggioli, Donald Rayfield, Virginia Llewellyn Smith, & Gleb Struve. Review: Slavic & East European J 24 (Spring 1980) 66-7.

486 Miles, Patrick & Harvey Pitcher, trs. Chekhov: The Early Stories, 1883-1888. London: Macmillan, 1983. Reviews: J of European Studies 13 (Dec 1983) 12-3; Studies in Short Fiction 20 (Fall 1983) 324-5; Times Literary Supplement, 24 Sep 1982, p. 1044.

487 Morton, Miriam, ed. & tr. Shadows and Light. N.Y.: Doubleday, 1968. 9 stories. Intro by Morton on "The Author and His Times."

488 Payne, Robert, tr. The Image of Chekhov: Forty Stories In The Order In Which They Were Written. N.Y.: Knopf, 1963. Intro by Payne.

489 Pitcher, Harvey & James Forsyth, trs. Chuckle with Chekhov. Cromer, Norfolk: Swallow House Books, 1975. A collection of Chekhov's early comic stories. Reviews: J of European Studies 20 (Dec 1976) 298-9; New Statesman, 13 Feb 1976, pp. 192-3.

490 ------. See also #486.

491 Rodale, J.I., ed. The Beggar and Other Stories. Emmaus, PA: Story Classics, 1949. 14 stories.

492 Rothschild's Fiddle and Other Stories. N.Y.: Modern Library, 1917. 14 stories. Review: Independent 93 (26 Jan 1918) 150-1.

493 Smith, Ursula, tr. The Thief and Other Tales. N.Y.: Vantage Pr, 1964.

494 Townsend, Rochelle S., tr. 11 stories in J.A. Hammerton, ed., The Masterpiece Library of Short Stories. London: Educational Book Co., 1920. Vol 12, pp. 307-79.

495 Wilks, Ronald, tr. In the Ravine and Other Stories. London: Penguin, 1981.

496 ------. The Kiss and Other Stories. London: Penguin, 1982. 10 stories. Intro by Wilks.

497 Wilson, Edmund, ed. The Peasants and Other Stories.N.Y.: Doubleday, 1956. 9 stories. Constance Garnett, tr. Preface by Wilson.

498 Yarmolinsky, Avrahm, tr. The Unknown Chekhov. N.Y.:Noonday Pr, 1954. Intro on Chekhov's life. First English translation of 18 stories, an early version of On the Harmfulness of Tobacco, two excerpts about the trip to Sakhalin, & two newspaper articles. Notes. Reviews: Atlantic 193 (Jun 1954) 78; Chicago Sunday Tribune, 11 Apr 1954, p. 8; Commonweal 60 (25 Jun 1954) 300; N.Y.Times Book R, 18 Apr 1954, p. 5; Saturday R (N.Y.) 37 (12 Jun 1954) 16; Time 63 (5 Apr 1954) 112.

Individual Stories (alphabetical by story title)

499 "An Acquaintance of Hers," New Age n.s. 13 (12 Jun 1913) 179-80.
500 "Anna on the Neck," in Norris Houghton, ed., Great Russian Short Stories (N.Y.: Dell, 1958) pp. 260-74.
501 "At a Country Cottage," English R 4 (Feb 1910) 385. Constance Garnett, tr.
502 "At a Country House," Touchstone (N.Y.) 7 (1920) 126-30, 168,172. Constance Garnett, tr.
503 "At the Call of the Siren," Gourmet 38 (Oct 1978) 30. D. Bider, tr.
504 "At the Cemetery," Athenaeum 153 (13 Aug 1920) 198. S.S. Koteliansky, tr.
505 "At the Mill," Chicago Jewish Forum 5 (1947) 245-8. Avrahm Yarmolinsky, tr.
506 "At the Post Office," Athenaeum 153 (13 Aug 1920) 198-9. S.S. Koteliansky, tr.
507 "An Awkward Situation," in A. E. Chamot, ed., Selected Russian Stories (London: Oxford Univ Pr, 1925). A.E. Chamot, tr.
508 "The Bastard," Double Dealer 6 (Jan 1924) 190-4. Jean Cutner, tr.
509 "The Beggar," Saturday Evening Post 243 (Winter 1971)87.
510 "The Bet," in Barrett H. Clark, ed., Great Short Stories of the World (N.Y.: McBride, 1928).
511 "The Bet," Golden Book 1 (1925) 651-4.
512 "The Bet," in Harry C. Schweikert, ed., Short Stories (N.Y.: Harcourt Brace, 1925).
513 "The Bet," in Thomas Seltzer, ed., Best Russian Short Stories (N.Y.: Boni & Liveright, 1917).
514 "Big Volodia and Little Volodia," Living Age 333 (1927) 910-7.
515 "The Biter Bit," Living Age 213 (1897) 879-82.
516 "The Biter Bit," Temple Bar 111 (May 1897) 104.
517 "Boa Constrictor and Rabbit," Harper's Bazaar, 1952. Avrahm Yarmolinsky. tr.
518 "Boa Constrictor and Rabbit," Nugget, Apr 1956, pp. 6-7.
519 Boys. London: Cohill, n.d. J. Riordan, tr.

520 "Bridegroom and Daddy," Mlle 74 (Dec 1971) 120. A. Ahuja Aks, tr.

521 "A Calculated Marriage," in Guy Daniels, ed., Russian Comic Fiction (N.Y.: New Amer Libr, 1970). Guy Daniels, tr.

522 "The Calumny," New Age n.s. 11 (17 Oct 1912) 591-2. Paul Selver, tr.

523 "A Carp's Love," Story 4 (May 1934) 3-5. William Simonoff, tr.

524 "The Chameleon," New Age n.s. 16 (31 Dec 1914) 220. Paul Selver, tr.

525 "Chat Between Our Special Correspondent and Prince Meshchersky," Soviet Literature no. 10 (1975) 143-8.

526 "The Chemist's Wife" New Age n.s.12 (27 Mar 1913) 502-4.

527 "The Chorus Girl," Golden Book 16 (1932) 113-6. Constance Garnett, tr.

528 "The Chorus Lady," Encore 3 (Mar 1943) 318-23. Bernard G. Guerney, tr.

529 "The Chorus Lady," in Bernard G. Guerney, ed.,A Treasury of Russian Literature (N.Y.: Vanguard, 1943). Bernard G. Guerney, tr.

530 "Chuckles," Spectator,10 Jan 1976, p.18. Benny Green,tr.

531 "The Conqueror's Triumph," Harper's Bazaar (Sep 1958). Frances H. Jones, tr.

532 "Country Holiday," New Statesman and Nation n. s. 15 (1938) 415. Marjorie Hatton, tr.

533 "The Culprit," in Guy Daniels, ed., Russian Comic Fiction (N.Y.: New Amer Libr, 1970). Guy Daniels, tr.

534 "Cure for Hard Drinking," Russian R (N.Y.) 8 (Oct 1949) 334-42. Anna Heifetz, tr.

535 "The Darling," in John Cournos, ed., A Treasury of Russian Life and Humor (N.Y.: Coward-McCann, 1943) pp.613-23. John Cournos, tr.

536 "The Darling," English R 20 (May 1915) 138-50. Constance Garnett, tr.

537 "The Darling," Fortnightly R 86 (1 Sep 1906) 560-8.

538 "The Darling," in Frances Newman, ed., The Short Story's Mutations from Petronius to Paul Morand (N.Y.: Huebsch, 1925) pp. 222-38. Frances Newman, tr.

539 "The Darling," in Thomas Seltzer,ed., Best Russian Short Stories (N.Y.: Boni & Liveright, 1917).

540 "The Darling," Soviet Literature no. 1 (Jan 1980) 28-38. R. Daglish, tr.

541 "Death of a Civil Servant," in Guy Daniels, ed., Russian Comic Fiction (N.Y.: New Amer Libr, 1970). Guy Daniels, tr.

542 "Death of a Government Clerk," Double Dealer 6 (Jan 1924) 7-11. Jean Cutner Stephens, tr.

543 "The Decoration," in Paul M. Fulcher, ed., Short Narratives (N.Y.: Century, 1928).

544 "A Defenseless Creature," in Guy Daniels, ed., Russian Comic Fiction (N.Y. New Amer Libr, 1970). G.Daniels,tr.
545 "Despair," Nation (London) 18 (1 Jan 1916) 505-7. Rochelle S. Townsend, tr.
546 "A Dialogue Between a Man and a Dog," Stratford J 4 (Jun 1919) 291-3. Eugene M. Kayden, tr.
547 "A Digression," in Alfred C. Ward, Aspects of the Modern Short Story (London: Univ of London Pr, 1925).
548 "A Drama," Egoist 3 (1 Jan 1916) 12-3. Natalie Andronikoff & John Hilton, trs.
549 "The Duel," in Four Great Russian Short Novels (N.Y.: Dell, 1959) pp. 275-383. N.H. Dole & Constance Garnett, trs.
550 "The Duel" in Tales vol 1 (N.Y.:Tales Publ Co., 1905).
551 "Dushechka," in Stephen Graham, ed., Great Russian Short Stories (N.Y.: Liveright, 1929). Rosa Graham, tr.
552 "Dushitchka," Pagan (N.Y.) 2 (1917) 3-11.
553 "An Encounter," Tomorrow 9 (1947) 12-7. Avrahm Yarmolinsky, tr.
554 "An Enigmatic Woman," Double Dealer 6 (Jan 1924) 7-11. Jean Cutner Stephens, tr.
555 "The Exclamation Mark," in Guy Daniels, ed.,Russian Comic Fiction (N.Y.: New Amer Libr, 1970). Guy Daniels,tr.
556 "Fat and Thin," Soviet Literature no. 1 (Jan 1980)206-8.
557 A Father. Boston: Branden, n.d. Isaac Goldberg, ed. R.E.C. Long, tr.
558 "First-Class Passenger," Golden Book 17 (1933) 131-6. Constance Garnett, tr.
559 "A Fishy Affair," New Statesman & Nation n.s. 9 (19 Jan 1935) 73-4. Hubert Butler, tr.
560 "The Flying Islands," Fantasy & Science Fiction (Apr 1959). Frances H. Jones, tr.
561 "Fugitive Coffins," Short Stories (Jul 1902) pp. 50-3. Grace Eldredge, tr.
562 "Genius," in Joel Chandler Harris, ed., The World's Wit and Humor vol 14 (N.Y.: R of Reviews, 1906).
563 "A Gentleman Friend," English R 4 (Feb 1910) 387. Constance Garnett, tr.
564 "Gooseberries," in Isai Kamen, ed., Great Russian Stories (N.Y.: Random House, 1959) pp. 237-46.
565 "A Happy Ending," Golden Book 7 (1928) 168-70. Constance Garnett, tr.
566 "A Happy Man," Golden Book 3 (1926) 845-7. Constance Garnett, tr.
567 "Heartache," in Janko Lavrin, ed., A First Series of Representative Russian Stories, Pushkin to Gorky (London: Westhouse, 1946). Walter Morison, tr.
568 "How to Win Other Men's Wives," Graphic 119 (31 Mar 1928) 510. Marianne Ribar & Charles Rideaux, trs.

569 "In a Foreign Land," in Paul Selver, ed., Anthology of Modern Slavonic Literature (London: Paul,Trench & Trubner, 1919). Paul Selver, tr.
570 "In Exile," in Joseph B. Eisenwein, ed., Short Story Masterpieces (Springfield, MA: Home Correspondence School, 1912) vol 16.
571 "In Exile," Fortnightly R 80 (1 Sep 1903) 529-35. R.E.C. Long, tr.
572 "In Exile," in Boris Ilyin et al, eds., The Writer's Art (Boston: Heath, 1950). Boris Ilyin, tr.
573 "In Exile," Lippincott's Monthly 90 (Sep 1912) 363-78. John Cournos, tr.
574 "In Moscow," in Louis S. Friedland, ed., Letters on the Short Story, the Drama & Other Literary Topics, by Anton Chekhov (London: Bles, 1924) pp. 315-23.
575 "In Search of Information," New Age n.s. 11 (4 Jul 1912) 229-30. Paul Selver, tr.
576 "In the Barber's Salon," New Age n.s. 21 (3 May 1917) 19-20. Paul Selver, tr.
577 "In the Coach House," Everyman 4 (26 Jun 1914) 331-2. C.J. Hogarth, tr.
578 "In the Court Room," in Leo Wiener,ed.,Anthology of Russian Literature (N.Y.: Putnam,1903) part 2, pp. 459-67.
579 "Ionych," Soviet Literature no. 1 (Jan 1980) 12-28. S. Henderson, tr.
580 "The Jealous Husband and the Intrepid Lover," Soviet Literature no. 10 (1975) 143-8. A. Miller, tr.
581 "Just for a Lark!" English R 6 (Nov 1910) 625-8.
582 "Kalchas," American Mercury 32 (Aug 1934) 394-7. Bernard G. Guerney, tr.
583 Kashtanka. Chicago: Imported Publications, n.d.
584 Kashtanka. London: Oxford Univ Pr, 1959. Charles Dowsett, tr. Illustrations by William Stobbs. Reviews: Booklist 58 (15 Feb 1962) 375; Bookmark 21 (Nov 1961) 44; Chicago Sunday Tribune, 12 Nov 1961, 2:18; Guardian, 16 Oct 1959, p. 12; Horn Book 38 (Feb 1962) 46; Library J 87 (15 Jan 1962) 329; N.Y.Herald-Trib Books, 12 Nov 1961, p. 8; N.Y.Times Book R, 12 Nov 1961,2:40; New Yorker 37 (18 Nov 1961) 231; San Francisco Chronicle, 3 Dec 1961, p. 36; Saturday R (N.Y.) 44 (16 Dec 1961) 23; Times Literary Supplement, 4 Dec 1959, p. 2.
585 "Kashtanka," New England Magazine 39 (Jan 1909) 564-77.
586 "The Kiss," Golden Book 10 (1929) 27-34. Constance Garnett, tr.
587 "The Kiss," in Isai Kamen, ed., Great Russian Stories (N.Y.: Random House, 1959) pp. 221-36.
588 "The Kiss," in Short Stories by Russian Authors (London: Dent, 1929) pp. 145-72. Rochelle S. Townsend, tr.
589 "La Cigale," in Robert Stallman & Ray B. West, eds., The Art of Modern Fiction (N.Y.: Rinehart, 1949).

590 "The Lady with the Dog," in Norris Houghton, ed., Great Russian Short Stories (N.Y.: Dell, 1958) pp. 242-59.

591 "The Lady with the Little Dog," in C.L. Cline, ed., The Rinehart Book of Short Stories (N.Y.: Holt, Rinehart & Winston, 1964). C.L. Cline, tr.

592 "Late Blooming Flowers," Ladies Home J 80 (Nov 1963) 74-7.

593 "A Lottery Ticket," Encore 12 (1947) 70-3. Bernard G. Guerney, tr.

594 "The Lottery Ticket," New Statesman 1 (3 May 1913)115-6. John Cournos, tr.

595 "The Man in a Case," International Literature (Moscow) no. 8 (1939) 53-61. Constance Garnett, tr.

596 "A Moscow Hamlet," Athenaeum 153 (31 Dec 1920) 882-4. S. S. Koteliansky, tr.

597 "Mouzhiks," in W. Somerset Maugham,ed., Tellers of Tales (N.Y.:Doubleday Doran, 1939) pp.614-39. Alec Brown,tr.

598 "My Life," in Russian Short Stories (London: Faber,1943) pp. 257-343.

599 My Life. London: Staples & Staples, 1943. E. R. Schimanskaya, tr.

600 "A Naughty Boy," in Paul M. Fulcher, ed., Short Narratives (N.Y.: Century, 1928).

601 "Newspaper Reports," Soviet Literature no. 10 (1975) 143-8. A. Miller, tr.

602 "The Night Before the Trial," American Mercury 63 (Dec 1946) 684-8. Anna Heifetz, tr.

603 "Night in the Cemetery," Mlle 74 (Dec 1971) 118-9. A. Ahuja Aks, tr.

604 "Old Age," Nation (London) 12 (8 Feb 1913) 779-80. Sasha Kropotkin, tr.

605 "On the Way," in Stephen Graham,ed., Great Russian Short Stories (N.Y.: Liveright, 1929). Marian Fell, tr.

606 "On the Way," in Boris Ilyin et al, eds., The Writer's Art (Boston: Heath, 1950). Boris Ilyin, tr.

607 "The Orator," in Janko Lavrin, ed., Russian Humorous Stories (London: Sylvan Pr, 1946).

608 "Out of Sorts," in Paul M. Fulcher, ed., Short Narratives (N.Y.: Century, 1928).

609 "Philosophy at Home," Short Stories (Oct 1891), pp. 64-72. Isabel F. Hapgood, tr.

610 "A Play," New Statesman 5 (18 Sep 1915) 566-8. Constance Garnett, tr.

611 "The Post," New Age n.s. 4 (8 Apr 1909) 481-2. Fanny Stepniak & Rochelle S. Townsend, trs.

612 "The Requiem," Golden Book 20 (1934) 203-6.

613 "A Russian Cabman," Everyman 1 (22 Nov 1912) 178-9.

614 "The Safety Match," in Sherwin Cody, ed., Continental Classics (N.Y.: Harper, 1909) vol 18, pp. 157-79.

615 "The Safety Match," in Julian Hawthorne, ed., Library of the World's Best Mystery and Detective Stories (N.Y.: R of Reviews, 1908).
616 "The Safety Match," in Janko Lavrin, ed., Russian Humorous Stories (London: Sylvan Pr, 1946).
617 "The Second Bet," Golden Book 14 (Aug 1931) 15-7. Janka Karsavina, tr.
618 "The Siren," American Mercury 64 (Mar 1927) 354-8. Avrahm Yarmolinsky, tr.
619 "The Sister," in Richard Garnett, ed., The Universal Anthology (London: Clarke, 1899) vol 31, pp. 398-403.
620 "A Slander," New Statesman 4 (6 Mar 1915) 535-6. Constance Garnett, tr.
621 "The Slanderer," N.Y.Call, 27 Dec 1914, magazine section. Rochelle S.Townsend, tr.
622 "The Slanderer," in William Patten, ed., Short Story Classics (N.Y.: Collier, 1907) vol 1. Herman Bernstein, tr.
623 "Sleepy," Golden Book 20 (1934) 709-14.
624 "Sleepy," in Russian Stories (N.Y.: Bantam, 1961). Gleb Struve & Mary Struve, trs.
625 "Sleepy Eye," Cosmopolitan 41 (Jun 1906) 151-6.
626 "Sleepy Head," International Socialist R (Chicago) 17 (1917) 492-4. R.E.C. Long, tr.
627 "Sorrow," Living Age 213 (1897) 882-5.
628 "Sorrow," Temple Bar 111 (May 1897) 108.
629 "The Speechmaker," in Guy Daniels, ed., Russian Comic Fiction (N.Y.: New Amer Libr, 1970). Guy Daniels, tr.
630 "The Stepmother," Soviet Literature no. 10 (1975) 143-8. A. Miller, tr.
631 "The Story of a Commercial Venture," New Statesman & Nation n.s. 6 (8 Jul 1933) 44-5.
632 "The Story of Natalia Vladimirovna," Everyman 4 (17 Jul 1914) 433-5. C.J. Hogarth, tr.
633 "A Street Scene in Russia," Canadian Magazine 24 (Apr 1905) 556-7.
634 "The Student," New Statesman 1 (16 Aug 1913) 594-5. John Cournos, tr.
635 "Surgery," Russian R (N.Y.) 8 (Oct 1949) 334-42. Anna Heifetz, tr.
636 "The Teetotallers," New Age n.s. 16 (26 Nov 1914) 94-5. Paul Selver, tr.
637 "A Terrible Night," Current Literature 42 (Jan 1907)112.
638 "The Terrible Wager," in Famous Russian Short Stories (South Croyden,England: Blue Book Co., n.d.) pp. 50-5.
639 "That Hateful Boy," English R 4 (Feb 1910) 390. Constance Garnett, tr.
640 "The Thieves," in A. E. Chamot, ed., Selected Russian Stories (London: Oxford Univ Pr, 1925). A.E. Chamot,tr.

641 Three Years. Moscow: Foreign Languages Publish. House, 1958. Rose Prokofieva, tr.
642 "To Speak or Be Silent," Nation (N.Y.) 179 (18 Sep 1954) 232. Leona Eisele, tr.
643 "A Trifle from Life," Golden Book 18 (1933) 235-8.
644 "Trouble," Russian R (N.Y.) 1 (May 1916) 218-24.
645 "The Trousseau," Touchstone (N.Y.) 1 (1917) 376-80. Constance Garnett, tr.
646 "An Unpleasantness," Charm (1952).Avrahm Yarmolinsky,tr.
647 "Unsuccess," New Statesman & Nation n.s. 9 (13 Apr 1935) 521. Marjorie Hatton, tr.
648 "An Upheaval," in Milton Crane, ed., Fifty Great Short Stories (N.Y.: Bantam, 1959) pp. 296-302.
649 "Useless Lessons," New Age n.s. 7 (13 Oct 1910) 564-5. Helen Brayne, tr.
650 "Vanka," in Isai Kamen, ed.,Great Russian Stories (N.Y.: Random House, 1959) pp. 217-20.
651 "Vanka," in Thomas Seltzer, ed., Best Russian Short Stories (N.Y.: Boni & Liveright, 1917).
652 "Vanka," World Review (Mt. Morris, IL) 7 (1928) 41.
653 "Vankya," [sic] in Eric Posselt, ed., The World's Greatest Christmas (N.Y.: Prentice-Hall, 1950). Eric Posselt, tr.
654 "A Visit to Friends," in Avrahm Yarmolinsky, tr., The Cherry Orchard (see #186). I.C. Chertok & Jean Gardner, trs.
655 "Ward No. 6," in Bernard G. Guerney, ed., The Portable Russian Reader (N.Y.: Viking, 1947). B. G. Guerney, tr.
656 "Ward No. 6," in Leo Hamilton & Vera von Wiren-Garczynski, eds., Seven Russian Short Novel Masterpieces (Popular Library, n.d.).
657 White Star. Drawings by N. Char. 1980.
658 "Who is to Blame?" in Guy Daniels, ed., Russian Comic Fiction (N.Y.: New Amer Libr, 1970). Guy Daniels, tr.
659 "A Wicked Boy," in Roger B. Goodman, ed., Seventy Five Short Masterpieces (N.Y.: Bantam,1961). Helen Reeve,tr.
660 Wife for Sale. London: Calder, 1959. David Tutaev, tr.
661 "Wife for Sale," in Three Great Classics (N.Y.: Arc, 1964). David Tutaev, tr.
662 The Wolf and the Mutt. Originally called "Belolobyy." N.Y.: McGraw-Hill, 1971. Guy Daniels, tr.
663 "Woman's Luck," Mlle 74 (Dec 1971) 121. A. Ahuja Aks,tr.
664 "A Work of Art," Encore 3 (Jan 1943) 5-8. B. Guerney,tr.
665 "The Work of Art," Golden Book 14 (1931) 402-4. Constance Garnett, tr.
666 "A Work of Art," New Age n.s. 11 (29 Aug 1912) 425-6. Paul Selver, tr.
667 "A Work of Art," Short Stories (Jan 1906) pp.53-6. Archibald J. Wolfe, tr.
668 "Zinotchka," Golden Book 21 (1935) 331-4.

Part II

Works about Anton Chekhov in English

Articles (alphabetical by author)

669 Aaron, J. "Three Sisters," Educational Theatre J 28 (Dec 1976) 556-7.

670 Academy 58 (3 Mar 1900) 175 (discusses Russian Academy of Letters).

671 Academy 79 (20 Aug 1910) 175 (Chekhov is a master of the short story).

672 Adler, Henry. London Mercury 39 (Nov 1938) 47-55 (Michel Saint-Denis showed the value of the Stanislavsky method in staging The Three Sisters).

673 ------. New English Weekly 9 (8 Oct 1936) 437 (the plays of Chekhov & Turgenev contain hidden social meaning).

674 Aiken, Conrad. Freeman 3 (6 Apr 1921) 90-2 (a detailed analysis of Chekhov's fictional technique).

675 ------. Freeman 3 (11 May 1921) 210-1 (Katherine Mansfield learned from Chekhov that a short story is not the narration of an action but the quintessence of a human life).

676 ------. Freeman 5 (21 Jun 1922) 357-8 (Chekhov's larger awareness makes his personality less noticeable in stories than is Katherine Mansfield's).

677 Aldanov, Marc. "Reflections on Chekhov," Russian R (N. Y.) 14 (Apr 1955) 83-92.

678 Allio, Rene. See #1322.

679 Argus, M.K. "Ivanov: Autobiographical Link," Saturday R (London) 49 (7 May 1966) 10.

680 Asahina, R. Hudson R 34 (Spring 1981) 99-104.

681 Athenaeum, 23 Jan 1920, p. 124; 6 Feb 1920, p. 191.

682 Atkinson, J. Brooks. N.Y.Times, 11 Mar 1928, 8:1.

683 ------. "Amazing Paradox," N.Y.Times, 8 Mar 1959, 2:1.

684 ------. "Enshrining Chekhov," N.Y.Times, 2 Jun 1929,8:1.

685 d'Auvergne, Jean. "The Moscow Art Theatre," Fortnightly R n.s. 95 (1 May 1914) 793-803.

686 Avengno, Hamilton. Xavier Univ Studies 1 (1961-62) 219.

687 Avilova, Lydia. "Chekhov in My Life," Soviet Literature no. 1 (Jan 1980) 7-90.

688 Azadovsky, K. & S. Vitale. "Chekhov in Berlin and Badenweiler," Soviet Literature no. 1 (Jan 1980) 132-9.

689 Babotchkine, B. See #1322.

690 Babula, William. "Three Sisters, Time, and the Audience," Modern Drama 18 (Dec 1975) 365-9.

691 Baehr, Stephen L. "Who Is Firs? The Literary History of a Name," Ulbandus R 2 (Fall 1979) 14-23.
692 Bailey, L.W. "From Wood Demon to Uncle Vanya," Drama no. 145 (Autumn 1982) 14-5.
693 Bakshy, Alexander. Drama, Feb 1919, pp. 31-61 (Moscow Art Theatre productions of Chekhov's plays).
694 Balmont, Constantine. Athenaeum, 2 Jul 1898, p.25; 1 Jul 1899, p. 26; 7 Jul 1900, p. 24.
695 Barber, John. "Acting Out of Character," Daily Telegraph (London), 17 May 1976, p. 9.
696 ------. "Chekhov and Hardy Caught by Change," Daily Telegraph (London), 28 Feb 1977, p. 9.
697 ------. "A More Cheerful Chekhov," Daily Telegraph (London), 12 Jun 1972, p. 9.
698 Barrault, J.L. See #1322.
699 Barricelli, Jean-Pierre. "Counterpoint of the Snapping String: Chekhov's The Cherry Orchard," California Slavic Studies 10 (1977) 121-36.
700 Basu, Amar & Sankar Basu. "Author's Voice in 'Ward No. 6'," Journal of the School of Languages 7 (1980 Monsoon-1981 Winter) 41-7.
701 Bateman, May. Fortnightly R n.s. 107 (1 May 1920)808-16.
702 Bates, Herbert E. Life and Letters Today 31 (Oct 1941) 4-21 (By not ridiculing his characters, Chekhov excels Maupassant as a short-story writer).
703 Bayuk, M. "Submissive Wife Stereotype in Anton Chekhov's 'Darling'," College Language Assn J 20 (Jun 1977)533-8.
704 Beckerman, Bernard. "Artifice of Reality in Chekhov and Pinter," Modern Drama 21 (Jun 1978) 153-61.
705 Beeson, B. Barker. "Anton Tchekhov, A Resume of His Works and His Career," Annals of Medical History n.s. 3 (1931) 603-18.
706 Belgion, Montgomery. "Verisimilitude in Tchekhov and Dostoievsky," Criterion 16 (Oct 1936) 14-32.
707 Benavente, S. See #1322.
708 Bentley, Eric. "Chekhov as Playwright," Kenyon R 11 (Spring 1949) 226-50.
709 Berdnikov, G. "Chekhov and Our Time," Soviet Literature no. 1 (Jan 1980) 3-11.
710 Bernstein, Herman. Nation (London) 75 (17 Jul 1902) 52.
711 Berthoff, A.E. "Recognizing and Interpreting Metaphor," Sewanee R 89 (Winter 1981) 57-82.
712 Bill, V.T. "Nature in Chekhov's Fiction," Russian R (N. Y.) 33 (Apr 1974) 153-66.
713 Birrell, Francis. Nation & Athenaeum 39 (4 Sep 1926) 640 (praises Komisarjevsky's staging of Chekhov's plays).
714 Bogayevskaya, K. "Tolstoy on Chekhov: Previously Unknown Comments," Soviet Literature no. 1 (1980) 40-4.
715 Bogdanovitch, L.A. de. Athenaeum, 3 Jul 1897, pp. 27-8 (discusses "The Peasants").

716 Booker, Christopher. "Mirror of Our Melancholy," Daily Telegraph (London), 26 Feb 1977, p. 10.
717 Bookman (N.Y.) 53 (Jun 1921) 343 (reviews Constance Garnett's translations).
718 ------. 54 (Feb 1922) 588 (reviews Reminiscences by Gorky, Bunin, and Kuprin).
719 ------. 62 (Oct 1925) 174 (resents D.S. Mirsky's attack on Chekhov).
720 ------. 62 (Jan 1926) 580-1.
721 ------. 62 (Feb 1926) 641, 700-1 (discusses Chekhov's plays in London).
722 Bordinat, Philip. "Chekhov's Two Great American Directors," Midwest Q 16 (Oct 1974) 70-84.
723 ------. "Dramatic Structure in Chekhov's Uncle Vanya," Slavic & East European J 16 (Fall 1958) 195-210.
724 Borker, David & Olga K. Garnica. "Male and Female Speech in Dramatic Dialogue:A Stylistic Analysis of Chekhovian Character Speech," Language & Style 13 (1980) 3-28.
725 Boyd, Ernest. Independent 116 (27 Feb 1926) 249 (resents D.S. Mirsky's attack on Chekhov).
726 Brahms, Caryl. "Chekhov, the Dramatist of Farewells," Times (London), 23 May 1966, p. 7.
727 Brandon, James R. "Toward a Middle View of Chekhov," Educational Theatre J 12 (Dec 1960) 270-5.
728 Brewster, Dorothy. "Chekhov in England and America," Masses & Mainstream 7 (Jul 1954) 35-41.
729 Brinton, Christian. Critic 45 (Oct 1904) 318-20 (obituary notice).
730 Bristow, Eugene K. "On Translating Chekhov," Q J of Speech 52 (Oct 1966) 290-4.
731 Brock, H. I. N.Y.Times, 28 Oct 1928, 5:16 (Moscow Art Theatre visit to America).
732 Brown, John Mason. "Chekhov as a Critic," Theatre Arts Monthly 9 (Jan 1925) 67.
733 Brustein, Robert S. "Ivanov," Hudson R 12 (Spring 1959) 94-101.
734 Bryden, Ronald. "Chekhov: Secret of The Sea Gull," Observer (London), 31 May 1970, pp. 10-20.
735 Bryusov, Valery. Athenaeum, 20 July 1901, p. 86; 3 Sep 1904, pp. 312-4.
736 Bunin, Ivan. "Chekhov," Atlantic 188 (Jul 1951) 59-63.
737 Burgum, E. "Chekhov the Optimist," VOKS Bulletin(Moscow) 3 (1954) 65-6.
738 Burnham, D. "Spokesman for the Central Importance of the Human Spirit," Commonweal 60 (25 Jun 1954) 300.
739 Burns, John F. N.Y.Times, 15 Jul 1984, 10:9 (Chekhov memorials in Yalta).
740 Cahan, Abraham. "The Mantle of Tolstoy," Bookman (N.Y.) 16 (Dec 1902) 328-33.

741 ------. Forum 28 (Sep 1899) 119-28 (first American appraisal of Chekhov's tales).
742 Calderon, George. "Beauties of Russian Literature," Proceedings of the Anglo-Russian Literary Society (London) 1905, pp. 22-3.
743 Calendar 3 (Oct 1926) 260 (review of D.S. Mirsky's Contemporary Russian Literature).
744 Campbell, Archibald Y. London Mercury 12 (Sep 1925) 551.
745 Canby, Henry Seidel. Atlantic 116 (Jul 1915) 60-8 (recommends Chekhov to American writers because of his "freedom").
746 Carpenter, Bruce. "Chekoviana," Theatre Time, Winter 1951, pp. 12-5.
747 Carr, E. H. "Chekhov: Twenty-Five Years After," Spectator 143 (20 Jul 1929) 72-3.
748 Carter, Huntly.Fortnightly R n.s.123 (2 Jan 1928) 58-71.
749 ------. New Age n.s. 10 (25 Apr 1912) 619.
750 Chambers, C. Plays and Players 26 (Mar 1979) 36 (Three Sisters in East Berlin).
751 Chances, Ellen. "Cexov and Xarms: Story/Anti-Story,"Russian Language J 36 (Winter-Spring 1982) 181-92.
752 Chekhov, Alexander. "My Brother at Home," Living Age 330 (10 Jul 1926) 115-7.
753 Chifrine, N. See #1322.
754 Childs, J. Rives. "Chekhov's 'The Bet'," South Atlantic Q 40 (Oct 1941) 397-400.
755 Christa, Boris. "The Interplay of Traditional and Symbolistic Elements in Chekhov's Last Plays," Australasian Universities Lang & Lit Assn Proceedings,1963, pp.20-1.
756 Chudakov, A. P. "The Poetics of Chekhov: The Sphere of Ideas," New Literary History 9 (Winter 1978) 353-80.
757 ------. "Newly Discovered Works by the Young Chekhov," Soviet Literature no. 10 (1975) 134-42.
758 Chukovsky, Kornei. "Friend Chekhov," Atlantic 180 (Sep 1947) 84-90.
759 Clark, Barrett H. Drama 13 (Jan 1923) 136-7 (Moscow Art Theatre productions of Chekhov's plays in Berlin).
760 ------. Drama 20 (May 1930) 234 (Chekhov's plays are quite dull).
761 Clemons, W. "Getting Chekhov Straight," Newsweek 81 (25 Jun 1973) 87.
762 Clurman, Harold. "The Sea Gull," TV Guide, 25 Jan 1975, 19-20.
763 Clyman, Toby W. "Chekhov's Victimized Women," Russian Language J 28 (Spring 1974) 26-31.
764 Collins, H. P. "Chekhov: The Last Phase," Contemporary R 186 (Jul 1954) 37-41.
765 Conrad, Joseph L."Cexov's 'An Attack of Nerves'," Slavic & East European J 13 (1969) 429-43.

766 ------. "Cexov's 'The Man in a Shell': Freedom and Responsibility," Slavic & East European J 10 (1966) 400-10.
767 ------. "Cexov's "Verocka": A Polemical Parody," Slavic & East European J 14 (Winter 1970) 465-74.
768 ------. "Sensuality in Cexov's Prose," Slavic & East European J 24 (Summer 1980) 103-17.
769 ------. "Unresolved Tension in Cexov's Stories,1886-88," Slavic & East European J 16 (Spring 1972) 55-64.
770 Conroy, Geraldine L. Modern Fiction Studies 24 (Autumn 1978) 355-67 (discusses translations of Chekhov's works by S.S. Koteliansky & Katherine Mansfield).
771 Corbin, John. N.Y.Times, 4 Feb 1923, 7:1.
772 Corrigan, Robert W. "Some Aspects of Chekhov's Dramaturgy," Educational Theatre J 7 (May 1955) 107-14.
773 ------. "Stanislavsky and the Playwright," Tulane Drama R 2 (Feb 1958) 62-70.
774 Cosmopolitan 41 (Jun 1906) 151-6 (discusses "Sleepy Eye").
775 Costa, O. See #1322.
776 Cournos, John. Criterion 15 (Oct 1935) 175-82 (Chekhov on the Soviet stage).
777 ------. Everyman 14 (6 Sep 1919) 517-8.
778 Courtney, W.L. Quarterly R 219 (Jul 1913) 80-103 (Chekhov can help English drama escape from its doldrums).
779 Critical Digest 28 (15 Nov 1976) 5 (A.B. Gurney identified as "an abounding Chekhovian playwriting talent").
780 Cross, A.G. "The Breaking String of Chekhov and Turgenev," Slavonic & East European R 47 (Jul 1969) 510-3.
781 Croyden, Margaret. "The Absurdity of Chekhov's Doctors," Texas Q 11 (Autumn 1968) 130-7.
782 Current Literature 42 (Jan 1907) 112-4 (discusses story "A Terrible Night").
783 Current Opinion 63 (Sep 1917) 192.
784 Curtin, Constance. "Cexov's 'Sleepy':An Interpretation," Slavic & East European J 9 (Winter 1965) 390-9.
785 Curtis, James M. "Spatial Form in Drama: The Sea Gull," Canadian-American Slavic Studies 6 (1972) 13-37.
786 Curtis, Penelope. "Chekhov," Quadrant 16(Jun 1972)13-22.
787 Deer, Irving. "Speech as Action in The Cherry Orchard," Educational Theatre J 10 (Mar 1958) 30-4.
788 Delp, W. E. "Goethe's Tasso in the Light of Chekhov," Comparative Literature Studies 12 (1944) 5-8.
789 Dewhurst, K. "Anton Chekhov:Pioneer in Social Medicine," J of the History of Medicine and Allied Sciences 10 (Jan 1955) 1-16.
790 Dial 65 (30 Nov 1918) 498-9 (effect of Russian revolution upon American readers).
791 Dillon, E.J. "Recent Russian Literature," R of Reviews 4 (Jul 1891) 79-83.

792 Dobree, Bonamy. "Drama and Values," New Statesman 14 (8 Nov 1919) 161-2.

793 ------. New Statesman 14 (3 Jan 1920) 379-80 (Chekhov's plays are dramatic for they are full of revelation).

794 ------. "Tchekov, King of Amateurs," Theatre (Bradford, England), Winter 1945-46, pp. 5-12.

795 Doyle, P.A. "Chekhov in Erin," Dublin R 241(Autumn 1967) 263-9 (Sean O'Faolain is seen as Chekhovian).

796 Dramatist 6 (Jul 1915) 590-1 (The Cherry Orchard is "the antithesis of drama").

797 Durkin, Andrew R. "Chekhov's Response to Dostoevski: The Case of Ward Six," Slavic R 40 (Spring 1981) 49-59.

798 Eaton, Walter Prichard. N.Y.Herald-Tribune Books, 17 Jan 1938, p. 3.

799 Eekman, T.A. "The Narrator and the Hero in Chekhov's Prose," California Slavic Studies 8 (1975) 93-129.

800 Efros, N. Russian R (London) 1 (1912) 141-52 (Moscow Art Theatre productions of Chekhov's plays).

801 Egri, Peter. "The Dramatic Function of the Mosaic Design in Chekhov's Late Plays," Acta Litteraria Academiae Scientarum Hungaricae 21 (1979) 45-68.

802 ------. "The Reinterpretation of the Chekhovian Mosaic Design in O'Neill's Long Day's Journey into Night,"Acta Litteraria Academiae Scientarum Hungaricae 22 (1980) 29-71.

803 ------. "The Short Story in the Drama: Chekhov and O'Neill," Acta Litteraria Academiae Scientarum Hungaricae 20 (1978) 3-28.

804 ------. "A Touch of the Story-Teller: The Dramatic Function of the Short Story Model in Chekhov's Uncle Vanya and O'Neill's A Touch of the Poet," Angol Filologiai Tanulmanyok 13 (1980) 93-115.

805 Ehre, Milton. "The Symbolic Structure of Chekhov's 'Gusev'," Ulbandus R 2 (Fall 1979) 76-85.

806 Elvgren, Gillette, Jr. "Peter Terson's Vale of Evesham," Modern Drama 18 (Mar 1975) 185-6 (Terson acknowledges his indebtedness to Chekhov).

807 Emeljanow, Victor. "Komisarjevsky Directs Chekhov in London," Theatre Notebook 37 (1983) 66-77.

808 Emmet, Alfred. "Head or Heart: The Actor's Dilemma," Theatre Q 5 (Jun-Aug 1975) 20 (3 of Emmet's most treasured theatrical moments, which show how complex and subtle human emotions are, came in the London productions of The Three Sisters in 1938, the Moscow Art Theatre Uncle Vanya in 1958, and The Three Sisters in 1958).

809 Erlich, Victor, ed. "Chekhov and West European Drama: A Symposium," Yearbook of Comparative Literature 12 (1963) 56-60.

810 Ermilov, V. "A.P. Chekhov," VOKS Bulletin (Moscow) 3 (1954) 29-34.
811 Esenwein, J. Berg. "Chekhov:Recorder of Lost Illusions," Lippincott's Monthly 90 (Sep 1912) 363-78.
812 Esterow, Milton."With Uncle Vanya from Stage to Screen," N.Y.Times, 24 Jun 1956, 2:5.
813 Everyman 12 (1 Jun 1918) 182 (Chekhov accurately depicts immaturity in the Russian character).
814 Evtushenko, E. "Steppe Has Spoken," Soviet Literature no. 1 (1979) 182-4.
815 Fagin, N. "In Search of an American Cherry Orchard," Texas Q 1 (Summer-Autumn 1958) 132-42.
816 Fagin, N. Bryllion. "Anton Chekhov: The Master of the Gray Short-Story," Poet Lore 32 (Autumn 1921) 416-24.
817 Falkland, Charles. "Tolstoy on Chekhov," Listener 8 (Sep 1932) 342.
818 Fallon, Gabriel. "Sea Change and Tchehov," Irish Monthly 68 (Jul 1940) 386-90.
819 Fausset, Hugh. "Tchehov as Lover," Bookman (London) 69 (1926) 315-6.
820 Fen, Elisaveta. "Getting to Know Chekhov," N.Y.Times, 5 Oct 1958, 2:3.
821 Fergusson, Francis. Bookman (N.Y.) 74 (Nov 1931) 298-9 (similarity between Chekhov and Paul Green).
822 Fernald, J. "Chekhov on the English Stage," VOKS Bulletin (Moscow) 86 (May-Jun 1954) 59-60.
823 ------. See #1322.
824 Ferrero, M. See #1322.
825 Filipp, Valerie. "Forms and Functions of Address in Cexov's Plays: A Suggested Classification," Russian Language J 116 (1979) 84-91.
826 FitzLyon, Kyril. Times Literary Supplement, 24 Sep 1982, p. 1044a (review of The Early Stories).
827 Flanagan, Hallie. Theatre Arts Monthly 12 (Jan 1928) 70 (review of 3 productions of The Proposal at Vassar).
828 Fludas, John. "Chekhovian Comedy: A Review Essay," Genre 6 (Sep 1973) 333-46.
829 Fodor, Alexander. "In Search of a Soviet Chekhov," J of Russian Studies 21 (1971) 9-19.
830 Fortnightly R n.s. 121 (1 Jan 1927) 143 (review of D.S. Mirsky's Contemporary Russian Literature).
831 Fovitzky, A.L. "Anton Tchekhoff as Teacher," N.Y.Times, 4 Feb 1923, 7:2.
832 Franklin, Olga. "Chekhov's Leading Lady," Listener 95 (1 Apr 1976) 418-9.
833 Freedman, Morris. "Chekhov's Morality of Work," Modern Drama 5 (May 1962) 83-93.
834 Freeman 4 (19 Oct 1921) 122 (Chekhov's Yalta home made into a museum).

835 Freeman, Gwendolen. Spectator 177 (29 Nov 1946) 588.
836 Freeman, John. London Mercury 14 (Oct 1926) 654 (review of D.S. Mirsky's Contemporary Russian Literature).
837 Freling, R. "New View of Dr. Dymov in Chekhov's 'The Grasshopper'," Studies in Short Fiction 16 (Summer 1979) 183-7.
838 Friedland, Louis S. Dial 63 (19 Jul 1917) 47-8.
839 Frost, Edgar L. "The Search for Eternity in Cexov's Fiction: The Flight from Time as a Source of Tension," Russian Language J 32 (1977) 111-20.
840 Frydman, Anne. "'Enemies': An Experimental Story," Ulbandus R 2 (Fall 1979) 103-19.
841 Fyfe, Hamilton. "Chekoff and Modern Russia," English R 24 (May 1917) 408-14.
842 Galsworthy, John. English R 55 (Nov 1932) 488-91.
843 Ganz, Arthur. "Arrivals and Departures: The Meaning of the Journey in the Major Plays of Chekhov," Drama Survey 5 (Spring 1966) 5-23.
844 Garnett, Edward. "Tchehov and His Art," Quarterly R 236 (Oct 1921) 257-69.
845 Gates, Barrington. Nation & Athenaeum 41(30 Apr 1927)116.
846 Gavrikova, I. "New Additions to the Chekhov Exhibits at the Museum of Literature," Soviet Literature no. 1 (Jan 1980) 140-2.
847 Gerhardi, William. "Anton Chehov: The Secret of His Literary Power," Forum 70 (Nov 1923) 2144-8.
848 ------. Listener 63 (21 Jan 1960) 121-2 (the space-time continuum in Chekhov).
849 Gerould, Daniel C. "The Cherry Orchard as Comedy," J of General Education 11 (Jan 1958) 109-22.
850 Gilman, Richard. "Broadway Critics Meet Uncle Vanya," Theatre Q 4 (Feb-Apr 1974) 67-72.
851 Gohdes, Clarence. South Atlantic Q 43 (Apr 1944) 209 (Chekhov is America's Poe and Hawthorne combined).
852 Goldberg, L. "Chekhov's Comedy The Cherry Orchard," Scripta Hierosolymitana 19 (1967) 100-25.
853 Gordon, Caroline. "Notes on Chekhov and Maugham," Sewanee R 57 (Summer 1949) 401-10.
854 Gorky, Maxim. "Anton Pavlovich Chekhov," Soviet Literature no. 1 (Jan 1980) 45-61.
855 ------. "Personal Recollections of Anton Pavlovich Chekhov," Independent 59 (10 Aug 1905) 299-304.
856 ------. "Recollections of Chekhov," Encore 3 (May 1943) 535-9.
857 ------. "Recollections of Chekhov," Freeman 3 (25 May, 1 Jun, 8 Jun, 1921) 251-2, 275-6, 298-300.
858 ------. "What Tchekhof Thought of It," English R 8 (May 1911) 256-66.
859 Gotman, Sonia K. "The Role of Irony in Cexov's Fiction," Slavic & East European J 16 (Fall 1972) 297-306.

860 Gould, Gerald. Observer (London), 8 Jan 1928, p. 7.
861 Graaf, Frances de. "Interpreting Chekhov To American Students," Bulletin of the American Assn of Teachers of Slavic & East European Languages 10 (1953) 42-5.
862 Graham, R. Gore. "Anton Chehov:The Myth of Objectivity," Socialist R (London) n.s. 28 (1928) 47-9.
863 Granville-Barker, Harley. Seven Arts, Sep 1917, p. 659.
864 Grein, J.T. "Komisarjevsky on Tchekhov," Illustrated London News 78 (16 Jan 1926) 104.
865 Grieve, C.M. New Age 37 (25 Jun 1925) 92 (review of D.S. Mirsky's Modern Russian Literature).
866 Griffith, Hubert. Fortnightly R 142 (Oct 1934) 437-45 ("Chekhov nearly played Shakespeare off the stage of his own theater").
867 ------. New Statesman & Nation n.s. 8 (15 Sep 1934) 325-6 (review of Moscow Art Theatre productions of Chekhov in Moscow).
868 Gruber, W.E. "Chekhov's Illusion of Inaction," College Language Assn J 20 (Jun 1977) 508-20.
869 Gruen, John. "The Avant-Garde Discovers Chekhov," N.Y. Times, 5 Jan 1975, 2:5.
870 Gulli Pugliatti, Paolo. "The Distribution of Implicit Information in the Opening Scenes of Dramatic Texts," Lingua e Stile 16 (1981) 481-93 (examples from Chekhov, Ibsen, and Osborne).
871 Gussow, Mel. "Peter Brook Returns to Chekhov's Vision," N.Y.Times, 9 Aug 1981, 4:3.
872 ------. "Theater: Three Sisters in Translation by Jarrell," N.Y.Times, 19 Feb 1984, p. 44.
873 Hagan, John. "Chekhov's Fiction and the Ideal of 'Objectivity'," PMLA 81 (Oct 1966) 409-17.
874 ------. "The Shooting Party, Chekhov's Early Novel: Its Place in His Development," Slavic & East European J 9 (1965) 123-40.
875 ------. "The Tragic Sense in Chekhov's Earliest Stories," Criticism 7 (Winter 1965) 52-80.
876 Hahn, Beverly. "Chekhov: The Cherry Orchard," Critical R (Melbourne) 16 (1973) 56-72.
877 ------. "Chekhov: The Three Sisters," Critical R (Melbourne) 15 (1972) 3-22.
878 Hainaux, R. See #1322.
879 Halward, Leslie. London Mercury 37 (Mar 1938) 515-8.
880 Hankin, St. John. Academy 72 (15 Jun 1907) 585 (Chekhov's plays avoid melodrama in favor of realistic character depiction).
881 Hanuszkiewicz, A. "Dialogue about Chekhov," Soviet Literature no. 2 (1978) 161-5.
882 Harris, H. J. "Shaw, Chekhov, & Two Great Ladies of the Theater," Shaw R 6 (1963) 96-9 (S.Bernhardt & E. Duse).

883 Harris, Jed. "Jed Harris Remembers His Uncle Vanya," N.Y.Times, 23 Jul 1972, 2:1.
884 Harris, W. Best. "Tchekov and the Russian Drama," Annual Reports & Transactions of Plymouth Institution and Devon & Cornwall Natural History Society 21 (1947-49) 141-50.
885 Harrison, John W. "Symbolic Action in Chekhov's 'Peasants' and 'In the Ravine'," Modern Fiction Studies 7 (Winter 1961) 369-72.
886 Harrop, John. Theatre Arts 8 (Autumn 1978) 89-91 (Harrop discusses the Actors Studio production of The Three Sisters in New York City in 1964).
887 Hatch, R. Nation (N.Y.) 181 (2 Jul 1955) 18-9.
888 Hayes, Richard. "Ibsen and Chekhov," Commonweal 62 (6 May 1955) 127.
889 Heath, Frederick. Bermondsey Book 5 (Mar-May 1928) 98-100 (Chekhov makes the commonplace fascinating).
890 Hellweg, J.D. & S.A. Hellweg. "The Sea Gull: A Communicative Analysis of Chekhovian Drama," Communication Q 30 (Spring 1982) 150-4.
891 Hesperian 4 (Oct-Dec 1905) 594 (says Chekhov defended Russia's "decadent" writers).
892 Hewitt, Barnard. "The Cherry Orchard," High School Thespian, Mar 1943, pp. 7-8.
893 Hichliffe, A. "Chekhov As I See Him," Soviet Literature no. 1 (Jan 1980) 196-9.
894 Hingley, Ronald. "Chekhov and the Art of Translation," Cambridge R, 1 May 1965.
895 ------. "Cutting Chekhov," Spectator 236(21 Feb 1976)26.
896 ------. "Two Anton Chekhovs," Times Literary Supplement, 7 May 1976, p. 556a.
897 Hoare, S. "Anton Tchehov," Golden Hind 2 (Oct 1923)9-14.
898 Holland, Peter. "The Dramatist as Doctor," Times Literary Supplement, 14 Nov 1980, p. 1306.
899 Holmberg, Arthur. Theatre J 31 (Dec 1979) 541-2.
900 Hood, Stuart. "The Englishman's Chekhov," Spectator, 1 Mar 1968, pp. 265-6.
901 Hopkins, Gerard. Chapbook 2 (Feb 1920) 25-32 (Turgenev excels Chekhov as a short-story writer).
902 Hoppe, Harry R. "Form in Chekhov's Short Stories," Univ of California Chronicle 34 (1932) 62-7.
903 Houghton, Norris. See #1322.
904 Howard, Leslie. N.Y.Times, 13 May 1951, 2:3.
905 Howarth, Herbert. "Chekhov on Work," Adelphi 12 (Aug 1936) 309-11.
906 Howe, Irving. Nation (N.Y.) 166 (22 May 1948) 581-3.
907 Hubbs, Clayton A. "Chekhov and the Contemporary Theatre," Modern Drama 24 (Sep 1981) 357-66.
908 ------. "Chekhovian Ritual in the Avant-Garde Theatre," Dissertation Abstracts International 32 (1972) 2692a.

909 ------. "The Function of Repetition in the Plays of Chekhov," Modern Drama 22 (Jun 1979) 115-24.
910 ------. & Joanna T. Hubbs. "The Goddess of Love and the Tree of Knowledge: Some Elements of Myth and Folklore in Chekhov's The Cherry Orchard," South Carolina R 14 (Spring 1982) 66-77.
911 Hunter, J. Hudson R 33 (Spring 1980) 39-57.
912 Hutchens, John. Theatre Arts Monthly 16 (Feb 1932) 98-100 (there are dangers in imitating Chekhov).
913 Ilyin, Eugene. "'Doctor' Chekhov," Plays & Players 8 (May 1960) 8-9.
914 Itallie, Jean-Claude van. "Chekhov's Characters Seem To Be Ourselves," N.Y.Times, 13 Feb 1977, 2:1.
915 Jackson, Robert Louis. "If I Forget Thee, O Jerusalem," Slavica Hierosolymitana (Jerusalem) 3 (1978) 55-67.
916 Jameson, Storm. Egoist 1 (16 Mar 1914) 116-7 (Chekhov pioneers in the search for new forms of drama).
917 Johnson, Alvin. New Republic 13 (17 Nov 1917) 12-4 (the tales of Chekhov explain the background of the Russian revolution).
918 Jones, W. Gareth. "Chekhov's Undercurrent of Time," Modern Language R 64 (Jan 1969) 111-21.
919 ------. "The Sea Gull's Second Symbolist Play-Within-The Play," Slavonic & East European R 53 (Jan 1975) 17-26.
920 Karlinsky, Simon. "Chekhov in English," N.Y.Times Book R, 26 Jul 1970, pp. 2, 20.
921 ------. "Nabokov and Chekhov: The Lesser Russian Tradition," Tri-Quarterly 17 (Winter 1970) 7-16.
922 ------. "Transmutation of a Master," Times Literary Supplement, 23 Jan 1981, pp. 93-4.
923 Katayev, V. "Understanding Chekhov's World," Soviet Literature no. 1 (Jan 1980) 171-6.
924 Katsell, J.H. "Character Change in Chekhov's Short Stories," Slavic & East European R 18 (Winter 1974) 377-83.
925 ------. "Chekhov's 'The Steppe' Revisited," Slavic & East European J 22 (Fall 1978) 313-23.
926 Kauffmann, Stanley. Theatre Q 4 (Aug-Oct 1974) 98 (discusses Uncle Vanya).
927 Kaun, Alexander. University R 10 (Winter 1943) 81.
928 Keeton, A.E. "Anton Tchehov," Academy & Literature 66 (9 Jan 1904) 40.
929 Kelson, John. "Allegory and Myth in The Cherry Orchard," Western Humanities R 13 (Summer 1959) 321-4.
930 Kendle, B. "Elusive Horses in The Sea Gull," Modern Drama 13 (May 1970) 63-6.
931 Kernan, Alvin. "Truth and Dramatic Mode in the Modern Theater: Chekhov, Pirandello & Williams," Modern Drama 1 (Sep 1958) 101-14.
932 Kinel, Lola. "The Crime of Translation," Story 12 (Jan 1938) 2-8.

933 King, Gertrude B. New Republic 3 (26 Jun 1915) 207 (The Cherry Orchard by the Moscow Art Theatre).

934 ------. New Republic 7 (8 Jul 1916) 256-8 (The Three Sisters by the Moscow Art Theatre).

935 Kitchin, Laurence. "Chekhov Without Inhibitions:The Moscow Art Theatre in London," Encounter 11 (Aug 1958) 68-72.

936 Kleine, D. W. "The Chekhovian Source of 'Marriage à la Mode'," Philological Q 42 (1963) 284-8.

937 Klitko, A."Chekhov and the Short Story in the Soviet Union Today," Soviet Literature no. 1 (Jan 1980) 143-8.

938 Knipper-Chekhova, Olga. "Marriage with a Genius," Golden Book 20 (Dec 1934) 710-2.

939 -------. "Memories of Chekhov," Living Age, Sep 1934, 58-62.

940 -------. N.Y.Times, 19 Mar 1944, 2:1 (she expresses appreciation for U.S. understanding of Chekhov).

941 Kobatake, M."Soliloquy and Modern Drama," Theatre Annual 18 (1961) 17-9.

942 Korpan, B. "Chekhov and Mann: An Overdue Debt," Sovremennik (Leeds) no. 9, pp. 4-17.

943 Koteliansky, S. S. "Reminiscences of Chekhov by Members of the Moscow Art Theatre," Spectator 135 (1925) 701.

944 Kott, Jan. "The Eating of The Government Inspector," Theatre Q 5 (Mar-May 1975) 26 (Gogol's St. Petersburg is echoed in the Moscow of Chekhov's Three Sisters).

945 Koun, K. See #1322.

946 Kozhevnikova, I. "Artists of Chekhov's Time," Soviet Literature no. 1 (Jan 1980) 200-5.

947 Kramer, Jane. New Yorker, 31 Oct 1983, pp. 132-3.

948 Kramer, Karl D. "Chekhov at the End of the Eighties: The Question of Identity," Etudes Slaves et Est-Europeennes 11 (1966) 3-18.

949 Kropotkin, Peter. Athenaeum, 7 Jul 1888, p. 26 (Chekhov compared to Zola).

950 Krutch, Joseph Wood. Nation 170 (15 Apr 1950) 354-5; 173 (22 Dec 1951) 554.

951 Kuhn, Reinhard. "The Debasement of the Intellectual in Contemporary Continental Drama," Modern Drama 7 (Feb 1965) 454-62.

952 Kuprin, Alexander. "To Chekhov's Memory," Freeman 3 (Aug 10, 17, 24, 31, 1921) 511-3, 535-7, 561-3, 583-5.

953 Kuranage, P. "Chekhov in Sri Lanka," Soviet Literature no. 2 (Feb 1980) 146-9.

954 Kuzmuk, V. A. "Vasilii Shukshin and the Early Chekhov," Soviet Studies in Literature 14 (Summer 1978) 61-78.

955 Laestadius, L. L. See #1322.

956 Lahr, John. "Chekhov and Pinter:The Bond of Naturalism," Drama R 13 (Winter 1968) 137-45.

957 Lakshin, V. "The Literary Heritage of Chekhov," Soviet Highlights, Mar 1960, pp. 1-13.
958 ------. "Unknown Note in the Hand of Chekhov," Soviet Literature no. 1 (Jan 1980) 128-31.
959 Lamm, Iudit. "Chekhov's Art of Writing," Studia Slavica Academiae Scientarum Hungaricae 26 (1980) 452-6.
960 Lantz, Kenneth A. "Chekhov and the Scenka," Slavic & East European J 19 (Winter 1975) 377-87.
961 -------. "Chekhov's 'Gusev': A Study," Studies in Short Fiction 15 (Winter 1978) 55-61.
962 Latham, Jacqueline. "The Cherry Orchard as Comedy," Educational Theatre J 10 (Mar 1958) 21-9.
963 Lau, J. S. M. "Ts'ao Yu, the Reluctant Disciple of Chekhov: A Comparative Study of Sunrise and The Cherry Orchard," Modern Drama 9 (Feb 1967) 358-72.
964 Lavrin, Janko. "Chekhov and Maupassant," Slavonic R 5 (Jun 1926) 1-24.
965 Lawson, John Howard. "Chekhov's Drama:Challenge to Playwrights," Masses & Mainstream 7 (Oct 1954) 11-26.
966 LeFleming, L.S.K. "The Structural Role of Language in Chekhov's Later Stories," Slavonic & East European R 48 (Jul 1970) 323-40.
967 Leong, Albert. "Literary Unity in Chekhov's 'Strakh'," J of Russian Studies 27 (1974) 15-20.
968 Lerman, L. "Cherry Orchard," Mlle 43 (May 1956) 130-1.
969 Lewis, F.R. "Anton Chekhov," London Q and Holborn R 160 (Oct 1935) 484-7.
970 Life "Chekhov and Fine Manners" 40 (7 Jun 1956) 136.
971 Lindstrom, T.S. Saturday R (N.Y.) 49 (19 Feb 1966)49-50.
972 Lippincott's Monthly 58 (Jul 1896) 102-8 (calls modern Russian literature decadent).
973 Literary Digest 28 (30 Apr 1904) 619-20 (Moscow Art Theatre production of The Cherry Orchard).
974 ------. 29 (13 Aug 1904) 194 (obituary notice).
975 ------. 29 (20 Aug 1904) 223-4 (Russian obit. notice).
976 Literature 1 (6 Nov 1897) 87 (discusses "The Peasants").
977 ------. 6 (24 Feb 1900)161-2 (Russ. Academy of Letters).
978 Littell, Robert. Theatre Magazine 51 (Jun 1930)18-9 (why Chekhov is considered a good dramatist).
979 Living Age 320 (26 Jan 1924) 190.
980 Lomunov, K. "Tolstoy, Chekhov, The Moscow Art Theatre," Soviet Literature no. 1 (Jan 1980)) 149-57.
981 Long, R.E.C. "Anton Tchekhoff," Fortnightly R n.s. 72 (1 Jul 1902) 103-18.
982 Luckett, Richard. "Chekhov's Sense of Decency," Spectator, 22 Sep 1973, pp. 376-7.
983 Lykiardopoulos, M. New Statesman Modern Theatre Supplement 3 (27 Jun 1914) 9-11.
984 McAfee, Helen. "Tchekhov and the Spirit of the East," North American R 204 (Aug 1916) 282-91.

985 MacCarthy, Desmond. New Statesman & Nation n.s. 13 (13 Mar 1937) 399.
986 McClintic, Guthrie. "Directing Chekhov," Theatre Arts 27 (Apr 1943) 212-5.
987 McDonald, J. "Productions of Chekhov's Plays in Britain Before 1914," Theatre Notebook 34 (1980) 25-36.
988 Macgowan, Kenneth. Freeman 6 (18 Oct 1922) 136-8 (Moscow Art Theatre productions of Chekhov's plays).
989 ------. Theatre Arts Monthly 8 (Apr 1924) 226.
990 Maichel, Karol. American Slavic & East European R 17 (1958)230-3 (review of Moscow ed. of Chekhov's works).
991 Majdalany, M. "Natasha Ivanovna,The Lonely Bourgeoise," Modern Drama 26 (Sep 1983) 305-9.
992 Manchester Guardian, 15 Nov 1929, p. 7.
993 Manderson, Sandra & Donald M. Fiene. "Chekhov's The Three Sisters," Explicator 36 (Winter 1978) 22-3.
994 Manheim, Michael. "Dialogue between Son and Mother in Chekhov's The Sea Gull and O'Neill's Long Day's Journey into Night," Eugene O'Neill Newsletter 6 (1982)24.
995 Mann, Thomas. "Anton Chekhov," Mainstream 12 (Mar 1959) 2-21 (Chekhov's gentle irony reminds us that the truth presented in interesting form refreshes the human spirit and prepares us for a better life).
996 ------. "The Stature of Anton Chekhov," New Republic 132 (16 May 1955) 23-5.
997 Markov, Paul. Modern Drama 2 (Dec 1959) 283-8 (Moscow Art Theatre productions of Chekhov's plays in Japan).
998 ------. Modern Drama 3 (Dec 1960) 373-5 (Moscow theaters produce Chekhov's plays for his centenary).
999 ------. See #1322.
1000 Marley, Donovan. "The Cherry Orchard," Impact (Allan Hancock College, Santa Maria, CA), May 1974, pp. 1-16.
1001 Marshall, Richard H., Jr. "Cexov and the Russian Orthodox Clergy," Slavic & East European J 7 (1963) 375-91.
1002 Martin, D.W. "Historical References in Chekhov's Later Plays," Modern Language R 71 (Jul 1976) 595-606.
1003 Martin, David. "Philosophy in Cechov's Major Plays," Welt der Slaven 23 (1978) 122-39.
1004 Matley, Ian M. "Chekhov and Geography," Russian R (N.Y.) 31 (Oct 1972) 376-82.
1005 Matthews, T.S. New Republic 59 (22 May 1929) 35-6.
1006 Matual, David. "Chekhov's 'Black Monk' & Byron's 'Black Friar'," International Fiction R 5 (Jan 1978) 46-51.
1007 Maxwell, D.E. "Chekhov's 'Steppe'," Slavic & East European J 17 (Summer 1973) 146-54.
1008 Meister, Charles W. "Chekhov: 100 Years After," Monument (Northern Ariz Univ, Flagstaff, AZ) 1 (Winter 1960) 5-10.

1009 ------. "Chekhov's Reception in England and America," American Slavic & East European R 12 (Feb 1953) 109-21.

1010 ------. "Comparative Drama: Chekhov, Shaw, Odets," Poet Lore 55 (Autumn 1950) 249-57.

1011 Mellquist, Jerome. "Chekhov and His One-Act Plays," One Act Play Magazine 2 (Mar 1939) 841-8.

1012 Melnick, Burton. "Theatre and Performance: The Cherry Orchard and Henry V," Tulane Drama R 11 (Summer 1967) 92-8.

1013 Mendelsohn, Michael J. "The Heartbreak Houses of Shaw and Chekhov," Shaw R 6 (Sep 1963) 89-95.

1014 Meyerhold, Vsevolod. "The Naturalistic Theatre and the Theatre of Mood," Tulane Drama R 4 (May 1960) 134-41.

1015 ------. Tulane Drama R 9 (Fall 1964) 24-5.

1016 Miles, Patrick. "The Chekhovs Offstage," Times Literary Supplement, 25 Apr 1980, p. 476.

1017 Miller, Jim W. "Stark Young, Chekhov, and the Method of Indirect Action," Georgia R 18 (1964) 98-115.

1018 Milyukov, Paul. Athenaeum, 6 Jul 1889, p.27; 5 Jul 1890 p. 26; 2 Jul 1892, p. 26; 1 Jul 1893, pp. 28-9; 7 Jul 1894, p. 23; 6 Jul 1895, p. 25; 4 Jul 1896, p. 26.

1019 Mirkovic, Damir. "Anton Pavlovich Chekhov and the Modern Sociology of Deviance," Canadian Slavonic Papers 18 (Mar 1976) 66-72 ("Ward No. 6" discovered labelling and the stigmatization process long before sociologists did).

1020 Mirsky, D.S. "Chekhov and the English," Monthly Criterion 6 (Oct 1927) 292-304.

1021 ------. London Mercury 3 (Dec 1920) 207-9.

1022 ------. Spectator 135 (7 Nov 1925) 824-6 (Moscow Art Theatre productions of Chekhov's plays).

1023 Moravcevich, Nicholas. "Chekhov and Naturalism: From Affinity to Divergence," Comparative Drama 4 (Winter 1970-71) 219-40.

1024 ------. "The Dark Side of the Chekhovian Smile," Drama Survey 5 (Winter 1966-67) 237-51.

1025 ------. "The Obligatory Scene in Chekhov's Drama," Drama Critique 9 (Spring 1966) 97-104.

1026 Mordaunt, Jerrold L.,ed. Proceedings: Pacific Northwest Conference on Foreign Languages, 20th Annual Mtg, 11-2 April 20 (1969) 94-102.

1027 Morfill,W.R. Cosmopolis 7 (Aug 1897) 348 (discusses "The Peasants").

1028 Morgan, Charles. N.Y.Times, 26 Sep 1926, 8:2 (Chekhov's triumph on the London stage).

1029 Morgan, Victor. "Chekhov's Social Plays and Their Historical Background," Papers of the Manchester Literary Club 64 (1938) 96-114.

1030 Moss, H. "Three Sisters," Hudson R 30 (Winter 1977) 525-43.
1031 Mudrick, M. Hudson R 27 (Spring 1974) 33-54.
1032 Murry, J. Middleton. Adelphi 1 (Aug 1923) 177-84 ("Hardy and Chekhov are the two truly religious writers of our time").
1033 -------. Athenaeum, 7 Jan 1921, pp. 11-2 (Chekhov was a consummate artist).
1034 -------. Nation & Athenaeum 31 (8 Apr 1922) 57-8 (gratitude for Constance Garnett's translations).
1035 Nabokoff, C. "Chekhov and His Plays," Contemporary R 125 (Mar 1924) 338-46.
1036 -------. "Chekhov on the English Stage," Contemporary R 129 (Jun 1926) 756-62.
1037 Nabokov, Vladimir. "On Chekhov," Atlantic 248 (Aug 1981) 19-23.
1038 Nagibin, Y. "Chekhov as an Editor," Soviet Literature no. 1 (Jan 1980) 112-9.
1039 Nagler, A.M. Theatre Research 2 (1960) 11-4 (first performance of The Sea Gull in St. Petersburg).
1040 Nathan, George Jean. American Mercury 56 (Jun 1943) 749 (Chekhov is no apostle of doom).
1041 ------. American Mercury 57 (Aug 1943) 236 (The Three Sisters is the leading money-earner in New York City).
1042 Nation (London) 15 (13 Jun 1914) 428 (review of Serge Persky's Contemporary Russian Novelists).
1043 ------. 20 (11 Nov 1916) 232.
1044 Nation (N.Y.) 79 (11 Aug 1904) 116 (obituary notice).
1045 ------. 92 (22 Jun 1911) 633.
1046 ------. 122 (19 May 1926) 561.
1047 ------. 129 (3 Jul 1929) 5 ("Chekhov: 25 Years After").
1048 Navrozov, Lev. Yale Literary Magazine 150 (1983) 74-88.
1049 Nazaroff, Alexander. N.Y.Times Book R, 17 Dec 1933, p. 8 (description of Chekhov's home life).
1050 -------. N.Y.Times Book R, 22 Oct 1939, p. 8 (Chekhov as a fun-loving youth).
1051 Nemirovich-Danchenko, Vladimir. N.Y.Times, 14 Oct 1928, 10:2 (letter concerning The Cherry Orchard).
1052 Nevins, Allan. N.Y.Eve Post Lit R, 5 Feb 1921, p. 3; 26 Nov 1921, p. 2.
1053 Newcombe, J.M. "Was Chekhov a Tolstoyan?" Slavic & East European J 18 (Summer 1974) 143-52.
1054 New Republic 5 (11 Dec 1915) 149.
1055 ------. 33 (10 Jan 1923) 163 (attacks chauvinism concerning the Moscow Art Theatre visit to New York).
1056 New Statesman 21 (5 May 1923) 112.
1057 -------. 26 (27 Mar 1926) 754 (review of D.S. Mirsky's Modern Russian Literature).
1058 ------. 34 (30 Nov 1929) 270 (review of Stephen Graham's Great Russian Short Stories).

1059 N.Y.Times, 12 Feb 1923, p. 13 (testimonial dinner in honor of Chekhov).
1060 ------. 30 Apr 1923, p. 11 (Olga Knipper-Chekhova reads Chekhov's works).
1061 ------. 17 Feb 1929, 9:4 (The Three Sisters performed by the Cartel des Quatres in Paris).
1062 ------. 3 Mar 1929, 8:3 (first performance of Platonov in Prague).
1063 ------. 15 Jul 1929, p. 7 (25th anniversary of Chekhov's death).
1064 ------. 10 Mar 1940, 12:6 (USSR issues Chekhov stamps).
1065 ------. 15 Jul 1944, p. 12; 16 Jul 1944, p. 3 (40th anniversary of Chekhov's death).
1066 ------. 23 Jun 1945, p. 10 (The Cherry Orchard).
1067 ------. 2 Jun 1960, p. 26; 24 Aug 1960, p. 33 (The Sea Gull in Bermuda by Assn of Producing Artists).
1068 ------. 8 Jan 1961, p. 84 (The Sea Gull in Stockholm by Ingmar Bergman).
1069 N.Y.Times Book R, 23 Jul 1922, p. 8 (Suvorin's daughter recalls Chekhov).
1070 Niedermoser, O. See #1322.
1071 Nightingale, Benedict. N.Y.Times, 12 Aug 1984, 2:3 (The Three Sisters in London, dir. by Lee Strasberg).
1072 Noyes, G.R. Nation (N.Y.) 107 (12 Oct 1918) 406 (Chekhov's one theme is the impotence of human nature).
1073 O'Bell, Leslie. "Chekhov's 'Skazka': The Intellectual's Fairy Tale," Slavic & East European J 26 (Winter 1981) 33-46.
1074 Observer (London), 20 Oct 1929, p. 13 (Chekhov's plays at the People's Theatre in Newcastle).
1075 O'Connor, Frank. "The Slave's Son," Kenyon R 25 (Winter 1963) 40-54 (an analysis of Chekhov's ideas).
1076 ------. "A Writer Who Refused to Pretend," N.Y.Times Book R, 17 Jan 1960, pp. 1, 24.
1077 O'Connor, G. "Uncle Vanya," Plays & Players 22 (Mar 1975) 34.
1078 O'Faolain, Sean. "On a Story by Tchekov," Life and Letters Today 17 (Autumn 1937) 60-9.
1079 Olgin, Moissaye. Bookman (N.Y.) 48 (Nov 1918) 356-64 (Chekhov's modesty gives him a charming style).
1080 Oliver, D.E. "Russian Literature: Anton Tchekoff," Papers of the Manchester Literary Club 42 (1916)188-207.
1081 Opulskaya, Lydia. Soviet Literature no. 10 (1975) 148-55 (review of Moscow ed. of Chekhov's complete works).
1082 Osipov, I. "Taking Chekhov's Itinerary to Sakhalin," U.S. Information Bulletin (Wash.D.C.) 6 (1946) 243.
1083 O'Toole, L.M. "Structure and Style in the Short Story: Chekhov's 'Student'," Slavonic & East European R 49 (Jan 1971) 45-67.
1084 Outlook (London) 12 (14 Nov 1903) 433.

1085 ------. 23 (13 Feb 1909) 226.
1086 Pachmuss, Temira. "Anton Chekhov in the Criticism of Zinaida Gippius," Etudes Slaves et Est-Europeennes 11 (1966) 35-48.
1087 Palmer, John. Saturday R (London) 112 (4 Nov 1911) 579.
1088 Palmer, Richard H. "The Aristocratic Motif in the Drama of Russia and the American South," Southern Q 17 (Fall 1978) 65-88.
1089 Paperny, Z. "Truth and Faith: Reading Chekhov's Rough Drafts and Notebooks," Soviet Literature no. 1 (Jan 1980) 104-11.
1090 Parker, David. "Three Men in Chekhov's Three Sisters," Critical R (Melbourne) 21 (1979) 12-23.
1091 Parry, Albert. "Dr. Anton Chekhov," Writer 68 (Sep 1955) 290, 322.
1092 Patrick, George Z. "Chekhov's Attitude towards Life," Slavonic & East European R 10 (Apr 1932) 658-68.
1093 Paul, Barbara. "Chekhov's Five Sisters," Modern Drama 14 (Feb 1972) 436-40.
1094 Pauls, John P. "Chekhov's Names," Names: J of the American Name Society (State Univ of N.Y., Potsdam) 23 (Jun 1975) 65-73.
1095 Pearson, Anthony G. "The Cabaret Comes to Russia: 'Theatre of Small Forms' as Cultural Catalyst," Theatre Q 9 (Winter 1980) 31-44 (Chekhov successfully developed the short popular farce or vaudeville).
1096 Pedereno, J. Sanchez. See #1322.
1097 Perry, Thomas S. North American R 196 (Jul 1912) 85-103 (despite seeming incoherence, Chekhov's plays have excellent unity).
1098 Phelps, William Lyon. "The Life and Art of Chekhov," Yale R n.s. 11 (1922) 399-406.
1099 ------. "The Poet's Dramatist," Nation (London) 30 (1921) 390-2.
1100 ------. Scribner's 81 (Jun 1927) 688.
1101 ------. Yale R n.s. 7 (Oct 1917) 189-91 (Chekhov had profound insight into child psychology).
1102 Pierce, Lucy F. "The Seagull Theatre of Moscow," Drama, Feb 1913, pp. 168-77.
1103 Pifer, Ellen. "Cexov's Psychological Landscapes," Slavic & East European J 17 (Fall 1973) 273-8.
1104 Plays & Players no. 367 (Apr 1984) 33-4 (The Three Sisters in Berlin).
1105 Poggioli, Renato. "Realism in Russia," Comparative Literature R 3 (1951) 253-67 (Chekhov, despite his objectivity, does not neglect ethics for esthetics).
1106 Pointon, R.M. "Checkov," Humberside 4 (Oct 1931) 39-48.
1107 Pollock, John. Fortnightly R n.s. 107 (1 Mar 1920) 390 (Chekhov's influence upon the Moscow Art Theatre was harmful).

1108 Popkin, Henry. "Chekhov: Self-Portrait," Commonweal 62 (24 Jun 1955) 310.
1109 ------. "Chekhov: The Ironic Spectator," Theatre Arts 36 (Mar 1952) 17, 80.
1110 Porter, Robert. "Hamlet and The Sea Gull," J of Russian Studies 41 (1981) 23-41.
1111 Priestley, J.B. Saturday R (London) 140 (17 Oct 1925) 446 (Chekhov's success grows out of his leaving crucial matters to inference).
1112 ------. Theatre Arts Monthly 14 (Aug 1930) 655-9 (like Shakespeare, Chekhov succeeds by artfully rendering character and atmosphere).
1113 Pritchett, V.S. New Statesman 55 (24 May 1958) 662-4.
1114 Public Opinion 33 (14 Aug 1902) 208-9 (Chekhov is the "painter of sordid life").
1115 ------. 37 (25 Aug 1904) 241 (historical survey of Russian drama).
1116 Quinn, Arthur Hobson. Scribner's 74 (Jul 1923) 66-7 (summary of Moscow Art Theatre visit to America).
1117 Quintus, John A. "The Loss of Dear Things: Chekhov and Williams in Perspective," English Language Notes 18 (Mar 1981) 201-6.
1118 Rahv, Philip. "The Education of Anton Chekhov," New Republic 133 (18 Jul 1955) 18-9.
1119 Reeve, F.D. "Tension in Prose:Chekhov's 'Three Years'," Slavic & East European J 16 (Summer 1958) 99-108.
1120 Remaley, Peter B. "Chekhov's The Cherry Orchard," South Atlantic Bulletin 38 (Nov 1973) 16-20.
1121 R of Reviews 26 (Jul 1902) 64 (Chekhov is the "prophet of despair").
1122 Rexroth, Kenneth. "Chekhov's Plays," Saturday R (N.Y.) 50 (8 Jul 1967) 18.
1123 Richart, R. See #1322.
1124 Rinear, D.L. "Kopit's Debt to Chekhov," Today's Speech 22 (Spring 1974) 19-23.
1125 Robinson, Harlow. N.Y.Times Book R, 3 Feb 1985, p. 18 (Yuri Trifonov is called "the Soviet Chekhov").
1126 Robinson, M. New Adelphi 1 (Mar 1928) 266-9 (Chekhov's tales condense much in little).
1127 ------. "Tchehov and Life," Adelphi 4 (May 1927) 683-7 (Chekhov always finds the light beyond the darkness).
1128 Roche, D. "On the High Road," L'Europe Nouvelle 17 (9 Jun 1934) 588.
1129 Ross, D. See #1322.
1130 Ross, David. "Why Chekhov?" N.Y.Times, 2 Oct 1955, 2:3; 9 Oct 1955, 2:1.
1131 Rossbacher, Peter. "Chekhov's Fragment 'Solomon'," Slavic & East European J 12 (Spring 1968) 27-34.

1132 ------. "The Function of Insanity in Cexov's 'The Black Monk' & Gogol's 'Notes of a Madman'," Slavic & East European J 13 (1969) 191-9.
1133 ------. "Nature and the Quest for Meaning in Chekhov's Stories," Russian R (N.Y.) 24 (Oct 1965) 387-92.
1134 ------. "The Thematic Significance of Four of Chekhov's Stylistic Devices," Proceedings: Pacific Northwest Conference on Foreign Lang, 21st Annual Mtg (1970) pp. 141 ff.
1135 Rosselli, J. "Wingless Sea Gull," Reporter 30 (4 Jun 1964) 34-5.
1136 Rudwin, Maximilian. Open Court 32 (Jul 1918) 401-3.
1137 Ruhl, Arthur. "'Bourgeois' Art in Red Russia," New Republic 34 (2 May 1923) 265-7.
1138 ------. "The Moscow Art Theatre," Collier's 59 (28 Jul 1917) 18-22.
1139 Rukalski, Zygmunt. "Anton Chekhov and Guy Maupassant: Their Views on Life and Art," Etudes Slaves et Est-Europeennes 5 (Spring-Summer 1960) 178-88.
1140 ------. "Human Problems of Maupassant and Chekhov," Etudes Slaves et Est-Europeennes 3 (Spring 1958) 80-4.
1141 ------. "Maupassant and Chekhov: Differences," Canadian Slavonic Papers 13 (Winter 1971) 374-402 (whereas Maupassant had contempt,Chekhov had pity for human sins).
1142 ------. "Maupassant and Chekhov: Similarities," Canadian Slavonic Papers 11 (Fall 1969) 346-58 (both are objective, economical, and insightful into human nature).
1143 ------. "Russian and French Writers on Politics and Public Opinion," Etudes Slaves et Est-Europeennes 6 (Spring-Summer 1961) 102-8.
1144 Sagar, Keith. "Chekhov's Magic Lake: A Reading of The Sea Gull," Modern Drama 15 (Mar 1973) 441-7.
1145 Saint-Gaudens, Homer. "The Russian Players," Critic 48 (Apr 1906) 318-23.
1146 Sampson, George. Bookman (London) 53 (Oct 1917) 8-14 (Chekhov's Russia is a country ready for change).
1147 Saturday R of Lit 39 (7 Apr 1956) 29 (Chekhov's life at Yalta).
1148 Sayers, Dorothy L. New Statesman & Nation n.s. 13 (27 Feb 1937) 324.
1149 Sayler, Oliver M. "Theory and Practice in Russian Theatres," Theatre Arts 4 (Jul 1920) 200-14.
1150 Schakowskoy, Zinaida. "Tchekov," Contemporary R 164 (Nov 1943) 296-300.
1151 Scharoff, P. See #1322.
1152 Schneider, Elisabeth. "Katherine Mansfield and Chekhov," Modern Language Notes 50 (Jun 1935) 394-7.
1153 Schneider, Isidor. "A Chekhov Anniversary," Soviet Russia Today 13 (Sep 1944) 27-8.

1154 Schwartz, Kessel. "La Gringa and The Cherry Orchard," Hispania 41 (Mar 1958) 51-5.
1155 Scott, V. "Life in Art: A Reading of The Sea Gull," Educational Theatre J 30 (Oct 1978) 357-67.
1156 Sedoy, A. "Chekhov's Taganrog," Soviet Literature no. 1 (Jan 1980) 62-9.
1157 Senanu, K.E. "Anton Chekhov and Henry James," Ibadan Studies in English 2 (1970) 182-97.
1158 Senderovich, Marena. "The Implicit Semantic Unities in Chekhov's Work of 1886-89," Dissertation Abstracts International 42 (Jun 1982) 5143a.
1159 Senelick, Laurence. "The Lake Shore of Bohemia: The Sea Gull's Theatrical Context," Educational Theatre J 29 (May 1977) 199-213.
1160 ------. "What is Chekhovian?" Prologue: Tufts Univ Theater 29 (Nov 1973) 1.
1161 Serban, M. See #1322.
1162 Sevastyanov, V. "Tribute to Chekhov," Soviet Literature no. 1 (Jan 1980) 191-5.
1163 Seyler, Dorothy U. "The Sea Gull and The Wild Duck: Birds of a Feather," Modern Drama 8 (Sep 1965) 167-73.
1164 Shakh-Azizova, Tatiana. "The Russian Hamlet," Soviet Literature no. 1 (Jan 1980) 157-63.
1165 Sherman, Stuart. N.Y.Herald-Tribune Books, 15 Nov 1925, pp. 1-3 (review of Chekhov's letters).
1166 Shishkoff, Paul. "I Knew Chekhov," Listener 20 (3 Nov 1938) 927-9.
1167 Shorter, Eric."Chekhov Through English Eyes In French," Drama no. 141 (Autumn 1981) 6-8 (The Cherry Orchard in Paris).
1168 ------. Drama no. 132 (Spring 1979) 23-4 (The Three Sisters in Paris).
1169 Shyer, Laurence. "Andrei Serban Directs Chekhov:The Sea Gull in New York and Japan," Theater Yearbook 13 (Winter 1981) 56-66.
1170 Silverman, R. N.Y.Times Book R, 21 Feb 1960, p.30 (discusses Chekhov as a moralist).
1171 Silverstein, Norman. "Chekhov's Comic Spirit and The Cherry Orchard," Modern Drama 1 (Sep 1958) 91-100.
1172 Simonson, Lee. Atlantic 143 (May 1929) 642 (Moscow Art Theatre productions of Chekhov's plays).
1173 Singleton, K.I. "Translator's Note on Uncle Vanya," Drama and Theatre 12 (Spring 1975) 127-9.
1174 Skidelsky, Berenice C. Book News Monthly 35 (Feb 1917) 240; 35 (Mar 1917) 273.
1175 ------. Book News Monthly 35 (Aug 1917) 458-9 (Chekhov's calm endings add to his power as a realist).
1176 ------. Book News Monthly 36 (Nov 1917) 89 (Chekhov's insight into human nature is profound).

1177 Slejskova, Nadezda. "The Illusion of Off-Stage Life in Theatre and Its Application to Chekhov's Drama: An Analysis of The Sea Gull," Dissertation Abstracts International 42 (Oct 1981) 1660a.
1178 Slonim, Marc. "Chekhov's Influence on Our Generation," Russian Language J 14 (1960) 25-32.
1179 ------. "Ivan Bunin on His Friend Chekhov," N.Y.Times Book R, 4 Mar 1956, p. 40.
1180 ------. "Lyrics and Satire out of Russia," Saturday R (N.Y.) 37 (Jun 1954) 16.
1181 Smith, J. Oates. "Chekhov and the Theatre of the Absurd," Bucknell R 14 (Dec 1966) 44-58.
1182 Smith, Virginia Llewellyn. "Stating the Problem," Times Literary Supplement, 1 Jul 1977, p. 799.
1183 ------. "Writing for Roubles," Times Literary Supplement, 31 Dec 1982, p. 1446.
1184 Smith, Winifred. Dial 61 (15 Aug 1916) 103-4.
1185 Sokolova, M. "Chekhov's Unknown Humorous Sketches in Budilnik," Soviet Literature no. 1 (Jan 1980) 120-7.
1186 Soulerzhitsky, L.A. "Reminiscences of Tchekhov by Actors of the Moscow Art Theatre," Spectator 135 (24 Oct, 7 Nov, 5 Dec, 1925) 701-2, 821-3, 1029-32.
1187 Soviet Literature, "Chekhov Through the Eyes of the Writers of the World," no. 1 (Jan 1980) 91-103.
1188 ------. "Literary Critics and Scholars Answer Our Questionnaire," no. 1 (Jan 1980) 184-90.
1189 ------. "Reminiscences of A.P. Chekhov by His Contemporaries," no. 4 (Apr 1949) 148-50.
1190 Spectator 104 (16 Apr 1910) 629 (review of Maurice Baring's Landmarks in Russian Literature).
1191 ------. 144 (25 Jan 1930) 129 (review of Stephen Graham's Great Russian Short Stories).
1192 Speirs, Logan. "I Shall Call the Play a Comedy: The Cherry Orchard," Oxford R no. 5 (Trinity 1967) 73-82.
1193 ------. "Tolstoy and Chekhov:'The Death of Ivan Ilyich' and 'A Dreary Story'," Oxford R no. 8 (Trinity 1968) 81-93 (there is a great emptiness in Tolstoy's story, but in Chekhov's story the old professor at least discovers himself).
1194 Stade, George. N.Y.Times Book R, 21 Nov 1982, p.12 (review of Leslie Epstein's novel Regina, showing parallels to The Sea Gull).
1195 Stanislavsky, Konstantin. Theatre Arts 42 (Dec 1958) 48-50 (excerpts from Stanislavsky's Legacy).
1196 States, Bert O. "Chekhov's Dramatic Strategy," Yale R 56 (Dec 1966) 212-24.
1197 Stein, W. "Tragedy and the Absurd," Dublin R 233 (Winter 1959-60) 363-82.
1198 Stephenson, Robert C. "Chekhov on Western Writers," Texas Univ Studies in English 30 (1951) 235-42.

1199 Stern, James. N.Y.Times Book R, 18 Apr 1954, p. 5.
1200 Stewart, Ian. "Portrait of a Marriage," Country Life 167 (17 Jan 1980) 150.
1201 Stowell, H.P. "Chekhov's 'The Bishop': The Annihilation of Faith and Identity Through Time," Studies in Short Fiction 12 (Spring 1975) 117-26.
1202 Strasberg, Lee. "Stanislavski and the Actors Studio," Theatre Q 8 (Spring 1978) 92 (Strasberg agrees that The Three Sisters by the Actors Studio in London in 1965 was a disaster, but he defends the production in New York City in 1964).
1203 Strongin, Carol. "Irony and Theatricality in Chekhov's The Sea Gull," Comparative Drama 15 (Winter 1981-82) 366-80.
1204 Stroud, T.A. "Hamlet and The Sea Gull," Shakespeare Q 9 (Summer 1958) 367-72.
1205 Stroyeva, M. "Everyone Has His Own Chekhov," Soviet Literature no. 2 (Feb 1980) 138-46.
1206 ------. "The Three Sisters at the Moscow Art Theatre," Tulane Drama R 9 (Fall 1964) 42-56.
1207 Strunsky, Rose. Forum 55 (Apr 1916) 444-5.
1208 Struve, Gleb. "Chekhov and Soviet Doublethink," New Leader, 22 Nov 1954, pp. 22-4.
1209 ------. "Chekhov in Communist Censorship," Slavonic & East European R 33 (Jun 1955) 327-41.
1210 ------. "On Chekhov's Craftsmanship: The Anatomy of a Story," Slavic & East European R 20 (Oct 1961) 465-76.
1211 Strzelecki, Z. See #1322.
1212 Styan, J.L. "The Delicate Balance: Audience Ambivalence in the Comedy of Shakespeare and Chekhov," Costerus 2 (1972) 159-84.
1213 ------. "The Idea of a Definitive Production of Chekhov In and Out of Period," Comparative Drama 4 (Fall 1970) 177-96.
1214 Sutton, Graham E. "Tchekov," Bookman (London) 70 (Apr 1926) 66-7 (Chekhov's influence upon English and Irish dramatists).
1215 Svoboda, J. See #1322.
1216 Szewcow, M. "Anatolij Efros Directs Chekhov's The Cherry Orchard," Theatre Q 7 (Summer 1977) 34-46.
1217 Taylor, Rachel A. Spectator 139 (10 Dec 1927) 1063.
1218 Tchekhov, Alexander. "Sketches from Anton Tchekhov's Childhood," New Age n.s. 39 (8 Jul 1926) 109.
1219 ------. "Tomorrow an Exam," T.P.Cassell's Weekly 6 (1926) 21.
1220 Telegraph (London), 18 Feb 1979, p. 14e.
1221 ------. 5 Mar 1979, p. 11a (discussion of dialogue in The Cherry Orchard).
1222 Theatre Arts 27 (Oct 1943) 603-6 (Nemirovich-Danchenko is quoted on The Three Sisters).

1223 Theatre Arts Monthly 12 (Jan 1928) 70.
1224 Theatre J 36 (Mar 1984) 107-8 (review of Uncle Vanya).
1225 Theatre Q 7 (Summer 1977) 24-32 (Anatoly Efros stages The Cherry Orchard and The Three Sisters in Moscow).
1226 Theatre Survey, "Chekhov's Reactions to Two Interpretations of Nina C. Hollosi," 24 (May-Nov 1983) 117-26.
1227 Thoms, Herbert. "Anton Chekhov, Physician and Literary Artist," J of the Amer Medical Assn 79 (1922) 1631-2.
1228 Time, "The Power of Negative Thinking," 65 (9 May 1955) 114.
1229 Times (London), 16 Jul 1904, p. 9c (obituary notice).
1230 ------. 18 Jul 1904, p. 6e (obituary article).
1231 ------. 15 Jul 1929, p. 15f (25th anniversary of Chekhov's death).
1232 ------. 14 Oct 1954, p. 10g (The Cherry Orchard in Paris).
1233 ------. 25 Apr 1956, p. 3d (forthcoming production of Platonov).
1234 ------. 26 May 1956, p. 8e (Bordeaux Platonov).
1235 ------. 18 Jun 1956, p. 5b (forthcoming The Sea Gull).
1236 ------. 3 Dec 1956, p. 5c (Platonov plans & rights).
1237 ------. 30 May 1958, p. 16a (article on Chekhov).
1238 ------. 23 Dec 1959, p. 9a (Chekhov centenary plans).
1239 ------. 4 Jan 1960, p. 14f (Chekhov centenary plans).
1240 ------. 16 Jan 1960, p. 9f (Chekhov on English stage).
1241 ------. 2 Feb 1960, p. 5c (Chekhov centenary plans).
1242 ------. 8 June 1960, p. 16d (plans for The Proposal).
1243 ------. 6 Jul 1960, p.4d (Chekhov centen. celebration).
1244 ------. 2 Jan 1961, p.12a (The Flowering Cherry plans).
1245 ------. 16 Mar 1961, p. 17b (translations of Chekhov).
1246 ------. 21 Sep 1961, p. 16d (The Cherry Orchard plans).
1247 ------. 8 Mar 1962, p. 16d ("The Swedish Match").
1248 ------. 24 May 1962, p. 17e (review of Select Tales).
1249 ------. 10 Oct 1962, p. 16e ("Woodman Spare That Cherry Orchard").
1250 ------. 12 Jan 1963, p. 4g (plans for The Proposal).
1251 ------. 3 Oct 1963, p. 15e (Chekhov biography).
1252 ------. 29 Oct 1963, p. 14c (Swiss The Three Sisters).
1253 ------. 21 Nov 1963, p. 19d (a book on Chekhov).
1254 ------. 14 Dec 1963, p. 11c (recording of Chichester Uncle Vanya).
1255 ------. 2 Jan 1964, p. 12b (plans for The Sea Gull).
1256 ------. 15 Jun 1964, p. 6a ("The Duel").
1257 ------. 1 Sep 1964, p. 13a (Chekhov's Lonely People).
1258 ------. 19 Nov 1964, p. 16e (Chekhov's plays analyzed).
1259 ------. 8 Feb 1965, p. 5c (The Three Sisters adapted).
1260 ------. 2 Nov 1965, p.13b (The Cherry Orchard in Rome).
1261 ------. 23 May 1966, p. 7b (article on Chekhov).
1262 ------. 12 Nov 1966, p.13c(The Three Sisters in Paris).

1263 ------. 11 Jun 1968, p. 6h (The Three Sisters in Moscow).
1264 ------. 17 Jul 1968, p. 6c (article on The Sea Gull).
1265 ------. 30 Nov 1968, p. 21a (article on The Sea Gull).
1266 ------. 25 Oct 1969, p. 3f (article on Chekhov).
1267 ------. 28 Mar 1970, p. 8e (Chekhov meets Tolstoy).
1268 ------. 11 Oct 1971, p. 10a (The Three Sisters plans).
1269 ------. 23 May 1976, p. 41 ("Portrait of the Artist as a Good Man").
1270 ------. 3 Jun 1976, p. 10 (biography of Chekhov).
1271 ------. 17 Dec 1976, p.15f(The Cherry Orchard,new tr.).
1272 ------. 7 Sep 1980, p. 43a (review of Five Plays).
1273 ------. 27 Jun 1982, p. 41a (review of The Early Stories, 1883-88).
1274 Times Educational Supplement (London),20 Jan 1978,p.20.
1275 Times Literary Supplement, 22 Jul 1904, p. 229 (obit).
1276 ------. 14 Jan 1915, p. 13c (review of Serge Persky's Contemporary Russian Novelists).
1277 ------. 14 May 1925, p. 331b (review of D.S. Mirsky's Modern Russian Literature).
1278 ------. 21 Oct 1926, p. 724c; 26 Jan 1928, p. 58d.
1279 ------. 14 Jun 1928, p. 451a; 30 Sep 1960, p. 629.
1280 ------. 23 Jan 1976, p. 79c (biography of Chekhov).
1281 ------. 6 Aug 1976, p. 988h (biography of Chekhov).
1282 "Tolstoy on Chekhov," Soviet Literature no. 1 (Jan 1980) 40-4.
1283 Toumanova, Nina A. "Chekhov and Kremlin," America 71 (23 Sep 1944) 596-7.
1284 Tovstonogov, Georgy. "Chekhov's The Three Sisters at the Gorky Theatre," Drama R 13 (Winter 1968) 146-55.
1285 Tracy, Robert. "A Cexov Anniversary," Slavic & East European J 4 (1960) 25-34.
1286 Trevor, William. Spectator, 15 May 1976, pp. 21-2.
1287 Trofimov, M.V. "Chehov's Stories and Dramas," Modern Language Teaching 12 (Nov 1916) 176-86.
1288 Trueblood, Charles K. Dial 68 (Feb 1920) 253-4 (Chekhov was an ironist who lacked Thomas Hardy's deep love of mankind).
1289 Uglow, J. Times Literary Supplement, 2 Sep 1983, p. 928 (review of Chekhov, 1981).
1290 Usmanov, L.D. "Some Observations on the Style of Chekhov's Later Stories," Soviet Studies in Literature 2 (Winter 1966) 26-33.
1291 Vassiliev, A. See #1322.
1292 Vergel, A. Gonzalez. See #1322.
1293 Vilar, J. See #1322.
1294 Vitins, Ieva. "Uncle Vanya's Predicament," Slavic & East European J 22 (Winter 1978) 454-63.

1295 VOKS Bulletin (Moscow) "50th Anniversary of Chekhov's Death, and Chekhov in Foreign Countries," 86 (May-Jun 1954) 21-68 (tributes to Chekhov by Mulk Raj Anand, E.B. Burgum, Maria Chekhova, A. D'Usseau, V.V. Ermilov, J. Fernald, K. Keshavarz, Olga Knipper-Chekhova, David Magarshack, Sean O'Casey, N. Silverskiold, & I. Soloviova).

1296 Volkov, Nikolai. "Emblem of the Seagull," Theatre World (London), Aug 1944, pp. 18-9.

1297 Wadsworth, P. Beaumont. "Tchekov at Yalta," Bookman (London) 84 (Apr 1933) 17-8.

1298 Walker, M. "Translating Chekhov," Landfall 11 (Jun 1957) 149-57.

1299 Walkley, A.B. "An Estimate of Anton Tchekhov," Vanity Fair (N.Y.) 25 (Jan 1926) 54, 114.

1300 Walton, M. New Theatre Magazine 8 (1967) 29-35.

1301 Warner, P. "The Axe in Springtime: Cherry Orchard," Theoria no. 10 (1958) 41-57.

1302 Warren, C. Henry. Outlook (London) 59 (11 Jun 1927)779.

1303 Webster, Margaret. "A Letter to Chekhov," N.Y.Times, 23 Jan 1944, 2:1.

1304 ------. Theatre Arts Monthly 22 (May 1938) 343-8.

1305 Weightman, John. "Chekhov and Chekhovian," Encounter 41 (Aug 1973) 51-3.

1306 Werth, Alexander. "Anton Chekhov," Slavonic R 3 (Mar 1925) 622-41.

1307 West, Jessamyn. "Secret of the Masters," Saturday R of Lit 40 (21 Sep 1957) 13 (Chekhov said a writer must be free, must "cast the slave out of himself").

1308 Wijnberg, N. See #1322.

1309 Willcocks, Mary P. "Tchehov," English R 34 (Mar 1922) 207-16.

1310 Williamson, C. "The Ethics of Three Russian Novelists," International J of Ethics 35 (Apr 1925) 230-7.

1311 Wilson, Arthur. "The Influence of Hamlet upon Chekhov's The Sea Gull," Susquehanna Univ Studies 4 (May 1952) 309-16.

1312 Wilson, Edmund. New Republic 25 (2 Feb 1921) 291.

1313 ------. "Seeing Chekhov Plain," New Yorker 28 (22 Nov 1952) 180-98.

1314 Winner, Thomas. "The Cexov Centennial Productions in the Moscow Theaters," Slavic & East European J 5 (1961) 255-62.

1315 ------. "Chekhov's Seagull and Shakespeare's Hamlet," Shakespeare Newsletter 4 (Dec 1954) 50.

1316 ------. "Chekhov's Seagull and Shakespeare's Hamlet: A Study of a Dramatic Device," American Slavic & East European R 15 (Feb 1956) 103-11.

1317 ------. "Chekhov's 'Ward No. 6' and Tolstoyan Ethics," Slavic & East European J 17 (Winter 1959) 321-34.

1318 ------. "Speech Characteristics in Chekhov's Ivanov and Capek's Loupeznik," American Contributions to the Fifth International Congress of Slavists (The Hague) 2 (1963) 403-31.
1319 ------. "Theme and Structure in Chekhov's 'The Betrothed'," Indiana Slavic Studies 3 (1963) 163-72.
1320 Witham, B.B. Educational Theatre J 27 (Oct 1975) 412-3.
1321 Woolf, Leonard. "Tchehov," New Statesman 9 (11 Aug 1917) 446-8 (Chekhov's stories leave a feeling of incompleteness, for he was bewildered by life).
1322 World Theatre (Chekhov Centenary Issue) 9 (Summer 1960) 11-48 (articles by Rene Allio, B. Babotchkine, J.L. Barrault, S. Benavente, N. Chifrine, O. Costa, J. Fernald, M. Ferrero, R. Hainaux, Norris Houghton, K. Koun, L.L. Laestadius, P. Markov, O. Niedermoser, J. Sanchez Pedreno, R. Richart, D. Ross, P. Scharoff, M. Serban, Z. Strzelecki, J. Svoboda, A. Vassiliev, A. Gonzalez Vergel, J. Vilar, & N. Wijnberg).
1323 Wright, A. Colin."Translating Chekhov for Performance," Canadian R of Comparative Lit 7 (Spring 1980) 174-82 (contrasts R. Hingley's translation of The Sea Gull with version done by Wright & Brenda Anderson for performance at Queen's Univ in Fall 1977).
1324 Yanagi, R. "Chekhov and Foreign Literature," Nippon-Russia-Bungakukai-Kaiho, no. 8 (Aug 1965).
1325 Yarros, Victor. Critic 40 (Apr 1902) 324 (Chekhov is Russia's best short-story writer).
1326 ------."Stagnation in Russian Literature," Dial 20 (16 Jan 1896) 39-40.
1327 Young, Stark. New Republic 25 (2 Feb 1921) 291.
1328 ------. New Republic 65 (21 Jan 1931) 274 (Moscow Art Theatre productions of Chekhov's plays).
1329 ------. New Republic 94 (13 Apr 1938) 305-6 (Constance Garnett's translation of The Sea Gull suffers from her lack of theater knowledge).
1330 ------. New Republic 94 (20 Apr 1938) 332-3 (Marian Fell's translation of The Sea Gull substitutes mistiness for natural dialogue).
1331 ------. New Republic 95 (8 Jun 1938) 130-1.
1332 ------. North American R 217 (Mar 1923) 343-52 (Chekhov's plays, like Shakespeare's, remain suspended mysteriously in one's experience).
1333 ------. North American R 219 (Jun 1924) 874-82 (Moscow Art Theatre productions of Chekhov's plays).
1334 ------. "Notes on Uncle Vanya," N.Y.Times, 29 Jan 1956, 2:3.
1335 ------. "Tea with Madame Tchehov," New Republic 34 (23 May 1923) 343-4.
1336 ------. Theatre Arts Monthly 22 (Oct 1938) 737-42 (its wide use has made Constance Garnett's translation of The Sea Gull harmful to Chekhov's intent).

1337 Zilboorg, Gregory. _Drama_ 2 (Nov 1920) 66-70 (after Ostrovsky, Chekhov is Russia's greatest dramatist).

1338 ------. _Drama_ 13 (Jan 1923) 127-30 (the Moscow Art Theatre visit to America).

1339 Zoshchenko, Mikhail. "On the Comic in Chekhov," _Soviet Studies in Literature_ 4 (Winter 1967) 408.

Bibliographies

1340 Adelman, Irving & Rita Dworkin, eds. _Modern Drama: A Checklist of Critical Literature on Twentieth Century Plays_. Metuchen, NJ: Scarecrow Pr, 1967.

1341 Boyer, Robert D. _Realism in European Theatre & Drama, 1870-1920: A Bibliography_. Westport, CT: Greenwood Pr, 1979.

1342 Breed, Paul F. & Florence Sniderman, eds. _Dramatic Criticism Index: A Bibliography of Commentaries on Playwrights from Ibsen to Avant-Garde._ Detroit: Gale Research Company, 1972.

1343 Coleman, Arthur & Gary R. Tyler, eds. _Dramatic Criticism, Vol Two:A Checklist of Interpretations Since 1940 of Classical And Continental Plays_. Chicago: Swallow Pr, 1971.

1344 Ettlinger, Amrei & Joan M. Gladstone, eds. _Russian Literature, Theatre, and Art_. Port Washington, NY: Kennikat Pr, 1971. Reprint of 1945 edition.

1345 Heifetz, Anna. "Bibliography of Chekhov's Works Translated into English and Published in America," _Bulletin of Bibliography_ 13 (1929) 172-6.

1346 ------. _Chekhov in English:A List of Works by and about Him_. Ed. & with a foreword by Avrahm Yarmolinsky. N.Y.: N.Y. Public Library, 1949.

1347 Hingley, Ronald. _The Oxford Chekhov_. London: Oxford Univ Pr, 1964-80. 9 vols. Bibliog in each vol. See #4.

1348 Horak, Stephen M. _Russia, the USSR, & Eastern Europe: A Bibliographic Guide to English Lang Publications:1975-80_. Littleton, CO: Libraries Unlimited, 1982.

1349 Line, Maurice B., et al. _Bibliography of Russian Literature in English Translation to 1945_. Totowa, NJ: Rowman, 1972. Reprint of 1963 edition.

1350 Magarshack, David. _Chekhov: A Life_. London: Faber,1952. Contains "Bibliographical Index of the Complete Works of Anton Chekhov," which has title of all Chekhov's writings between 1880 and 1904, with the original Russian date of publication, plus dates and translators of all English works.

1351 Palmer, Helen. _European Drama Criticism: 1900-1975_. 2nd ed. Hamden, CT: Shoe String Pr, 1977.

1352 Patterson, Charlotte A. _Plays in Periodicals_. Boston: Hall, 1970.

1353 Salem, James M. A Guide to Critical Reviews. 2nd ed. Part III: Foreign Drama, 1909-1977. Metuchen, NJ: Scarecrow Pr, 1979.
1354 Simmons, Ernest J. Chekhov: A Biography. Boston: Little, Brown, 1962. Has archive materials and bibliogs in both English and Russian.
1355 Yachnin, Rissa. The Chekhov Centennial in English: A Selective List of Works by and about Him, 1949-60. N.Y.: New York Public Library, 1960.
1356 Zenkovsky, Serge & David L. Armbruster. Guide to the Bibliographies of Russian Literature. Nashville: Vanderbilt Univ Pr, 1970.

Books on Chekhov (alphabetical by author)

1357 Avilov, Lydia. Chekhov in My Life. Tr. with an intro by David Magarshack. London: Lehmann, 1950. The wife of an official in the Ministry of Education, Avilov describes her friendship with Chekhov, a relationship she felt developed into mutual love. Reviews: Manchester Guardian, 25 Apr 1950, p. 4; New Statesman & Nation 40 (8 Jul 1950) 43; Spectator 184 (9 Jun 1950) 794; Times Literary Supplement, 19 May 1950, p. 311.
1358 ------. Reprint of #1357. N.Y.: Harcourt Brace, 1950. Reviews: Booklist 46 (15 Jul 1950) 352; Chicago Sunday Tribune, 2 Jul 1950, p.4; Commonweal 52 (4 Aug 1950) 415; Kirkus R 18 (1 Jun 1950) 320; Library J 75 (15 Jun 1950) 1043; N.Y. Herald-Tribune Book R, 18 Jun 1950, p. 4; N.Y.Times Book R, 18 Jun 1950, p.12; New Yorker 26 (24 Jun 1950) 94; Saturday R of Lit 33 (8 Jul 1950) 13; Theatre Arts 34 (Sep 1950) 96.
1359 ------. Excerpt of #1357 (tr. by V. Roussin) in Soviet Literature no. 1 (1980) 70-90.
1360 Barricelli, Jean-Pierre, ed. Chekhov's Great Plays: A Critical Anthology. N.Y.: New York Univ Pr,1981. Footnotes. Index. Critical articles by Jean-Pierre Barricelli, Philip Bordinat, Eugene Bristow,Francis Fergusson, Michael Heim, Robert Louis Jackson, Simon Karlinsky, Jerome Katsell, Sonia Kovitz, Karl D. Kramer, Nicholas Moravcevich, Nils Ake Nilsson,Louis Pedrotti, Richard D. Risso, Laurence Senelick, Maurice Valency, and Ieva Vitins. Reviews: Choice 19 (Mar 1982) 928; Slavic R 62 (Jan 1984) 110-1; Theatre J 34 (Dec 1982) 559-61; World Literature Today 57 (Winter 1983) 128.
1361 Bitsilli, Peter M. Chekhov's Art: A Stylistic Analysis. Tr. by Toby Clyman and Edwina Cruise. Ann Arbor: Ardis Publications, 1983. Footnotes. Index. Chekhov was influenced by many writers, such as Gogol,Lermontov, and

Turgenev, and in turn influenced many others, including Alain-Fournier and Thomas Mann. An impressionist, Chekhov presents images in a non-sequential order. In his characters we recognize ourselves, and we feel a mystical oneness with the universe. But his plays fail because the characters are acted upon rather than being the active agents required by the theater.

1362 Brahms, Caryl (pseudonym of Doris Caroline Abrahams). Reflections in a Lake:A Study Of Chekhov's Four Greatest Plays. London: Weidenfeld & Nicholson, 1976. Bibliog. Chronological table. Quotations from Chekhov's letters describe his writing his four main plays. Chekhov combines his own inner truth with outward appearances, so each performance is less a play than an experience. In some magical way his plot line seems to spin itself out of the characterization, which is so intense that even servants are interesting characters in themselves. Review: J of European Studies 10 (Sep 1980) 221-2.

1363 Bruford, Walter H. Anton Chekhov. London:Bowes & Bowes, 1957. Brief biography (62 pp) relates Chekhov's plays and stories to events in his life. Brief bibliog. Reviews: American Slavic & East European R 17 (Feb 1958) 132; Library J 82 (Aug 1957) 1922; N.Y.Times, 22 Dec 1957, p. 12.

1364 ------. Chekhov and His Russia: A Sociological Study. London: Paul,Trench & Trubner, 1948. Bibliog. Index. Chekhov's Russia is described in detail in terms of the people, the church, the economy, the government, and the professions. Chekhov is seen as a realistic writer and a humanitarian. Chekhov's writings constantly illustrate social conditions. Reviews: Book R Digest, Nov 1948; N.Y.Herald-Trib Weekly Book R 15 Aug 1948, p. 11; Spectator 180 (18 Jun 1948) 744.

1365 Reprint of #1364. Hamden, CT: Archon Books, 1971. Review: Choice 8 (1971) 1184.

1366 Bullins, Ed. Anton Chekhov and the Drama of Mood. 1977. Review: College Language Assn J 20 (Jun 1977) 521-32.

1367 Chekhova, Maria P. The Chekhov Museum in Yalta. Tr. by Molly Perelman. Moscow: Foreign Languages Publishing House, 1958. A pictorial guide through Chekhov's Yalta house, now a museum of his memorabilia. Brief intro by his sister Maria.

1368 Chudakov, A.P. Chekhov's Poetics. Tr. by Edwina Jannie Cruise & Donald Dragt. Ann Arbor: Ardis Publications, 1983. Chekhov's early stories are full of the narrator's emotions and value judgements. His later stories strain everything through the consciousness of the central character. Using quantifying data, Chudakov shows how Chekhov pioneered in fusing dialogue, exposition, and setting into an organic whole. He was the first writer to incorporate an environmental concern into his ethical system. An impressionist, Chekhov was the father of modern drama. His plays show the artistic importance of the commonplace: "Everything merges into an eternal whole and nothing can be separated." Index. Notes.

1369 ------. The Poetics of Chekhov: The Sphere of Ideas. 1977. Tr. by J. Graffy. Review: New Literary History 9 (Winter 1978) 353-80.

1370 Chukovsky, Kornei. Chekhov the Man. Tr. by Pauline Rose. London: Hutchinson, 1945. Little critical comment but much adulation of Chekhov as a humanitarian. Chekhov's chief theme is the struggle between the will and the lack of will-power in humans. Reviews: Life & Letters; and the London Mercury and Bookman 47 (Nov 1945) 118-9; Spectator 176 (4 Jan 1946) 18.

1371 Debreczeny, Paul & Thomas Eekman, eds. Chekhov's Art of Writing: A Collection of Critical Essays. Columbus,OH: Slavica Publishers, 1977. Intro by Ronald Hingley. Index. Notes. Essays by Ellen Chances, Charanne Clark, Joseph L. Conrad, Phillip A. Duncan, Jerome H.Katsell, Karl D. Kramer, David E.Maxwell, Nicholas Moravcevich, Marena Senderovich, Savely Senderovich, Susan S. Smernoff, H. Peter Stowell, & Thomas Winner. Review: Slavic & East European J 23 (Spring 1979) 130-2.

1372 Eekman, Thomas, ed. Anton Cechov, 1860-1904. Some Essays. Leiden: Brill, 1960. Notes. Six essays in German, five in Russian, three in French, and the following six in English: Thomas Eekman finds Chekhov a Westernizer, thoroughly familiar with the high points of European culture. George Ivask states that, in Chekhov, clergymen tend to be average persons who are more sensitive and open-minded than other people. Ralph E. Matlaw believes that the rigorous structure demanded by the novel did not suit Chekhov's essentially miniaturist skills. Nils Ake Nilsson feels that Chekhov's careful stage directions concerning intonation help him achieve a rhythm in keeping with the varied emotional atmosphere he builds. Charles B. Timmer finds that as Chekhov drops the bizarre (the element that makes man conscious of his existence as a dilemma) in his fiction, he increasingly uses it in his plays. Thomas G. Winner sees that no one intellectual system, not even science or art, was sufficient, in Chekhov's opinion, to account for the intracacies of the human personality.

1373 Ehrenburg, Ilya. Chekhov, Stendhal and Other Essays. Leningrad: Iskusstvo, 1962. Harrison E. Salisbury, ed.

1374 ------. Chekhov, Stendhal And Other Essays. Tr. by Anna Bostock, Yvonne Kapp, & Tatiana Shebunina. London:MacGibbon & Kee, 1962. Chekhov has influenced writers all over the world. People quote many different plays and stories as their special favorite. Chekhov's modesty is very becoming. When he condemns, he does so in such a gentle fashion that an insensitive person might miss the point. He was constantly hostile to inhumanity. He detested cruelty and vulgarity, and he hated to see beauty destroyed. One could build up a catalog of virtues by listing the things he opposed (pp.11-77). Reviews: Book R Digest, Sep 1963; Christian Sci Monitor, 1 Aug 1963, p. 11; Critic 22 (Aug 1963) 82; Library J 88 (Aug 1963) 2908; N.Y.Herald-Tribune Books, 30 Jun 1963, p. 4; N.Y.Times Book R, 7 Jul 1963, p. 5; Saturday R of Lit 46 (17 Aug 1963) 17; Times Literary Supplement, 11 May 1962, p. 340; Virginia Q R 40 (Winter 1964) 22.

1375 Emeljanow, Victor, ed. Chekhov: The Critical Heritage. London: Routledge & Kegan, 1981. Bibliog. Index. An anthology of play reviews and critical notices of Chekhov in England and the United States from 1891 to 1945. A long intro by Emeljanow summarizes Chekhov criticism in England and the United States. The appendix provides cast lists of Chekhov play productions in London and New York City up to 1945. Review: Times Literary Supplement, 2 Sep 1983, p. 928c.

1376 Eng, J. van der, Jan M. Meyer & Herta Schmidt. On the Theory of Descriptive Poetics:Anton P. Chekhov as Story-Teller and Playwright. Lisse: Peter de Ridder Pr, 1978. Bibliog.

1377 Ermilov, Vladimir. Anton Pavlovich Chekhov, 1860-1904. Moscow: Foreign Languages Publishing House, 1956. Tr. by Ivy Litvinov. Notes. Extensive biography gives the background of many stories and plays. Chekhov uses the beauty of nature not to belittle man but as a constant reproach to the ugliness, injustice, and triviality of human relations. His democratic spirit is seen in how he raises "little" people to a lofty place. His works often show how hard it is for a poor person to rise to higher social status by means of artistic creation. He wrote to his brother that "the salt of life consists in dignified protest." Artistic talent was inextricably bound up with high ethical standards, he felt. But although he stood for liberal and humane values, like most of the Russian intelligentsia he remained apart from any revolutionary change.

1378 ------. Reprint of #1377. London: Sidgwick, 1957.

1379 Garnett, Edward. Chekhov and His Art. London: 1929.

1380 Gerhardi, William. Anton Chehov: A Critical Study. London: Cobden-Sanderson, 1923. Gerhardi analyzes five factors: Chekhov's unique effect; Chekhov's sensibility or personality; the life factors that produced that sensibility; how Chekhov's style expressed his sensibility; and characteristic excerpts from Chekhov's writings that perfectly express that sensibility. Reviews: Bookman (London) 66 (May 1924) 133-4; London Mercury 9 (Jan 1924) 326; Nation & Athenaeum 34 (8 Dec 1923) 380; New Statesman 25 (20 Jun 1925) 284; Spectator 131 (8 Dec 1923) 902; Times Literary Supplement, 6 Dec 1923, p. 841b.

1381 ------. Reprint of #1380. N.Y.: Duffield,1923. Reviews: American Mercury 2 (May 1924) 127; Bookman (N.Y.) 59 (Apr 1924) 226-7; Forum 71 (Mar 1924) 412-3; McNaught's Monthly 1 (Mar 1924) 178; Nation (N.Y.) 118 (4 Jun 1924) 656-7; New Republic 38 (26 Mar 1924) 129-30; N.Y.Times Book R, 6 Jan 1924, p. 4.

1382 ------. Reprint of #1380. London: Duckworth, 1928.

1383 ------. New ed. of #1380. London: McDonald, 1974. Preface by Michael Holroyd.

1384 ------. Reprint of #1383. N.Y.: St. Martin's Pr, 1975.

1385 Gilles, Daniel. Chekhov: Observer Without Illusion. N.Y.: Funk & Wagnalls, 1967. Tr. from the French by Charles L. Markman. Bibliog. Index. Notes. This biography relates Chekhov's life experiences to his works. It is particularly good on Chekhov's changing attitude towards Tolstoy, and on Chekhov's various amorous interests. Reviews: Best Sellers 29 (1 Jun 1969) 90; Book World, 20 Apr 1969, p. 4; Library J 93 (15 Nov 1968) 4286; N.Y.Times Book R, 19 Jan 1969, p. 36; Slavic & East European J 14 (Spring 1970) 90-2.

1386 Goldstone, Herbert, ed. Chekhov's The Cherry Orchard. Boston: Allyn & Bacon, 1965. The Cherry Orchard, tr.by Stark Young. 21 letters by Chekhov about this play. Bibliog. Critical articles and reviews by Leonid Andreyev, Eric Bentley, W.H. Bruford, Harold Clurman,Robert W. Corrigan, Irving Deer, N.E. Efros, Francis Fergusson, William Gerhardi, Maxim Gorky, Richard Hayes, Gertrude Besse King, Jacqueline Latham, David Magarshack, Margaret Marshall, Vsevolod Meyerhold, Nils Ake Nilsson, Konstantin Stanislavsky, Charles B. Timmer, Virginia Woolf, and Stark Young.

1387 Gorchakov, N., ed. Anton Pavlovich Chekhov in the Theatre. Moscow: 1955.

1388 Gorky, Maxim. Reminiscences. N.Y.: Dover, 1946. Has reminiscences of Leonid Andreyev, Alexander Blok, Chekhov, and Leo Tolstoy.

1389 ------. Reminiscences of Anton Tchekhov. Tr. by S.S. Koteliansky & Leonard Woolf. London: Hogarth Pr, 1921. Gorky praises Chekhov for his honesty, accurate observation, and modesty.

1390 ------. Reminiscences of Tolstoy, Chekhov, & Andreyev. London: Hogarth Pr, 1934. "Reminiscences of Chekhov" tr. by S.S. Koteliansky & Leonard Woolf. "The Gorky-Chekhov Correspondence" & "Chekhov in Gorky's Diary" ed. by Aron Krich.

1391 ------. Reprint of #1390. N.Y.: Viking, 1959.

1392 ------, & Ivan Bunin & Alexander Kuprin. Reminiscences of Anton Tchekhov. Tr. by S. S. Koteliansky & Leonard Woolf. London: Hogarth Pr, 1921.

1393 ------. Reprint of #1392. N.Y.: Huebsch, 1921. Reviews: Bookman (N.Y.) 54 (Feb 1922) 588; Freeman 4 (1 Mar 1922) 592-4; Nation (N.Y.) 114 (5 Apr 1922) 400; N.Y. Times Book R, 1 Jan 1922, p. 2.

1394 Gottlieb, Vera. Chekhov and the Vaudeville: A Study of Chekhov's One-Act Plays. Cambridge: Cambridge Univ Pr, 1982. Bibliog. Index. Notes. Chekhov's short plays are classified and analyzed as farce-vaudevilles, dramatic studies, one-act plays, and one-act monologues. Seen as growing out of his stories, they are evaluated as a stage in the development of his more mature dramatic technique, and as an insight into his philosophy of life. Appendices contain translations of two little-known one-act plays: A Forced Declaration and Dishonourable Tragedians And Leprous Dramatists. Reviews: Slavic & East European J 27 (Summer 1983) 262-4; Times Literary Supplement, 31 Dec 1982, p. 1446.

1395 Hahn, Beverly. Chekhov: A Study of the Major Stories and Plays. Cambridge: Cambridge Univ Pr, 1977. Bibliog. Chronological table. Index. Notes. Influenced by Tolstoy, Chekhov helped develop the novella as a literary form. Time is a protagonist in his works. Change, even in temperament and sensibility, subtly accompanies time's passage. In the theater, Chekhov's contribution lay in his successfully transferring to the stage the emotional realism he was able to depict in the short story. With deep understanding he renders feminine psychology: he seems repulsed by both trivial domesticity and primitive female aggression, but he sympathetically portrays strong and cultured women who find civilized ways to protest against a confining environment. Review: Times Literary Supplement, 1 Jul 1977, p. 799.

1396 Hingley, Ronald. Chekhov: A Biographical and Critical Study. London: Allen & Unwin, 1950. Bibliog. Index. Notes. The facts of Chekhov's life are used to help the reader understand and appreciate the stories and plays. Appendix lists Chekhov's translated stories in chronological order. Reviews: Library J 76 (1951) 1030; N.Y.Times Book R, 3 Jun 1951, p. 5; Russian R (N.Y.) 10 (Oct 1951) 321; Virginia Q R 27 (Oct 1951) 604-8.

1397 Revised ed. of #1396. London: Allen & Unwin, 1966. No notes or appendix. Review: Choice 3 (1967) 1021.

1398 ------. A New Life of Anton Chekhov. London: Oxford Univ Pr, 1976. Appendices on Chekhov's works and on Chekhov in English. Bibliog. Index. Notes. This biography sheds much light on Chekhov's art. Based on Russian sources, it explains Chekhov's relationship to the many journals that published his stories. Suggesting that perhaps he was undersexed, it shows Chekhov treating women with affectionate condescension. No Marxist, yet opposed to the inhumanity of czarist Russia, Chekhov had little use for "liberals" who were as doctrinaire from the left as those they opposed on the right. Attempting to debunk the image of Chekhov as a paragon of virtue, Hingley nevertheless concludes that he was a man of extraordinary gentleness, kindness, and modesty. Reviews: New Statesman, 14 May 1976, p. 649; N.Y.Times Book R, 20 Jun 1976, p. 1; Spectator 236 (15 May 1976) 21-2.

1399 Hulanicki, Leo & David Savignac, eds. & trs. Anton Cexov as a Master of Story-Writing. The Hague: Mouton, 1976. Bibliog. Index. Notes. Nine Soviet literary critics discuss Chekhov's art. A. A. Cicerin finds Chekhov using a deliberate vagueness in order to suggest more ideal realms of beauty and justice. A. B. Derman says that Chekhov's meaning is buried in a subtext, which can be found by a close reading of his endings. E.S. Dobin believes that slight details often carry deep literary, psychological, and social meanings. V.V. Golubkov finds a lyrical quality in the stories, due to emotional phrases, repetitions, and near-poetic expressions. V. Laksin feels that a tiny fragment in a story makes it possible to imagine the whole fate of a character. Vadim Nazarenko analyzes Chekhov's imagery as coming from a vivid pictorial sense rather than from conventional figures of speech. G.N. Pospelov states that the ennui of Chekhov's characters arises not so much from personal dissatisfaction as from political repression. Viktor Shklovsky believes that the suffering of Chekhov's heroes remains unavenged. V.V. Vinogradov sees in Chekhov's dialogue great depth and subtlety in delineating social and class distinctions. Reviews: Mod Fict Studies 23 (Winter 1977) 690-3; Slavic & East European J 22 (Spring 1978) 86-7; Slavic & East European R 56 (Apr 1978) 314-5.

1400 Jackson, Robert Louis, ed. Chekhov: A Collection of Critical Essays. Englewood Cliffs, NJ: Prentice-Hall, 1967. Bibliog. Notes. Critical articles on Chekhov's writings by S. D. Balukhaty,G. Berdnikov, Dmitri Chizhevsky, Charles du Bos, Boris Eichenbaum, Francis Fergusson, John Gassner, Maxim Gorky, Leonid Grossman, Robert Louis Jackson, Vsevolod Meyerhold, Nils Ake Nilsson, A. Skaftymov, M. N. Stroeva, and V. Yermilov. Review: Choice 5 (1968) 966.

1401 Katzer, Julius, ed. Anton Chekhov: 1860-1960. Moscow: Foreign Language Publishing House, 1960.

1402 Kirk, Irina. Anton Chekhov. Edited by Charles Moser. Boston: Hall, 1981. Bibliog. Chronology. Index. Notes. This brief biography combines the author's critical insights with those of other critics. Chekhov's tales are praised for objectivity, and for the creation of atmosphere from setting. In his plays a growing artistry is detected, from broad farcical effects to serious drama employing symbols, mood, and sub-text. Review: Modern Language R 77 (Jul 1982) 764-5.

1403 Koteliansky, S. S., ed. & tr. Anton Tchekhov: Literary and Theatrical Reminiscences. London: Routledge, 1927. 6 stories. Plays: On the Harmfulness of Tobacco, Tatyana Riepin. Chekhov's autobiography, chronology, and diary. Index. Articles and reminiscences by Leonid Andreyev, Mme. V. S. Boutov, Ivan Bunin, Alexander Chekhov, Ivan Chekhov, Michael Chekhov, N.Efros, Maxim Gorky, V. I. Kachalov, V. Korolenko, Alexander Kuprin, L. M. Leonidov, Mme. M. P. Lilin, Mme. E. P. Muratov, V. I. Nemirovich-Danchenko, Y. Sobolev, L. A. Soulerzhitsky,K.S. Stanislavsky, A.S. Suvorin, Leo Tolstoy, and A. L. Vishnevsky. Reviews: Adelphi 4 (Jun 1927) 767; Manchester Guardian, 21 Jun 1927, p. 9; Monthly Criterion 6 (Aug 1927) 183; Nation and Athenaeum 41 (30 Apr 1927) 116; New Statesman 29 (14 May 1927)152; Observer (London), 15 May 1927, p. 6; Saturday R (London) 143 (9 Apr 1927) 565; Times Literary Supplement, 21 Apr 1927, p. 277a.

1404 Reprint of #1403. N.Y.: Doran, 1927. Reviews: Booklist 24 (Nov 1927) 66; Bookman (N.Y.) 65 (Aug 1927) 714; Boston Transcript, 28 May 1927, p. 3; Dial 83 (Dec 1927) 527; Forum 78 (Oct 1927) 635; N.Y.Evening Post, 23 Jul 1927, p. 8; N.Y.Times Book R, 12 Jun 1927, p. 14; Saturday R of Lit 4 (24 Sep 1927) 133-4.

1405 Reprint of #1403. N.Y.: Haskell House, 1974.

1406 Kramer, Karl D. The Chameleon and the Dream: The Image of Reality in Cexov's Stories. The Hague: Mouton,1970. Bibliog. Index. Notes. Chekhov's early parodies show his serious interest in mastering his craft. Seeking inner action, Chekhov abandoned formula plots of external action. His villain is the unfeeling person. A chameleon is a person who instantly changes his behavior as he perceives the other person's social status as being above or below his own. In portraying chameleons, Chekhov satirizes a society in which rank and bribes play so important a part. A world of constant change is one lacking permanent moral values. Chekhov sympathized with the dreamer (not the daydreamer) who has a vision of a better world, one with more permanent moral values. Chekhov's impressionism led to ambiguity, which was itself on a path away from realism and toward symbolism, which permits varied levels of actuality unified by a single image.

1407 Laffitte, Sophie. Chekhov: 1860-1904. N.Y.: Scribner, 1973. Tr. from the French by Moura Budberg & Gordon Latta. Brief biography stresses Chekhov's life more than his works. Bibliog. Index. Notes. Reviews: Comparative Drama 10 (Spring 1976) 86-8; J of European Studies 5 (Dec 1975) 383-4.

1408 Lucas, Frank L. The Drama of Chekhov, Synge, Yeats and Pirandello. London: Cassell, 1963. Bibliog. Index. A summary of the plots of Chekhov's plays. Defying Aristotle, Chekhov substitutes unity of mood for unity of action. The most Western of Russia's great writers, Chekhov is far more of a world figure than John Millington Synge, though both used similar almost classical simplicity. Chekhov's nearly scientific objectivity contrasts with the personal subjectivism of William Butler Yeats. Luigi Pirandello's disguised philosophy would have seemed too pedantic to Chekhov. But Chekhov's ideas--the need for irony, for compassion, for hard work, for stoical indifference--seem more limited than the revolutionary questioning found in the plays of Henrik Ibsen (pp. 1-146). Review: Drama n.s. no. 74 (Autumn 1964) 36-9.

1409 Magarshack, David. Chekhov the Dramatist. London: Lehmann, 1952. Appendix on Act IV of Ivanov. Chronological list of Chekhov's plays. Index. Notes. Based upon original Russian sources, this book gives good background material on Chekhov's farces. Quoting from previously untranslated letters, Magarshack shows that Chekhov wrote plays with specific actors in mind, and that he felt that a play was not completed until it had been revised after rehearsals. A number of similarities between Greek drama and Chekhov's plays are given. Most directors,including Stanislavsky, warp Chekhov's intent by stressing pessimistic moodiness rather than the positive ideas and ideals in the plays. Chekhov moved from conventional direct-action drama to lyrical indirect-action plays.

1410 ------. Reprint of #1409. N.Y.: Auvergne Publishers, 1951. Reviews: Library J 77 (1952) 900; Russian R (N.Y.) 12 (Apr 1953) 126-7; Saturday R of Lit, 24 May 1951, p. 32.

1411 ------. Reprint of #1409. N.Y.: Hill & Wang, 1960.

1412 Magarshack, David. Chekhov: A Life. London: Faber,1952. Lengthy biography based on many Russian sources.Stresses Chekhov's effort to write a comprehensive novel, and to secure recognition as a writer of comedies rather than tragedies. Bibliog contains the title of everything Chekhov published from 1880 to 1904; given are English and Russian titles, dates of publication, publishers, and translators. Index. Review: New Statesman & Nation 44 (15 Nov 1952) 577.

1413 ------. Reprint of #1412. N.Y.: Grove, 1953. Reviews: American Slavic & East European R 14 (Apr 1954) 267-9; Books of the Month (British Book Center, N.Y.C.), Feb 1953, p. 34; Library J 78 (15 Oct 1953) 1849; Nation (N.Y.) 177 (19 Sep 1953) 235; New Republic 129 (12 Oct 1953) 19; N.Y.Herald-Trib Book R, 29 Nov 1953, p. 7; N.Y.Times, 13 Sep 1953, p. 6; New Yorker 29 (19 Sep 1953) 120; Saturday R of Lit 36 (19 Sep 1953) 19; Time 62 (28 Sep 1953) 90.

1414 ------. Reprint of #1412. Westport, CT: Greenwood Pr, 1970.

1415 ------. The Real Chekhov: An Introduction to Chekhov's Last Plays. London: Allen & Unwin, 1972. Index. Magarshack feels that directors ruin Chekhov's plays by ignoring his intention in writing the plays. The Sea Gull deals with the nature of creative art. The Three Sisters shows how slowly necessary change comes. Uncle Vanya portrays both selfish and unselfish idealism. In Chekhov's opinion, The Cherry Orchard should be played as "gay and light-hearted comedy."

1416 ------. Reprint of #1415. N.Y.: Barnes & Noble, 1973.

1417 Markov, Pavel A. The First Studio Sullerzhitsky-Vacktangov-Tchekhov. Tr. by Mark Schmidt. N.Y.: Group Theatre, 1934.

1418 Melchinger, Siegfried. Anton Chekhov. Tr. from the German by Edith Tarcov. N.Y.: Ungar, 1972. Bibliog. Index. Biography stresses Chekhov's humanitarianism. It gives special attention to his youth, when as a high-spirited amateur actor, Chekhov's improvisations were very popular with the crowd. Review: Slavic R 32 (Dec 1973) 852-3.

1419 Nemirovsky, Irene. A Life of Chekhov. Tr. from the French by Erik de Mauny. London: Grey Walls Pr, 1950. A novelist, Nemirovsky writes this brief biography as if it were a novel. Based upon facts, it has many references to Chekhov's letters and stories. Reviews: New

Statesman & Nation 40 (8 Jul 1950) 43; Spectator 184 (9 Jan 1950) 794.

1420 Reprint of #1419. N.Y.: Haskell House, 1974.

1421 Nielsen, Marit B. Two Women Characters in Cexov's Work and Some Aspects of His Portrayal of Women. Oslo: Universitetet, 1975.

1422 Nilsson, Nils Ake. Studies in Chekhov's Narrative Technique: "The Steppe" and "The Bishop". Stockholm: Almqvist & Wiksell, 1968. Bibliog. Notes. In an early work "The Steppe," settings are important both as suggestive backdrops and as independent descriptions. A late work like "the Bishop" uses landscapes only in the first sense. Also, whereas Nature seems indifferent to man in the early stories, in the later ones Nature is seen as more of a nurturing factor to man.

1423 Peace, Richard A. Chekhov: A Study of the Four Major Plays. New Haven: Yale Univ Pr, 1983. Index. Notes. Chekhov's dramatic art is typically Russian. He uses symbols iconographically, both to suggest deeper meanings and to escape censorship. Usurpation is both his theme and his method. Treplev tries to usurp Trigorin's role; Natasha usurps the Prozorovs; Lopakhin usurps the Ranevskys. Daydreams usurp action; mood encroaches on plot; and direct statement is replaced by indirect commentary. Reviews: Choice 21 (Dec 1983) 580; Times Literary Supplement, 27 Apr 1984, p. 471.

1424 Pitcher, Harvey. The Chekhov Play:A New Interpretation. London: Chatto & Windus,1973. Index. Notes. As a dramatist Chekhov is not a social historian nor an ironic depicter of human isolation, but the greatest portrayer of human emotion. He shows the emotional network existing among a group of people: the complex and sensitive interconnections that we form with persons around us--these connections alone are meaningful in life. Charting the intricate communication network, Chekhov has his characters interrelate by such subtle means as a pause, a tune, a tone of voice. His plots are centrifugal: the audience concentrates not so much on the characters' fates as on the way they open up feelings about life in general and our relationship to the world we inhabit. Reviews: Contemporary R 224 (Feb 1974) 108-9; Drama no. 111 (Winter 1973) 83; Times Literary Supplement, 8 Feb 1974, p. 122.

1425 Reprint of #1424. N.Y.: Harper & Row, 1973. Reviews: Book R Digest, 1974, p. 963; Choice 10 (1973) 1557; Library J 98 (1973) 3637.

1426 ------. Chekhov's Leading Lady: A Portrait of the Actress Olga Knipper. London: Murray, 1979. Bibliog. Index. Notes. This biography not only sheds much light on Chekhov's life but also clearly depicts the emotional triangle consisting of Chekhov, his wife, and his sister Masha. Reviews: Contemporary R 235 (Dec 1979) 333-4; Times Literary Supplement, 25 Apr 1980, p. 476.

1427 Reprint of #1426. N.Y.: Franklin Watts, 1980. Review: Russian R (N.Y.) 39 (Jul 1980) 369-70.

1428 Priestley, J.B. Anton Chekhov. London: International Profiles, 1970. Bibliog. Chronological table. A brief biography, with many photographs of Chekhov. Chekhov's influence on short-story writers has not been good, since they cannot achieve his unique economy and restraint. But in the theater his influence has been profound. With "the most delicate antennae in Russian literature," he was a master of creating deep effects with few strokes. Moreover, as a person Chekhov is the model for a new kind of man: skeptical, pragmatic, but always humane.

1429 Rayfield, Donald. Chekhov: The Evolution of His Art. London: Elek Books, 1975. Bibliog. Index. Notes. Relying upon recently published letters, reminiscences and research into Chekhov's medical background, this book shows how Chekhov's plays and stories interrelate. Review: New Statesman, 13 Feb 1976, pp. 192-3.

1430 Reprint of #1429. N.Y.: Barnes & Noble, 1975.

1431 Saunders, Beatrice. Tchehov the Man. London: Centaur Pr, 1960. Bibliog.Index. Detailed social background of Chekhov's life, more biography than criticism. Stress is upon Chekhov as a humanitarian: "If ever a man's nobility of soul was apparent it was in this man."

1432 Shestov, Leon. Anton Tchekhov and Other Essays. London: Maunsel, 1916. Tr. by S.S. Koteliansky and J.M. Murry. Repressive czarism killed hope within Chekhov, but by creating lasting works of art out of the negative experience, Chekhov proved the supremacy of man's spirit over its own hopelessness. It is sad that Chekhov's only hero is the hopeless man (pp 3-60). Reviews: Athenaeum, Apr 1917, p. 200; Times Literary Supplement, 26 Jan 1917, p. 40b.

1433 Reprint of #1432. New intro by Sidney Monas. Ann Arbor: Univ of Mich Pr, 1966. Reviews: Choice 5 (1968) 202; Russian R (N.Y.) 26 (Jan 1967) 97; Saturday R of Lit, 11 Jun 1966, p. 57.

1434 Simmons, Ernest J. Chekhov: A Biography. Boston: Little Brown, 1962. The fullest and best biography of Chekhov in English. Based on many original Russian sources. Extensive bibliog. Index. Notes. Reviews: Canadian Forum 43 (Sep 1963) 140; Chicago Sunday Tribune, 28 Oct 1962, p. 2; Christian Sci Monitor, 25 Oct 1962, p. 7; Commonweal 77 (11 Jan 1963) 411-2; Library J 87 (15 Oct 1962) 3669 & 88 (Jul 1963) 2785; Nation

(N.Y.) 195 (1 Dec 1962) 378; New Statesman 66 (25 Oct 1963) 582; N.Y.Herald-Tribune Books, 21 Oct 1962,p.5; N.Y.Times Book R, 21 Oct 1962, p. 1; New Yorker 39 (2 Mar 1963) 138; Reporter 27 (6 Dec 1962) 55-6; Russian R (N.Y.) 22 (Apr 1963) 202; Saturday R (N.Y.) 45 (24 Nov 1962) 28; Slavic & East European J 7 (Fall 1963) 313-6; Slavic R 22 (1963) 591-5; Time 80 (19 Oct 1962) 94; Times Literary Supplement, 11 Oct 1963, p. 799; Virginia Q R 39 (Winter 1963) 135; Yale R 52 (Mar 1963) 20.

1435 Smith, Virginia Llewellyn. Anton Chekhov and the Lady with the Dog. London: Oxford Univ Pr, 1973. Foreword by Ronald Hingley. Bibliog. Index. Notes. Anna Sergeyevna, the lady with the dog in Chekhov's story by that name, is symbolic of the ideal love that Chekhov could envision but not embrace. In Chekhov's later work, this ideal love became increasingly identified with a quasi-mystical faith in the future of mankind. Review: Russian R (N.Y.) 33 (Jul 1974) 339-41.

1436 Speirs, Logan. Tolstoy and Chekhov. Cambridge: Cambridge Univ Pr, 1971. Notes. Intro treats of relationship between the two great writers. Sections are then devoted to Tolstoy; Chekhov's stories;Chekhov's plays. Reviews: Choice 8 (Sep 1971) 842; Encounter 37 (Sep 1971) 80; N.Y.Times Book R, 18 Apr 1971, p. 41; Times Literary Supplement, 4 Jun 1971, p. 650.

1437 Stowell, H. Peter. Literary Impressionism, James and Chekhov. Athens, GA: Univ of Georgia Pr,1980. Bibliog. Index. Notes. Henry James and Chekhov followed similar patterns of the most advanced literary impressionism. In impressionism, perception is the progressive creation of the perceiver. Literary impressionists deliberately skirt reality, reflecting modern life. What results is "the dissolution of plot, the broken cycle of causality, the relativism of time and space, and the perceptual subjectivity of characters" (p. 20). In his writings, "Chekhov fused subjective with objective time, space with time, and successive moments with duration" (p. 157). "Literary impressionists discovered modernism: what is rendered is the mood, sense, feel, and atmosphere that exists between perceiver and perceived, subject and object" (p. 244). Review: Comparative Literature Studies 19 (Spring 1982) 77-9.

1438 Styan, J.L. Chekhov in Performance: A Commentary on the Major Plays. Cambridge: Cambridge Univ Pr, 1971. Bibliog. Notes. A detailed stage history of productions of The Cherry Orchard, The Sea Gull, The Three Sisters, and Uncle Vanya by many directors.

1439 Talento, Louis V. Anton Chekhov: The Three Sisters; The Cherry Orchard. N.Y.: Barnes & Noble Book Notes, 1970.

1440 Toumanova, Nina A. Anton Chekhov: The Voice of Twilight Russia. N.Y.: Columbia Univ Pr, 1937. Bibliog. Index. Chekhov's life viewed in the light of its milieu. The revised version of a doctoral dissertation. Reviews: Adelphi 14 (Oct 1937) 19-20; Harper's 174 (Feb 1937) "Among the New Books"; New Republic 90 (3 Mar 1937) 116-7; New Statesman & Nation n.s. 14 (11 Sep 1937) 380-2; N.Y.Times Book R, 24 Jan 1937, p.3; Slavonic & East European R 15 (Apr 1937) 717-8; Spectator 159 (19 Nov 1937) 20-2; Time 29 (18 Jan 1937) 75; Time & Tide 18 (11 Sep 1937) 1202; Virginia Q R 13 (Summer 1937) 440-3.

1441 Tulloch, John. Chekhov: A Structuralist Study. London: Macmillan, 1980. Index. Notes. A revised doctoral dissertation, this study asserts that Chekhov's outlook as an environmental doctor determined and shaped his literary themes. His two main types of characters are the impractical visionary and the inauthentic hero (one who escapes boredom through such inauthentic avenues as adultery or alcoholism). Review: Times Literary Supplement, 14 Nov 1980, p. 1306.

1442 Urbanski, Henry. Chekhov as Viewed by His Russian Literary Contemporaries. Wroclaw, Poland: Wroclaw Univ Pr, 1979. A revised doctoral dissertation. Bibliog.

1443 Valency, Maurice. The Breaking String: The Plays of Anton Chekhov. London: Oxford Univ Pr, 1966. Bibliog. Index. Notes. A study of the interrelationship between Chekhov's stories and plays. Wisdom counseled indifference to life, but life's vital principle impelled one to action. In this tension, impossible to resolve, lay Chekhov's artistic dynamic. Chekhov developed a dramatic polyphony unparalleled in theatrical history. He best portrayed the transition from the old age to the new. The golden string that connected man to his father on earth and his Father in heaven has been snapped--the result has been both world-shaking and soul-shaking. Reviews: N.Y.Times Book R, 2 Apr 1967, p. 26; Russian R (N.Y.) 26 (Jul 1967) 305; Virginia Q R 43 (Spring 1967) 74.

1444 Watson, Ian. Chekhov's Journey. London: Gollancz, n.d.

1445 Wellek, Rene & Nonna D. Wellek, eds. Chekhov: New Perspectives. Englewood Cliffs, NJ: Prentice-Hall, 1984. Bibliog. Chronology. Index. Notes. Eric Bentley analyzes the craftsmanship of Uncle Vanya. Beverly Hahn interprets The Three Sisters sensitively. Simon Karlinsky provides a biographical sketch. David Magarshack presents The Cherry Orchard as a comedy. Harvey Pitcher gives a fresh introduction to Chekhov's plays. Donald Rayfield points out how Chekhov's fictional art merged with his dramatic technique. Thomas Winner relates The Sea Gull to Hamlet.

1446 Wexford, Jane. Monarch Notes on Chekhov's Plays and Stories. N.Y.: Monarch Pr, 1965.

1447 Winner, Anthony. Characters in the Twilight: Hardy, Zola, and Chekhov. Charlottesville: Univ Pr of Virginia, 1981. Index. Notes. Chekhov asked: "Have I no ideology? Aren't many stories a protest against lying?" Chekhov not only avoids answers--he shows the pathos of badly framed questions. Hardy shows mankind as prey to forces beyond its control. Zola depicts modern individuals victimized by amoral extremities.Chekhov shows that the individual is partly to blame, but is nevertheless to be pitied, for he is us. Reviews: Comparative Literature 34 (Fall 1982) 379-80; Modern Fiction Studies 28 (Summer 1982) 255-9.

1448 Winner, Thomas G. Chekhov and His Prose. N.Y.: Holt, Rinehart & Winston, 1966. Index. Notes. Winner analyzes Chekhov's prose style from the standpoint of its diction, its relation to other Russian writers, and its relation to Chekhov's life. Using many Russian sources, Winner shows Chekhov's seminal influence upon the modern short story. Reviews: Book R Digest, Aug 1966; Nation (N.Y.) 202 (6 Jun 1966) 684-6; N.Y. R of Books 7 (18 Aug 1966) 20; Russian R (N.Y.) 26 (Jul 1967) 305; Saturday R of Lit 49 (19 Feb 1966) 50; Virgina Q R 42 (Summer 1966) 103.

1449 Yoder, Hilda V.Dramatizations of Social Change: Heijermans' Plays as Compared with Selected Dramas by Ibsen, Hauptmann and Chekhov. The Hague: Nijihoff, 1978.

Books with Chekhov Material (alphabetical by authors)

1450 Agate, James. The Contemporary Theatre. N.Y.: Blom, 1969. Reprint of 1927 ed. Review of The Three Sisters at the Barnes Theatre in London, directed by Theodore Komisarjevsky (pp. 55-9).

1451 ------. First Nights. N.Y.: Blom, 1971. Reprint of 1934 ed. Review of The Cherry Orchard at the Old Vic Theatre in London on 9 Oct 1933 (pp. 214-7).

1452 ------. More First Nights. N.Y.: Blom, 1969. Reprint of 1937 ed. Reviews of The Three Sisters at the Old Vic Theatre in London on 12 Nov 1935, and of The Sea Gull at the New Theatre in London on 20 May 1936 (pp. 189-94, 272-6).

1453 ------, ed.English Dramatic Critics: An Anthology 1660-1932. N.Y.: Hill & Wang, 1958. Review by Desmond MacCarthy of Uncle Vanya production by the Stage Society in London in May 1914 (pp. 300-6).

1454 Aiken, Conrad P. Collected Criticism. London: Oxford Univ Pr, 1968. Chekhov's tales have the quality of natural actuality. He avoids literary tricks. His characters are more complex than those of Maupassant. Chekhov and Henry James are at opposite literary poles: James uses conscious art, Chekhov unconscious art (pp. 148-52).

1455 Allen, Walter. The Short Story in English. Oxford: Clarendon Pr, 1981. Chekhov's influence is seen upon Conrad Aiken, H.E.Bates, Morley Callaghan, Leslie Halward, Katherine Mansfield, and Frank O'Connor (pp. 136, 138, 165-8, 174, 201-2, 209, 216-8, 262, 275).

1456 Alpatov, Mikhail. The Russian Impact on Art. N.Y.: Philosophical Library, 1950. Creator of the Russian short story, Chekhov uses chance occurrences to show life's mysterious flow. Whereas Maupassant found life to be meaningless, Chekhov's all-pervading love of life saved him (and his work) from despondency (pp. 273-6).

1457 Andrew, Joe. Writers and Society During the Rise of Russian Realism. Atlantic Highlands, NJ: Humanities Pr, 1980. Chekhov asks: "What great question is answered in Anna Karenina or Eugene Onegin?" None. They are great works, he says, because they formulate the questions of life correctly (p. 22).

1458 Bakshy, Alexander. The Path of the Modern Russian Stage and Other Essays. London: Palmer & Hayward, 1916. The Moscow Art Theatre discovered Chekhov's dramatic secret to be to bring out numerous small details, all related to the "main sentiment" of the play (pp. 38-43).

1459 Baring, Maurice. Landmarks in Russian Literature. N.Y.: Macmillan, 1910. Chekhov's plays reveal "the poetry of everyday life." He goes beyond other dramatists in his ability to avoid artifical devices like the chorus, the raisonneur, monologues, and asides, but showing us in a gesture or a tune a deeply concealed emotion. His tales are outstanding for their humor, pathos, and simplicity (pp. 263-99).

1460 ------. An Outline of Russian Literature. London: Butterworth, 1915. Chekhov's humor and humanity keep his pessimism from being intolerable. In his plays, beneath the surface triviality, one hears "the still sad music of humanity" (pp. 243-7).

1461 Barrault, Jean-Louis. The Theatre of Jean-Louis Barrault. Tr.from the French by Joseph Chiari. N.Y.: Hill & Wang, 1961. The Cherry Orchard is the most universal of Chekhov's plays, since all people are subject to the corrosive influence of time, which is the play's theme (pp. 104-11).

1462 Bates, Alfred, ed. The Drama. London: Smart & Stanley, 1903. "A first-rate artist in an inferior style. In his tales we find a strange assemblage of neurotics and lunatics" (vol 18, pp. 158-60).

1463 Bates, Herbert E. The Modern Short Story. London: Nelson, 1942. "Tchehov and Maupassant" (chap. 4).

1464 Beach, Joseph Warren. American Fiction, 1920-1940. N.Y.: Macmillan, 1941. Chekhov's depth of characterization gives readers a heightened interest in living. Each person is portrayed with such individuality that he has a dignity and an importance of his own (pp. 310-4).

1465 Becker, George J. Master European Realists of the Nineteenth Century. N.Y.: Ungar, 1982. Chekhov's significant contribution to realism is his ability to convey simultaneously a physical environment and the accompanying emotional states of the characters in that environment (pp. 202-38).

1466 Beckerman, Bernard. Dynamics of Drama: Theory and Method of Analysis. N.Y.: Knopf, 1970. Instead of using linear narrative, Chekhov's plays use spatial simultaneity, that is, several strands of action converge on the stage at one time, giving the plays unusual depth (pp. 101-12).

1467 Bellinger, Martha Fletcher. A Short History of the Drama. N.Y.: Holt, 1927. Only Chekhov and John Millington Synge, among naturalistic dramatists, have captured "the classical tragic note" (pp. 149-50).

1468 Bennett, Arnold. Books and Persons. N.Y.: Doran, 1917. Chekhov has achieved "absolute realism" (pp. 117-9, 321-4).

1469 ------. The Journals of Arnold Bennett, 1896-1928.N.Y.: Viking, 1933. Chekhov's deep influence upon Bennett's short fiction is shown (pp. 320, 632, 660-1, 727, 729, 766, 789).

1470 ------. The Savour of Life. N.Y.: Doubleday Doran,1928. Bennett praises Chekhov's breadth of interest and excellent "landscapes", and says he "did as much as any writer to hasten the Russian revolution" (pp. 128-9, 138).

1471 ------. Things That Have Interested Me. London: Chatto & Windus, 1921. Compared to Maupassant, Chekhov had better observation, wider interests and sympathies, and greater vividness. The Frenchman was superior, however, in economy, technique, and in "the emotional power of rendering a given situation" (pp. 195-7).

1472 ------. Things That Have Interested Me, Third Series. N.Y.: Doran, 1926. Bennett was disappointed at the poor public reception of The Cherry Orchard as staged at the Lyric Theatre in London in 1925, but then, as both public and critical recognition came to Chekhov, Bennett saw it as a sure sign of the evolution of dramatic taste in London (p. 14).

1473 Bennett, Benjamin. Modern Drama and German Classicism: The Renaissance from Lessing to Brecht. Ithaca, NY: Cornell Univ Pr, 1979. Chekhov's plays are not true tragicomedy; rather, he portrays futile sociability (pp. 168-70, 312-4).

1474 Bentley, Eric. In Search of Theater. N.Y.: Knopf, 1953. "Craftsmanship in Uncle Vanya" (pp. 342-64).

1475 -------. The Life of the Drama. N.Y.: Atheneum, 1972. Chekhov and Ibsen are the greatest psychological dramatists. Like Ibsen, Chekhov celebrated individuality more than individualism. Chekhov even used traditional villains, that is, those who drive the action towards catastrophe (pp. 54-9).

1476 ------. The Playwright as Thinker. N.Y.:Meridian Books, 1955. Chekhov said: "You must not lower Gogol to the people, but raise the people to the level of Gogol." True, he called for a People's Theater, but it was to be one guided by taste and intelligence (pp. 249-51).

1477 Berlin, Normand. The Secret Cause: A Discussion of Tragedy. Amherst: Univ of Mass Pr, 1981. Chekhov's plays surpass those of John M. Synge, since Synge ignores the deep inner secret cause of tragedy. Beckett is Chekhov's heir. Waiting for Godot echoes the "waiting for Moscow" found in The Three Sisters (pp. 109-24).

1478 Berman, Morton & Sylvan Barnet & William Burto, eds. Types of Drama. Boston: Little,Brown, 1972. Chekhov wanted to have The Cherry Orchard staged as a comedy, but Stanislavsky insisted it was a tragedy. "Perhaps neither of the men fully wanted to see the resonant ambiguities in the play" (pp. 489-92).

1479 Block, Anita. The Changing World in Plays and Theatre. Boston: Little,Brown, 1939. It is "false" to think of Chekhov merely as a creator of lasting characters and a perfected dramatic technique. His subject matter and underlying social philosophy transcend his character portrayals as completely as Ibsen's social concepts dwarf his own technique. There is no more damning portrayal of czarist Russia than Chekhov's plays (p. 69).

1480 Bogard, Travis & William I. Oliver, eds. Modern Drama: Essays in Criticism. London: Oxford Univ Pr, 1965. Chekhov's plays have a "mysterious quality of affirmation." His comedy celebrates man's capacity to endure (Robert W. Corrigan, "The Drama of Anton Chekhov," pp. 73-98).

1481 Boyarski, Y. & N. Chuskin, eds. Fortieth Anniversary of the Moscow Art Theatre. Moscow: USSR in Construction, 1938. Has material on The Cherry Orchard,The Sea Gull, and The Three Sisters.

1482 Brereton, Geoffrey.Principles of Tragedy. Coral Gables: Univ of Miami Pr, 1968. In his tragicomedy, Chekhov created a new dramatic idiom, possibly the finest achievement of realism (pp. 214-24).

1483 Brewster, Dorothy & Angus Burrell. Dead Reckonings in Fiction. N.Y.: Longmans,Green, 1924. Chekhov and Katherine Mansfield are alike in selecting certain "instants of realization" in their characters' lives as the material for the story rather than the full narrative. Chekhov used felicitous imagery in building atmosphere. Chekhov and Mark Twain had similar spiritual outlooks on the essential tragedy of man's loneliness (pp. 43, 54, 49-50, 85-6, 99).

1484 ------. Modern Fiction. N.Y.: Columbia Univ Pr, 1934. Chekhov dispensed with plot structure and climax. He refused to place people into categories; each was an individual with an importance and a dignity of his own. Seeing the depths of his achievement, other writers have followed suit (pp. 348-87).

1485 Brook, Peter. The Empty Space. N.Y.:Avon, 1968. Chekhov gives, not a slice of life,but many slices exquisitely arranged. He shows life's coincidences and alienations; each dissonance provokes us to thought (pp. 71-2).

1486 Brooks, Cleanth. Understanding Drama. N.Y.: Henry Holt, 1945. In terms of esthetic distance, Chekhov holds himself aloof from his dramatic characters, never sentimentalizing them. Thus we never quite identify with them, but rather view them from a distant vantage point, with a mixture of pity and ironic understanding (pp. 489-502).

1487 Brooks, Van Wyck. On Literature Today. N.Y.: Dutton, 1941. Chekhov accurately confessed that a major weakness in all of his writings was the lack of an overpowering purpose (pp. 11-2).

1488 Brown, Edward J. Russian Literature Since the Revolution. N.Y.: Collier Books, 1963. Chekhov taught Isaac Babel the art of elevating the funny story to the level of irony (p. 117).

1489 Brown, John Mason. Broadway in Review. N.Y.: Norton, 1940. The Surry Players at the Longacre Theatre did not capture the relevance of The Three Sisters' seeming irrelevancies (pp. 230-3).

1490 ------. Two on the Aisle. N.Y.: Norton, 1938. The Cherry Orchard is perennially new because it intentionally does not iron out the characters' complexities. Thus an actor finds new meaning and depth in a role each time he plays it (pp. 84-8).

1491 Bruckner, A. A Literary History of Russia. London: Unwin, 1908. Chekhov stands high above other tellers of tales. His pessimism would be unbearable except for his deep sympathy, his purified humaneness, and his modest but inexhaustible power of creating always living and ever fresh characters. His plays are merely dramatized short stories (pp. 532-9).

1492 Brustein, Robert S. The Culture Watch: Essays on Theatre and Society, 1969-1974. N.Y.: Knopf, 1975. Treplev in The Sea Gull was right; it is not a question of new form or old form in drama but of sincere expression springing from the writer's soul. The Actors Studio production of The Three Sisters at the 1965 World Theatre Festival failed because the actors did not subordinate personal mannerisms to the character requirements (pp. 85, 154-5).

1493 ------. Seasons of Discontent: Dramatic Opinions, 1959-1965. London: Cape, 1965. On its visit to the United States, the Moscow Art Theatre missed Chekhov's farce in The Cherry Orchard but captured The Three Sisters' poignant archaism (pp. 165-8).

1494 ------. The Theatre of Revolt. Boston: Little,Brown, 1962. Although Chekhov is the gentlest, subtlest, and most dispassionate of all great modern dramatists, beneath the surface lie depths of moral fervor and revolt. Chekhov has the deepest humanity of all modern playwrights. He couples sweetness of temper with toughness of mind (pp. 137-79).

1495 Bunin, Ivan. Memories and Portraits. Tr. by Vera Traill and Robin Chancellor. N.Y.: Doubleday, 1951. Chekhov discusses writing problems and his personal life with his friend Bunin (pp. 31-58).

1496 Calder, Angus. Russia Discovered: Nineteenth Century Fiction from Pushkin to Chekhov. London: Heinemann, 1976. "Literature and Morality: Leskov, Chekhov, late Tolstoy" (pp. 238-75).

1497 Caputi, Anthony, ed. Modern Drama. N.Y.: Norton, 1966. Critics' comments and letters by Chekhov concerning The Three Sisters (pp. 363-91).

1498 Carmichael, Joel. A Cultural History of Russia. N.Y.: Weybright & Talley, 1968. Tchaikowsky's music is a counterpart of Chekhov's writing, "a sort of twilight yearning corresponding to something in the atmosphere of the epoch" (pp. 120, 185, 196, 224).

1499 Carpenter, Bruce. The Way of the Drama. N.Y.: Prentice-Hall, 1929. Though most Russian writers lack a sense of form, Chekhov had an excellent feeling for form, acquired from reading French writers (pp. 159-60).

1500 Carter, Huntly. The New Theatre and Cinema of Soviet Russia. N.Y.: International Publishers, 1925. Moscow Art Theatre productions of Chekhov's plays from 1917 to 1923 (pp. 270-3).

1501 Chandler, Frank W. Aspects of Modern Drama. N.Y.: Macmillan, 1916. Chekhov's deep pessimism grew out of the extreme repression of his period (passim).

1502 ------. Modern Continental Playwrights. N.Y.: Harper, 1931. Strong in characters and manners, Chekhov's plays are "refined realism". Chekhov's relationship to the Moscow Art Theatre is discussed (pp. 84, 92).

1503 Cheney, Sheldon. The Art Theater. N.Y.: Knopf, 1925. A description of how Stanislavsky staged Chekhov's plays (pp. 47, 120, 226).

1504 Chiari, Joseph. Landmarks of Contemporary Drama. London: Jenkins, 1965. Chekhov imposes subtle form in his plays through a highly complex, poetic imagination. Realism is made translucent, with no deception or mask to make it something else (pp. 30-9).

1505 Chukovsky, Kornei. His Nameless Love: Portraits of Russian Writers. Tr. by Julius Katzer. Moscow: Progress Publishers, 1974.

1506 Cizevskij, Dmitrij. History of Nineteenth Century Russian Literature. Vol II: The Age of Realism. Tr. by Richard N. Porter. Ed. by Serge A. Zenkovsky. Nashville: Vanderbilt Univ Pr, 1974. Chekhov was a realist blended with impressionism (pp. 148-52, 200-1).

1507 Clardy, Jesse V. & Betty S. Clardy. The Superfluous Man in Russian Letters. Wash. DC: Univ Pr of America, 1980. The Cherry Orchard and The Three Sisters discussed (pp. 83-95).

1508 Clark, Barrett H. The Continental Drama of Today. 2nd ed. revised. N.Y.: Holt, 1915. Chekhov's plays fall short of perfection "through their too great insistence upon character in the abstract" (pp. 59-65).

1509 ------. A Study of the Modern Drama. N.Y.: Appleton-Century, 1938. Chekhov's long plays would have been more effective as tales or novels but his farces were clearly "of the theater" (pp. 56-62).

1510 ------, & George Freedley, eds. A History of Modern Drama. N.Y.: Appleton-Century, 1947. Much material is given on Chekhov's early dramatic writings (H. W. L. Dana, chapter on "Russia").

1511 Clay, James H. & Daniel Krempel. The Theatrical Image. N.Y.: McGraw-Hill, 1967. In The Cherry Orchard Chekhov's stage directions are not so much lists of technical details as they are images designed to create the appropriate atmosphere (pp. 114-8).

1512 Clurman, Harold. Lies Like Truth. N.Y.: Macmillan, 1958. The Phoenix Theatre production of The Sea Gull in 1954 suffered from acting imperfections. The Uncle Vanya directed by David Ross had good acting, but the staging and the mood of the play were at times inexcusably trite (pp. 131-5).

1513 Collins, Joseph. Taking the Literary Pulse. N.Y.:Doran, 1924. See pp. 281-2.

1514 Conrad, Joseph. Letters from Joseph Conrad, 1895-1924. Ed. by Edward Garnett. Indianapolis: Bobbs-Merrill, 1928. The famous novelist calls Chekhov's work "very great" (pp. 277, 283).

1515 Corrigan, Robert W., ed. Theatre in the Twentieth Century. Characteristically failing to understand the relationship of the actor to the playwright, Stanislavsky misinterpreted Chekhov's plays (pp. 182-91).

1516 ------, and James L. Rosenberg, eds. The Context and Craft of Drama. San Francisco: Chandler, 1964. No modern playwright is more respected and less understood than Chekhov. His plays reflect as few others do the spirit of our time. He was conscious of man's existential loneliness. But he never abdicated his sense of responsibility for human life. As a man Chekhov cared deeply for fellow humans; as an artist he practiced complete objectivity. "It is the fusion of these two characteristics that makes his work great" (Corrigan, "The Plays of Chekhov," pp. 139-67).

1517 Courtney, William L. The Development of Maurice Maeterlinck and Other Sketches of Foreign Writers. London: Richards, 1904. Chekhov was exploring the uses of symbolism in drama at the same time as Maeterlinck, but in different ways (passim).

1518 Cowell, Raymond. Twelve Modern Dramatists. London: Pergamon Pr, 1967. In Uncle Vanya Chekhov allows meaning and emotional power to emerge very gradually (pp. 36-8).

1519 Cubeta, Paul M. Modern Drama for Analysis. 3rd ed. N.Y.: Holt, Rinehart & Winston, 1962. In The Cherry Orchard Chekhov sacrifices realism to focus attention on atmosphere. He subtly blends pity and amusement towards his feckless characters (pp. 322-8).

1520 Das, G.K. and J. Beer, eds. E.M. Forster: A Human Exploration. N.Y.: N.Y. Univ Pr, 1979. J. McConkey, "Two Anonymous Writers, E.M. Forster and Anton Chekhov" (pp. 231-44).

1521 Davie, Donald, ed. Russian Literature and Modern English Fiction. Chicago: Univ of Chicago Pr, 1965. The British intelligentsia have made a cult of Chekhov, but for two very bad reasons: his ethical system is purely negative and his prose style is mediocre. He also cannot be considered a heroic person, for he had neither the will nor the strength to rebel (D.S. Mirsky, "Chekhov and the English," pp. 203-13).

1522 Davies, Ruth. The Great Books of Russia. Norman: Univ of Oklahoma Pr, 1968. "Chekhov: The Axe to the Tree" (pp. 309-45).

1523 Dickinson, Thomas H. An Outline of Contemporary Drama. Boston: Houghton Mifflin, 1927. In Chekhov's plays the surface symbolism suggests a deep tragic undercurrent. The only naturalistic playwright whose art excelled that of Chekhov was Gerhart Hauptmann (pp. 117, 159, 234-5).

1524 Dobree, Bonamy. The Amateur and the Theatre. London: Hogarth Pr, 1947. Chekhov's protest against "stagey" acting calls for a new naturalism in acting (p. 16).

1525 Drew, Elizabeth. Discovering Drama. N.Y.: Norton, 1937. The Cherry Orchard created a new type of social comedy, using comic irony that is both implicit and gentle (p. 164).

1526 ------. The Modern Novel. N.Y.: Harcourt Brace, 1926. In fiction "the school of Chekhov" has made psychology its engrossing interest. Chekhov had illustrated something of the impulses, desires, and emotions which can be released into consciousness in an instant of time (pp. 247-8).

1527 Driver, Tom F. Romantic Quest and Modern Query. N.Y.: Delacorte, 1970. Chekhov utterly broke with the Aristotelian tradition in drama. He organically fused the laughable and the lamentable in a type of tragicomedy that can achieve a deeper irony than can "pure" comedy or tragedy (pp. 217-48).

1528 Dukes, Ashley. Drama. N.Y.: Henry Holt, 1927. Chekhov ignored the structure of the "well made" play to capture the beauty that comes from detailed character portrayal (pp. 111-12).

1529 -----. Modern Dramatists. Chicago: Sergel, 1913. By no means a great dramatist, Chekhov nonetheless gives us accurate pictures of modern life (pp. 190-210).

1530 -----. The Youngest Drama. Chicago: Sergel, 1924. Chekhov is the greatest naturalist among playwrights. His chief achievements are the creation of atmosphere and the slow revelation of character. Initially the British public had been puzzled by Chekhov's plays, not perceiving the sort of preparation Chekhov used for his plot incidents (pp. 20-1).

1531 Elsom, John. Post-War British Theatre. London: Routledge & Kegan Paul,1976. Chapter 3 contrasts Chekhov's drama with the "well made" play.

1532 Elton, Oliver. Essays and Addresses. London: Arnold, 1939. Chekhov's indeterminate endings are not the sign of a subdued passivity, but an honest refusal to pretty up life in order to be popular. This is no exclusively Russian phenomenon, but can also be found in the British writers George Eliot, George Gissing, and Thomas Hardy (pp. 118-50).

1533 Erlich, Victor. Russian Formalism, History--Doctrine. The Hague: Mouton, 1955. Chekhov introduced into Russian literature elements of low farce and the feuilleton (passim).

1534 ------, ed. Twentieth-Century Russian Literary Criticism. Tr. by Carol A. Palmer. New Haven: Yale Univ Pr, 1975. Peter M. Bitsilli, "From Chekhonte to Chekhov" (pp. 212-8).

1535 Esslin, Martin. The Theatre of the Absurd. Garden City, N.Y.: Doubleday Anchor, 1961. Influenced by Chekhov, Arthur Adamov uses disconnected dialogue in his plays. Like Chekhov, Eugene Ionesco moved steadily away from realism. Chekhov shows paradox as one of life's absurdities (pp. 67-9, 77, 80, 306).

1536 Farrell, James T. The League of Frightened Philistines, and Other Papers. N.Y.: Vanguard, 1942. Chekhov is a part of the great tradition of world literature, without whose presence the world would have been spiritually poorer. Gorky was right in saying that Chekhov's main message is the admonition:"It is shameful to live like that" (pp. 61, 71, 80-1).

1537 Fennell, John, ed. Nineteenth-Century Russian Literature. Berkeley: Univ of Calif Pr, 1973. M.H. Shotton, chapter on Chekhov (pp. 293-346).

1538 Fergusson, Francis. The Idea of a Theater. N.Y.:Doubleday, 1953. The Cherry Orchard is "a theater-poem on the suffering of change." The action is complete, with the beginning, middle,and end called for by Aristotle. Chekhov seems slight compared to Sophocles, but "he sees much more in the little scene of modern realism than Ibsen does." Chekhov "reduced the dramatic art to its ancient root, from which new growths are possible" ("Ghosts and The Cherry Orchard: The Theater of Modern Realism" pp. 159-90).

1539 Fernald, John. Sense of Direction. N.Y.: Stein and Day, 1968. Stanislavsky missed Chekhov's unique mixture of comedy and tragedy (pp. 80-93, 101-9).

1540 Floyd, V., ed. Eugene O'Neill: A World View. N.Y.: Ungar, 1979. Peter Egri, "The Use of the Short Story in O'Neill's and Chekhov's One-Act Plays" (pp. 115-44).

1541 Freedman, Morris. The Moral Impulse: Modern Drama from Ibsen to the Present. Carbondale: Southern Illinois

Univ Pr, 1967. The Cherry Orchard explores the tension between illusion and reality. Work is Chekhov's prescription for a better future (pp. 31-44).

1542 Freedman, Morris, ed. Essays on the Modern Drama. Boston: Heath, 1964. Francis Fergusson writes on The Cherry Orchard, Stark Young on The Sea Gull, and David Magarshack on "Chekhov the Dramatist" (pp. 19-55).

1543 Galsworthy, John. Candelabra. N.Y.: Scribner, 1933. Chekhov has the knack of making the commonplace fascinating (pp. 253-8).

1544 Ganz, Arthur. Realms of the Self: Variations on A Theme in Modern Drama. N.Y.: N.Y. Univ Pr, 1980. In his four mature plays Chekhov evokes, by symbolic suggestion, a visionary realm in which the longing of the self may be satisfied. Buried in his plays is the romantic image of the fatal enchantress and the knight errant she holds in thrall (pp. 37-56).

1545 Garnett, Edward. Friday Nights. N.Y.: Knopf, 1922. Chekhov is peculiarly modern because he unites a scientific objectivity with an esthetic consciousness. Although he deserves praise for his unselfishness and his struggle against lies and human stupidity, he was but one of thousands of Russians who labored conscientiously even in a very repressive political environment (pp. 39-66).

1546 Gaskell, Ronald. Drama and Reality: The European Theatre Since Ibsen. London: Routledge & Kegan Paul,1972. Chekhov's sense of reality grows out of his feeling for light, sound, and space (pp. 94-8).

1547 Gassner, John. Directions in Modern Theatre and Drama. N.Y.: Holt, Rinehart & Winston, 1966. Chekhov was a flexible realist who had such a sure sense of theater that he could use symbolism and dramatic counterpoint to achieve symphonic effects, as he did in The Three Sisters (pp. 107-8, 185-6).

1548 ------. Dramatic Soundings. N.Y.: Crown, 1968. In Olivier's Uncle Vanya, put on by the new National Theatre in London, the first half dragged because of too much British restraint, but Michael Redgrave's acting livened up the production toward the end (pp. 537-8).

1549 ------. Masters of the Drama. N.Y.: Dover, 1945. Chekhov achieved a poetry of emotions and environment by alternating the motifs of despair and hope. The secret strength of his plays is their "portentous hunger for life and positiveness" (pp. 495-517).

1550 ------. Theatre at the Crossroads. N.Y.: Holt, Rinehart & Winston, 1960. The excellent production of Uncle Vanya by David Ross shows how naturalness and truth can become a consuming experience as poetic as it is real. Chekhov's influence upon the American theater is shown (pp. 188-93, 289-91).

1551 ------, ed. A Treasury of the Theatre: From Henrik Ibsen to Arthur Miller. N.Y.: Simon & Schuster, 1950. Chekhov maintained a delicate balance between regret for the loss of old values and joy for the dawn of a new day. His detachment enabled him to "equalize pathos and humor, and to render a probing account of the contradictions of human character" (pp. 205-6).

1552 Gerhardi, William. Memoirs of A Polyglot. N.Y.: Knopf, 1931. Replying to D.H. Lawrence's charge that Chekhov's writing contained "disintegrating cells" which emitted a doleful twang as they burst, Gerhardi said that Chekhov's honesty prevented him from employing a cheap or sentimental note of reconciliation. Nevertheless, Chekhov achieves deep reconciliation; as he declared, "It would be strange not to forgive" (pp. 227, 288).

1553 Gielgud, John. Stage Directions. N.Y.: Capricorn, 1966. Gielgud describes his playing roles in Chekhov's plays since 1924 (pp. 85-93, 140-1).

1554 Gifford, Henry. The Novel in Russia. London: Hutchinson Universal Library, 1964. Chekhov was a classical realist, striving always for detachment, lucidity, and assertion of human values (pp. 125-34).

1555 Giles, Steve. The Problem of Action in Modern European Drama. Stuttgart: Hans-Dieter Heinz, 1981. Action in The Cherry Orchard, The Sea Gull, and The Three Sisters is discussed (pp. 211-59).

1556 Gilliatt, Penelope. Unholy Fools. N.Y.: Viking, 1973. John Gielgud's production of Ivanov in 1965 was an oddly one-note performance that merged on melodrama (pp. 336-8).

1557 Gilman, Richard. Common and Uncommon Masks. N.Y.: Random House, 1971. In their New York City production of The Cherry Orchard the Moscow Art Theatre was too obvious and too operatic (pp. 284-7).

1558 ------. The Making of Modern Drama. N.Y.: Farrar,Straus & Giroux, 1974. Chekhov had a marvelous capacity for making his plays yield exactly the consciousness he wants, excluding whatever would disturb the balance by being false or irrelevant (pp. 115-56).

1559 Goldberg, Lea. Russian Literature in the Nineteenth Century. Jerusalem: Magnes Pr, 1976. Tr. by Hillel Halkin. It is difficult to describe Chekhov's peculiar effect, since he employs a serious type of humor (pp. 148-57).

1560 Goldman, Emma. The Social Significance of the Modern Drama. Boston: Badger,1914. A modern Turgenev, Chekhov shows in The Sea Gull the triumph of an idealist who would rather die than give up his ideals (pp. 283-93).

1561 Gordon, Caroline & Allen Tate, eds. The House of Fiction. N.Y.:Scribner, 1950. The symbolism in the story "On the Road" is clear: we may be so blinded by our own concerns that we cannot see each other clearly (pp. 97-9).

1562 Gorky, Maxim. On Literature. Moscow: Foreign Languages Publishing House, 1956. Tr. by Ivy Litvinov. "Anton Chekhov" contains reminiscences by Chekhov about literature and life (pp. 278-91).

1563 Gosse, Edmund. Books on the Table. London: Heinemann, 1921. Chekhov's letters show keen and comic observation as well as objective melancholy. They help throw light on the mind of Russia, "a mysterious continent" still relatively unknown to western Europeans (pp. 69-74).

1564 Granville-Barker, Harley. The Exemplary Theatre. London: Chatto & Windus, 1922. Moscow Art Theatre productions of Chekhov's plays show that they are not undramatic (p. 229).

1565 ------. On Dramatic Method. London: Sidgwick & Jackson, 1931. The form of Chekhov's plays comes from each character's elucidating the play's central theme (p. 186).

1566 Guthke, Karl. Modern Tragicomedy. N.Y.: Random House, 1966. The Cherry Orchard embraces not only extreme comedy and extreme tragedy but also the middle ground between the two. It was the tragicomic in Chekhov that appealed to Thomas Mann (pp. 22, 66, 79, 140).

1567 Guthrie, Tyrone. A Life in the Theatre. N.Y.: McGraw-Hill, 1959. Guthrie describes how he acted in and directed many Chekhov plays (passim).

1568 Hapgood, Elizabeth R., ed. & tr. Stanislavski's Legacy. N.Y.: Theatre Arts Books, 1958. "Chekhov's Influence on the Art Theatre," "Memories of Chekhov," and "Messages about The Cherry Orchard" (pp. 81-126).

1569 Hapgood, Isabel F. A Survey of Russian Literature, with Selections. N.Y.: Chautauqua Pr, 1902. Although Chekhov's tales are full of humor and brilliant wit, his fame has been surpassed by the rapid rise of Maxim Gorky's literary star (pp. 266-7).

1570 Hare, Richard. Russian Literature from Pushkin to the Present Day. London: Methuen, 1947. Chekhov spins finished masterpieces out of a formless flux. Although "they never achieve the monumental architecture of Tolstoy, they remain wonderful mosaics of incident and impression." His plays have such delicate artistic touches that unless they are presented with unerring accuracy, they seem boring and pointless (pp. 169-80).

1571 Hauser, Arnold. The Social History of Art. N.Y.: Vintage, 1958. Chekhov's impressionism is compared to the painting technique of Degas (vol 4, p. 209).

1572 Hayman, Ronald. Theatre and Anti-Theatre: New Movements Since Beckett. London: Oxford Univ Pr, 1979. Stanislavsky describes how he prepared to direct The Sea Gull autocratically, telling each actor how to dress, speak, move, and think (p. 179).

1573 Hingley, Ronald. The Russian Mind. N.Y.: Scribner,1977. The young Chekhov was castigated by the "intellectual" critic N.K. Mikhaylovsky, who said that Chekhov should have hewed to a "cause". Chekhov's response: "Under the banner of learning, art, and freedom of thought, Russia will one day be ruled by such toads and crocodiles as were unknown even in Spain under the Inquisition" (pp. 232-42).

1574 ------. Russian Writers and Society, 1825-1904. N.Y.: McGraw-Hill, 1967. Russian life as depicted by the major Russian writers, including Chekhov (pp. 37-9,84-7, 117-20, 159-60).

1575 Hogan, Robert and Sven Molin, eds. Drama: The Major Genres. N.Y.: Dodd Mead, 1962. Chekhov uses choral effects, such as verbal duets and ensembles, effectively in his plays (pp. 397-404).

1576 Holloway, John. Narrative and Structure: Exploratory Essays. Cambridge: Cambridge Univ Pr, 1979. Chekhov's narrative technique is contrasted with the techniques of Henry James and D.H. Lawrence (pp. 53-74).

1577 Jameson, Storm. Modern Drama in Europe. London: Collins, 1920. Chekhov goes beyond Shaw and the drama of ideas to question life's values and forms. He has two weaknesses: his style insufficiently captures his characters' spirit of protest, and his deep probing wearies itself so that no strength remains to carry the weight of the misery and despair it uncovered. Nevertheless, his characters show the courage to face and master disillusion (pp. 245-53).

1578 Janacek, Gerald, ed. Andrew Belyy: A Critical Review. Lexington, KY: Univ of Kentucky Pr, 1978. Zoya Yurieff shows the relationship of Belyy's He That Is Come to Treplev's playlet in The Sea Gull (pp. 44-55).

1579 Jarrell, Randall. Third Book of Criticism. N.Y.: Farrar, Straus & Giroux, 1965. Discussion of "Ward No. 6" (pp. 235-78).

1580 Kazin, Alfred. Contemporaries. Boston: Little,Brown, 1962. Chekhov is praised for showing that prose can be as profound a revelation of human existence as is poetry (pp. 469-74).

1581 ------. On Native Grounds. N.Y.: Reynal & Hitchcock, 1942. The parallel between The Cherry Orchard and Ellen Glasgow's novel The Sheltered Life is shown (p. 263).

1582 Kerr, Walter. Thirty Plays Hath November. N.Y.: Simon & Schuster, 1969. Chekhov shows us that, at base, all comedy is sad (pp. 151-8).

1583 Kitchin, Laurence. Mid-Century Drama. London: Faber & Faber, 1962. The Moscow Art Theatre performs Chekhov's plays in London in 1958 (pp. 130-42, 201-3).

1584 Komisarjevsky, Theodore. Myself and the Theatre. N.Y.: Dutton, 1930. The famous director describes his successful production of Chekhov's plays based upon the Stanislavsky method: "I evolved the way to convey Chekhov's inner meaning and made the rhythm of the 'music' of the play blend with the rhythm of the movements of the actors" (pp. 135-41).

1585 Kronenberger, Louis. The Last Word. N.Y.: Macmillan, 1972. Because of his sharp insight, Chekhov deserves a place among the great aphorists (pp. 225-44).

1586 ------. The Republic of Letters. N.Y.: Knopf, 1955. Chekhov is the truest artist among modern dramatists. His plays lack classic form but they have the perspective and proportion that only humor can supply, a result of his extraordinary sanity (pp. 178-204).

1587 ------, ed. The Best Plays of 1954-55. N.Y.: Dodd Mead, 1958. Andre Josset reviews Jean-Louis Barrault's production of The Cherry Orchard at Theatre Marigny in Paris (p. 37).

1588 Kropotkin, Peter. Ideals and Realities in Russian Literature. N.Y.: Knopf, 1915. Chekhov's psychological realism, especially as it depicts the intelligentsia, will profoundly influence world fiction. The distinctive features of his tales--gentleness, minute observation, and lack of idealization--are repeated in his plays (passim).

1589 Krutch, Joseph Wood. Modernism in Modern Drama. Ithaca: Cornell Univ Pr, 1966. Chekhov laughs at his characters but still has affection for them. We know that their present is unsatisfactory, and we even have fears for their future (pp. 68-77).

1590 Kunitz, Joshua. Russian Literature and the Jew. N.Y.: Columbia Univ Pr, 1929. Kunitz shows how Jews are handled in Chekhov's writings (pp. 108-16).

1591 Lahr, John. Astonish Me: Adventures in Contemporary Theatre. N.Y.: Viking Pr, 1973. "Pinter and Chekhov: The Bond of Naturalism" (pp. 67-82).

1592 Lamm, Martin. Modern Drama. N.Y.: Philosophical Libr, 1953. A study combining biography and criticism of Chekhov (pp. 194-215).

1593 Larkin, Maurice. Man and Society in Nineteenth-Century Realism. Totowa, NJ: Rowman & Littlefield, 1977. How medicine influenced Chekhov's writings (pp. 134-8, 152-74).

1594 Lavrin, Janko. From Pushkin to Mayakovsky. London: Sylvan Pr,1948."The Dramatic Art of Chekhov"(pp. 174-91).

1595 ------. An Introduction to the Russian Novel. N.Y.: McGraw-Hill, 1947. Chekhov influenced Russian writers Vladimir Lidin, Boris Zaitsev, and Mikhail Zoshchenko (pp. 178-9, 211, 214).

1596 ------. Russian Literature. London: Benn, 1927. Chekhov is morbidly aware that our existence has lost its organic wholeness. He shows that when life is no longer rooted in deeper values, it disintegrates into philistinism and vulgarity (pp. 57-64).

1597 ------. Russian Writers. N.Y.: Van Nostrand, 1954. In his plays Chekhov deviates from traditional realism in order to create atmosphere through such effects as symbolism and impressionism (pp. 216-30).

1598 ------. Studies in European Literature. London: Constable, 1929. Both Chekhov and Maupassant show great discipline, economy, and a graphic eye for details. Whereas Maupassant permits his disgust at man's ignoble behavior to show in cynicism and aloofness, Chekhov transmutes his disillusion into a poetic sadness. By his integrity and his freedom, Chekhov made "one of the greatest efforts since Pushkin to liberate Russian prose from its moralizing, social, and didactic thraldom" (pp. 156-92).

1599 Lawrence, D.H. The Letters of D.H. Lawrence. Ed. by Aldous Huxley. Just as a Russian audience had finally been found for Chekhov's plays, so too would they eventually find a British audience (p. 103).

1600 Leaska, Mitchell. The Voice of Tragedy. N.Y.: Robert Speller, 1963. Because of Chekhov's magnanimity, an elusive spirituality emanates from his works (pp. 231-41).

1601 Le Gallienne, Eva. At 33. N.Y.: Longmans Green, 1934. The Stanislavsky method at work in the staging of Chekhov's plays at the Civic Repertory Theatre in New York City (p. 201).

1602 Lewis, Allen. The Contemporary Theatre. N.Y.: Crown, 1962. Chekhov's characters are multi-dimensional, seen from all angles. Where Shaw's characters discuss the social system, Chekhov's characters are the social system (pp. 59-80).

1603 Lewis, B. Roland. The Technique of the One-Act Play. Boston: Luce, 1918. One-act plays like Chekhov's The Proposal might introduce an entertainment form far better than conventional vaudeville material (p. 15).

1604 Lewis, Robert. Slings and Arrows. N.Y.: Stein & Day, 1984. In a London production of The Three Sisters in 1965 George C. Scott threatened Lee Strasberg with bodily injury for his poor direction of the play.

1605 Lindstrom, Thais. A Concise History of Russian Literature. N.Y.: N.Y. Univ Pr, 1966. This brief biographical sketch states that Chekhov gave the modern short story its present form (pp. 202-15).

1606 Lynd, Robert. Books and Authors. London: Cobden-Sanderson, 1922. If ever a writer had a genius for faith in the decency of man, it is Chekhov. This it is that provides catharsis from the very serious emotions that he arouses (passim).

1607 ------. Old and New Masters. London: Cobden-Sanderson, 1919. Sympathy and disgust live in curious harmony in Chekhov's stories. He united truth and tenderness, like a doctor making his rounds in a sick world, one he cares for deeply (pp. 171-7).

1608 Mabley, Edward. Dramatic Construction. Philadelphia: Chilton Book Company, 1972. A brief analysis of dramatic technique in The Cherry Orchard (pp. 139-52).

1609 MacCarthy, Desmond. Drama. N.Y.: Blom, 1971. Reprint of 1940 London ed. Chekhov's gentle irony gives us the courage to face life's futility and frustration. The Ranevskys are found in English country houses, too! (pp. 84-90, 118-30, 174-7).

1610 ------. Humanities. London: Oxford Univ Pr, 1954. Reviews of the Stage Society production of Uncle Vanya in 1914, and of the Lyric Theatre production of The Cherry Orchard in 1925 (pp. 71-82).

1611 ------. Theatre. London: Oxford Univ Pr, 1955. Chekhov overlooks the event-plot to penetrate deeper to the life-plot. His dialogue captures the broken communication pattern of everyday life better than does that of any other dramatist (pp. 98-104).

1612 McCarthy, Mary. Mary McCarthy's Theatre Chronicles, 1937-1962. N.Y.: Noonday Pr, 1963. "Shaw and Chekhov," a reprint from #1613 (pp. 39-45).

1613 ------. Sights and Spectacles, 1937-1956. N.Y.: Farrar, Straus & Cudahy, 1956. There is a coldness and poverty in even the best work of Shaw that keeps him from equalling Chekhov's best. Yet in The Three Sisters the characters are all a little hollow, and their dreams of nobility and hard work have in them an element of pretense (pp. 39-45, 57-62).

1614 McConkey, James. To a Distant Island. N.Y.: Dutton, 1984. McConkey draws parallels between his own spiritual search and Chekhov's (passim).

1615 Macgowan, Kenneth and Robert Edmond Jones. Continental Stagecraft. N.Y.: Harcourt Brace, 1922. Chekhov creates something between realism and expressionism, "a realism of the spirit." The perfection of the Moscow Art Theatre's performance of Chekhov's plays reminds us that we can never expect such high dramatic art in America until we too have permanent theater companies employing the repertory system (pp. 8-16).

1616 Mackenzie, Compton. Literature in My Time. London: Rich & Cowan,1933. Like Dostoevsky, Chekhov was a great influence upon English intellectuals (pp. 151-2, 218-9).

1617 Macleod, Joseph. Actors Cross the Volga. London: Allen & Unwin, 1946. MacLeod traces the rise of the Moscow Art Theatre, and the roles played by Chekhov and Gorky in that rise (pp. 92-114).

1618 Mais, S. P. B. Why We Should Read --. N.Y.: Dodd Mead, 1921. Chekhov's main feature is incurable optimism (pp. 292-311).

1619 Mann, Thomas. Last Essays. N.Y.: Knopf, 1959. Tr. from German by Richard and Clara Winston and Tania and James Stern. Chekhov's modesty kept back recognition of his art. Chekhov ridiculed the self-righteousness of "progressives" (pp. 178-203).

1620 Mansfield, Katherine. Journal of Katherine Mansfield. Ed. by J. Middleton Murry. N.Y.: Knopf, 1941. Feeling that she shared Chekhov's temperament, she shows how Chekhov influenced her life and work. She agreed with Chekhov that stories must vary greatly in length, depending upon their goal. Such stories of his as "In Exile" and "Missing" she called "frankly incomparable" (pp. 223, 233-4, 253-4).

1621 ------. The Letters of Katherine Mansfield. Ed. by J. Middleton Murry. N.Y.: Knopf, 1936. She agrees with Chekhov that an artist's job is not to solve problems but to state them accurately. In her later illness, she feels that she and Chekhov had been condemned persons (pp. 215,376,416,440-1,473,475,480,500,505).

1622 ------. Novels and Novelists. N.Y.: Knopf, 1930. Chekhov is used as the standard for comparison as Mansfield reviews novels and stories for the Athenaeum (pp. 80-1, 92, 137, 311).

1623 Mantle, Burns. American Playwrights of Today. N.Y.: Dodd Mead, 1929. The dramatist George Kelly disliked strict adherence to a plot formula, since the theme of a play is "those who live and those who die." His idea of good theater, thus, was The Three Sisters, the best play he had ever seen (p. 29).

1624 ------, and Garrison P. Sherwood, eds. The Best Plays of 1909-19, and the Yearbook of the Drama in America. N.Y.: Dodd Mead, 1934. Also, yearbooks from 1920 to date (passim). See, for example, The Best Plays of 1939-40, p. 446.

1625 Marble, Annie Russell. A Study of the Modern Novel. N.Y.: Appleton, 1928. Chekhov has influenced Maurice Baring, Virginia Woolf, and other stream-of-consciousness writers (pp. 50, 94-5).

1626 Masaryk, Tomas G. The Spirit of Russia. Ed. & tr. by George Gibian. London: Allen & Unwin, 1967. Chekhov was a decadent, perhaps due to a physical disability. Although he was a skeptic, he realized the value of faith for modern man (vol 3, pp. 299-304).

1627 Mathewson, Rufus W., Jr. The Positive Hero in Russian Literature. N.Y.: Columbia Univ Pr, 1958. Chekhov shows the alienated man just as modern European realism shows the anti-hero. Chekhov insisted that the artist needed to accurately state, not solve, life's problems (pp. 119-20, 143).

1628 Maugham, W. Somerset. East and West. N.Y.: Garden City Pub. Co., 1934. Chekhov excels over Maupassant because of his readability, good beginnings, atmosphere, and in showing characters' spirits communing with one another (preface, pp. ix-xiv).

1629 ------. The Summing Up. N.Y.: Literary Guild, 1938. Chekhov was a very good short story writer but his influence has been bad. Everyone tries to copy his Russian melancholy and futility. Maugham prefers stories with a tightly knit plot and a climactic conclusion--just what Chekhov lacks (pp. 207-9).

1630 ------,ed. Tellers of Tales. N.Y.:Doubleday Doran,1939. More than any other author, Chekhov gives the reader a sense of life's mystery. Chekhov's stories linger in the memory longer than most other stories, because his characters have something left unsaid, as if to suggest untold depths of secrecy (intro, pp. xxi-xxiii).

1631 Maurina, Zenta. Profiles of Russian Writers. Memmingen: Maximilian Dietrich, 1968. Contains essays on Chekhov and on other Russian writers (passim).

1632 Mazour, Anatole G. Russia Past and Present. N.Y.: Van Nostrand, 1951. With true artistic vision, Chekhov's writings foreshadow the coming changes in Russia (pp. 236-7).

1633 Michaud, Regis. The American Novel Today: A Social and Psychological Study. Boston: Little, Brown, 1928. Chief among influences upon the modern American novel are the Russian writers, especially Andreyev, Chekhov, and Dostoevsky (p. 23).

1634 Miller, Anna I. The Independent Theatre in Europe: 1887 to the Present. N.Y.: Long & Smith, 1931. Chekhov drew much of his inspiration for creating his characters from the actors of the Moscow Art Theatre (p. 339).

1635 Miller, Nellie B. The Living Drama. N.Y.: Century,1924. See pp. 211-4.

1636 Millett, Fred B. Contemporary American Authors. N.Y.: Harcourt Brace, 1944. Chekhov is the chief overseas influence upon American short story writers. Lack of plot structure in his stories is more than compensated for by "incomparable skill in conveying character and suggesting tone by the smallest number of telling strokes" (p. 90).

1637 ------, & Gerald Eades Bentley. The Art of the Drama. N.Y.: Appleton-Century, 1935. A true realist, Chekhov minimizes plot development, climax, and denouement. His dialogue is the most realistic in modern drama. He gives us "the incoherence, the desultoriness,the self-absorption of actual conversation" (pp. 148, 229).

1638 ------. The Play's the Thing. N.Y.: Appleton-Century, 1936. By showing the slight significance that the play action has upon the characters, Chekhov achieves "a sense of the persistence of the character through time that is infrequently created by even the best realistic drama" (p. 481).

1639 Mirsky,D.S. Contemporary Russian Literature, 1881-1925. N.Y.: Knopf, 1926. Chekhov uses lyrical and musical architectonics rather than straight-line linear plots. But his tales are written in a language "devoid of all raciness and nerve." His dialogue is undifferentiated, partly because his characters do not "feel ideas", as do those of Dostoevsky (pp. 84-95).

1640 ------. Modern Russian Literature. London: Oxford Univ Pr, 1925. Chekhov is the supreme artist of Russian fiction, because of his artistic conscience, sense of proportion, and unified effect. But his work suffers from a lack of moral judgment. His period was hurt by "the Chekhov frame of mind," identified with doing nothing to abolish an unjust social system (pp. 85-91).

1641 Moderwell, Hiram K. The Theatre of Today. N.Y.: Lane, 1914. Chekhov's plays are drama for the sake of character, which is often revealed in an indirect gossamer manner (passim).

1642 Monroe, N. Elizabeth. The Novel and Society: A Critical Study of the Modern Novel. Chapel Hill: Univ of North Carolina Pr, 1941. Chekhov is one of the main influences upon Virginia Woolf, but she lacks the sense of life's holiness that underlies his work (pp. 195-201).

1643 Moses, Montrose & John Mason Brown, eds. The American Theatre as Seen by Its Critics, 1752-1934. N.Y.: Norton, 1934. John Corbin describes the Moscow Art Theatre staging Chekhov's plays in New York (pp. 178-84).

1644 Moss, Howard. Writing Against Time. N.Y.: Morrow, 1969. Chekhov's great victory was to discover that the best style is to have none. Chekhov and Henry James were the last great dramatizers of the unconscious (pp. 72-87, 154-68).

1645 Muchnic, Helen. An Introduction to Russian Literature. N.Y.: Doubleday, 1947. Pushkin presents a well-ordered world, but Chekhov reflects the confusion and chaos of modern times. Both are objective realists, unlike Tolstoy and Dostoevsky (pp. 223, 253).

1646 Mudford, Peter. The Art of Celebration. London: Faber & Faber, 1979. Chekhov is like Thomas Hardy in that his mastery comes from a quality perceived within people. Chekhov celebrated life's goodness, not only in what people are, but in what they intend (pp. 110-22).

1647 Mudrick, Marvin. The Man in the Machine. N.Y.: Horizon, 1977. Chekhov was a Wunderkind, a brilliant and unpretentious personality who was unspoiled by success--yet his personality does not coincide with his role as a writer (pp. 153-77).

1648 Muller, H.J. The Spirit of Tragedy. N.Y.: Knopf, 1956. "The Realism of Chekhov" (pp. 283-93).

1649 Muller, Joachim, ed. Gestaltung-Umgestaltung. Writings in Honor of the 75th Birthday of Herman A. Korff. Leipzig: Koehler & Amelang, 1957. Walter H. Bruford, "Goethe & Tschechow as Liberal Humanists" (pp.118-28).

1650 Munk, E., ed. Stanislavski and America. N.Y.: 1966. M. N. Stroeva, The Three Sisters at the Moscow Art Theatre," tr. by E.R. Hapgood.

1651 Murry, John Middleton. Aspects of Literature. London: Collins, 1920. Chekhov's letters help us understand his art, which is best seen in his marvelous unity. He felt that life was too sacred to be re-arranged for artistic purposes. He saw sufficient beauty in all of life to trust it to transfigure the specific ugliness or squalor that he might depict (pp. 76-80).

1652 ------. Discoveries. London: Collins, 1924. Chekhov's tales suggest a subtle but profound unity in the universe. Murry believes William Gerhardi was correct in placing Chekhov "far in advance" of James Joyce and Marcel Proust, for his work is "a resolution of their illimitable intellectualism" (pp. 76-7, 81-101).

1653 Nabokov, Vladimir. Lectures on Russian Literature. Ed. by Fredson Bowers. N.Y.: Harcourt Brace Jovanovich, 1981. A detailed analysis is given of "In the Ravine" and The Sea Gull (pp. 245-95).

1654 Nathan, George Jean. The Theatre Book of the Year,1942-1943. N.Y.: Knopf, 1943. A review of The Three Sisters as produced by Katherine Cornell & Guthrie McClintic in New York City in 1942 (pp. 174-7).

1655 ------. The Theatre Book of the Year,1943-1944. Rutherford, NJ: Fairleigh Dickinson Univ Pr, 1972. Reprint, with new material, of 1944 ed. A review of The Cherry Orchard as performed at the National Theatre in New York City in 1944 (pp. 221-5).

1656 Nemirovich-Danchenko, Vladimir. My Life in the Russian Theatre. Tr. by John Cournos. Boston: Little,Brown, 1936. The co-founder of the Moscow Art Theatre describes his relations with Chekhov (chapters 1-5).

1657 Reprint of #1656. London: Bles, 1968. Intro by Josh Logan & chronology by Elizabeth R. Hapgood.

1658 Nicol, Bernard de Bear, ed.Varieties of Dramatic Experience. London: Univ of London Pr, 1969. As a dramatist Chekhov is a cross between a naturalist and an absurdist (pp. 175-91).

1659 Nicoll, Allardyce, ed. World Drama from Aeschylus to Anouilh. Rev. ed. N.Y.:Barnes & Noble, 1976. Chekhov's poetic realism invests the particular with universal attributes. Future theater historians may rate him as the best of modern dramatists (pp. 577-607, 682-718).

1660 Noyes, George R. Masterpieces of the Russian Drama. N.Y.: Appleton, 1933. Chekhov's tone is that of elegiac poetry. His genius lies in interesting us in the tragicomedy of petty undistinguished lives (intro).

1661 Oates, Joyce Carol. The Edge of Impossibility: Tragic Forms in Literature. N.Y.: Vanguard, 1972. Chekhov's use of the inexplicable, the ludicrous, and the paradoxical prefigures similar effects in the Theater of the Absurd (pp. 115-37).

1662 Ober, William B. Boswell's Clap and Other Essays. Carbondale: Southern Illinois Univ Pr, 1979. Chekhov said that his study of medicine gave him an enriched knowledge and an extended range of observation. It kept him from scientific mistakes and from hostility towards science. It also gave him few illusions about life (pp. 193-205).

1663 O'Brien, Edward J. The Advance of the American Short Story. N.Y.: Dodd Mead, 1923. Chekhov, Poe, and Henry James achieve unity of effect by suggesting their themes initially, and remaining true to the initial suggestion (p. 85).

1664 ------, ed. The Best Short Stories of 1917, and the Yearbook of the American Short Story. Boston: Small & Maynard, 1918. Also, yearbooks to date. The 1917 yearbook first recognized Chekhov's greatness, attributing it to his ability to capture every Russian mood with subtle artistry and creative vision (passim).

1665 O'Casey, Sean. Blasts and Benedictions. N.Y.:Macmillan, 1967. Chekhov is not for one nation but for all mankind. The loveliness and strength of Chekhov's nature add glory to the life of man (pp. 42-5).

1666 O'Connor, Frank. The Lonely Voice. N.Y.: Bantam, 1968. Unlike Katherine Mansfield, Chekhov shows not simply human loneliness but a profound moral probing into the reason for it (pp. 83-4).

1667 O'Faolain, Sean. The Short Story. N.Y.: Devin-Adair, 1951. Chekhov is praised for his hatred of sham, ironic detachment, optimism, personal integrity, and preference for simple people (pp. 76-105).

1668 Olgin, Moissaye. A Guide to Russian Literature. N.Y.: Harcourt Brace & Howe, 1920. Chekhov's classical sense of beauty, shocked by modern barbarism, ended in poetic melancholy (passim).

1669 Orr, John. Tragic Drama and Modern Society: Studies in the Social & Literary Theory of Drama from 1870 to the Present. London: Macmillan, 1981. "The Everyday and the Transient in Chekhov's Tragedy" (pp. 57-83).

1670 O'Toole, L. Michael. Structure, Style, and Interpretation in the Russian Short Story. New Haven: Yale Univ Pr, 1982. "The Black Monk" is analyzed for character and "The Peasants" for setting (pp. 161-79, 204-20).

1671 Palmer, John. The Future of the Theatre. London: Bell, 1913. Great influences upon recent British drama have been the plays of Chekhov, Ibsen, & Tolstoy (passim).

1672 Peace, Richard A. The Enigma of Gogol. Cambridge: Cambridge Univ Pr, 1981. Chekhov was deeply influenced by Gogol (pp. 52,89,150,191,204,247,299,321,330,337).

1673 Peacock, Ronald. The Poet in the Theatre. N.Y.: Harcourt Brace, 1946. Exquisite sensitivity gave Chekhov the genius to reveal precisely those moments when persons are "spiritually awake." He avoided explicit moralizing, but his plays abound in moral aspiration. He pioneered in developing a dramatic form organic to his milieu and his purpose (pp. 94-104).

1674 Perry, F. M. Story Writing: Lessons from the Masters. N.Y.: Holt, 1926. Chekhov shows a character at a quintessential moment, when all he stood for would be tested and revealed. He usually uses a single character as his center of interest, which helps him give his stories compactness and force (pp. 76-99).

1675 Perry, Henry T. Masters of Dramatic Comedy and Their Social Themes. Cambridge: Harvard Univ Pr, 1939. Chekhov's themes are art in The Sea Gull, work in Uncle Vanya, ancient and modern life in The Three Sisters, and a carefully articulated pattern of love and art, tradition and education, and business and science in The Cherry Orchard (pp. 338-58).

1676 Persky, Serge. Contemporary Russian Novelists. Freeport, NY: Books for Libraries Pr, 1968. Reprint of 1913 ed. A critical discussion of Chekhov's stories and plays. Typically Russian are Chekhov's humor and mysticism, the latter based upon the emptiness that can be found deep in the human soul (pp. 40-75).

1677 Peschel, Enid R., ed. Medicine and Literature. N.Y.: Neale Watson, 1980. Stephen Grecco, "A Physician Healing Himself: Chekhov's Treatment of Doctors in the Major Plays" (pp. 3-10).

1678 Phelps, William Lyon. Essays on Russian Novelists. N. Y.: Macmillan, 1911. Despite Chekhov's formlessness, his works show subtle interpretation of Russian people and combine the real and the fantastic with Gogol's charm (pp. 237-40).

1679 Phillips, D.Z. Through a Darkening Glass. South Bend: Notre Dame Univ Pr, 1982. It is wrong for Logan Speirs to inject his own moral position ("there is no final answer to the problem of death") into a comparative literary judgment between Tolstoy and Chekhov (pp. 51-63).

1680 Playfair, Nigel. The Story of the Lyric Theatre, Hammersmith. London: Chatto & Windus, 1925. In 1911 most London playgoers found Chekhov boring, but by now he is a classic. Much of the credit for this change goes to critics who kept pioneering for Chekhov's new kind of drama (pp. 215-7).

1681 Poggioli, Renato. The Phoenix and the Spider. Cambridge: Harvard Univ Pr, 1957. Chekhov's stories use pathos, counterpoint, and symbolism to create a somber yet beautiful world (pp. 109-30).

1682 Pritchett, V.S. The Myth Makers. N.Y.: Random House, 1979. A brief biographical sketch stating that Chekhov's comedy lay in the collision of solitudes (pp. 37-49).

1683 Prusek, Jaroslav. The Lyrical and the Epic: Studies of Modern Chinese Literature. Bloomington: Indiana Univ Pr, 1980. Many similarities in theme and technique are found in the writings of Chekhov and of Yeh Shao-chün (pp. 178-94).

1684 Rahv, Philip. Essays on Literature and Politics, 1932-1972. Boston: Houghton Mifflin, 1978. Chekhov's letters give us a chance to see his growth as a person and as a writer (pp. 227-31).

1685 Redmond, James, ed. Drama and Symbolism. Cambridge:Cambridge Univ Pr, 1982. Peter Holland, "Chekhov and the Resistant Symbol"; Laurence Senelick, "Chekhov and the Irresistible Symbol"; Leigh Woods, "Chekhov and the Evolving Symbol" (pp. 228-58).

1686 Reeve, Franklin D. The Russian Novel. London: Muller, 1966. Analysis of "Three Years" (pp. 274-301).

1687 Reinert, Otto, ed. Classic Through Modern Drama. Boston: Little,Brown, 1970. "Chekhov has been blamed for a whole tradition of unstructured insignificance in modern drama." True, his plot is not a chain of causally linked events. He catches life in a "carefully crafted succession of little individual epiphanies and moments of social discord, some pathetic, some funny." Time is the enemy in Chekhov's plays, as in life, "and one measure of the greatness of Chekhov's art is the way in which he turns that fact into matter of moral relevance" (pp. 570-8).

1688 ------. Six Plays. Boston: Little,Brown, 1973. Chekhov builds drama by a kind of pointillism. "If we look too close we see only specks of reality, but at a distance a pattern emerges." He makes heavy demands upon the reader. "Few great playwrights gain more from performance than he" (pp. 315-23).

1689 -----, & Peter Arnott, eds. Twenty-Three Plays. Boston: Little,Brown, 1978. Charlotta, the governess in The Cherry Orchard, might be a character in a modern absurdist play, for she shows the contemporary person's existential agony. "The point of Chekhov's 'absurdity' is the more general one that art always 'is' and does not 'mean'" (pp. 579-85).

1690 Reiter, Seymour. World Theater: The Structure and Meaning of Drama. N.Y.: Horizon Pr, 1973. In The Three Sisters Chekhov invented a new plot structure, one in which none of the most interesting characters is the character central to the plot. The plot revolves around Natasha, as close to a villainess as can be found in Chekhov's plays (pp. 17, 202-3).

1691 Richards, Dick, ed. The Curtain Rises. London: Frewin, 1966. Caryl Brahms states that one should see a Chekhov play many times, for each production brings out a new value hidden in the play (pp. 35-7).

1692 Rodgers, B.F., Jr. Philip Roth. Boston: Hall, 1977. Shows Roth's use of Chekhov as a literary model (passim).

1693 Rose, William and J. Isaacs. Contemporary Movements in European Literature. London: Routledge, 1928. Arnold Bennett was one of the first English writers to see how the imperceptible loading of the dice in Chekhov's seemingly plain statements molds the material of life, without distorting it, into complex forms of beauty (pp. 10, 13).

1694 Saint-Denis, Michel. Theatre: The Rediscovery of Style. N.Y.: Theatre Arts Books, 1960. After the visit of the Moscow Art Theatre to Paris in 1922 French critics no longer made fun of Russian drama. His first experience with realism came when he directed The Three Sisters in 1938 with John Gielgud's company (pp.41,45).

1695 Sayler, Oliver M. The Russian Theatre. N.Y.: Brentano, 1922. Playing Chekhov's plays, the Moscow Art Theatre achieved a "spiritualized realism" by a deliberate holding back or minimization, in which the impression within the spectator is all the more vivid for his having to conclude the emotional effect for himself. "Ordinary" scenes can build into an overpowering cumulative effect (pp. 47-52).

1696 Seidel, Michael and Edward Mendelson, eds. Homer to Brecht. New Haven: Yale Univ Pr, 1977. Walter Reed states that Ibsen tried to reclaim tragedy in Hedda Gabler but Chekhov transcends both tragedy and comedy in The Cherry Orchard (pp. 317-35).

1697 Seltzer, Daniel, ed. The Modern Theatre: Readings and Documents. Boston: Little,Brown, 1967. Stanislavsky's director's notebook for The Sea Gull is given. Jean-Louis Barrault discusses The Cherry Orchard from a director's viewpoint. S.D. Balukhaty describes the sets for Stanislavsky's The Sea Gull (pp. 203-15, 288-94, 368-70).

1698 Senelick, Laurence, ed. Russian Dramatic Theory from Pushkin to the Symbolists. Austin: Univ of Texas Pr, 1981. Chekhov was one of the first Russian writers to be attracted to symbolism. His comments on his plays were practical ones, not meant to be used as the basis for a comprehensive theory of drama (intro, pp. xxxv-xlv, 83-92, 204-7, 243-4, 274-5, 303-4).

1699 Shaw, George Bernard. Heartbreak House, Great Catherine, and Playlets of the War. N.Y.: Brentano, 1919. Shaw indicates his great admiration for Chekhov's plays (preface to Heartbreak House).

1700 Shedd, Robert G. and Haskell M. Block, eds. Masters of Modern Drama. N.Y.: Random House, 1962. Aware that he was "sinning terribly against the rules of the stage," Chekhov built two kinds of plays: those with no protagonist, and those in which every character is a protagonist. Chekhov's characters are his main concern. His "finest achievement was to reveal the comedy of their pathetic attempts to guard themselves against their common enemy, time" (pp. 173-4, 195).

1701 Sherman, Stuart. Critical Woodcuts. N.Y.: Scribner, 1927. Even though his dispassion misled Mirsky into considering Chekhov a pessimist, Chekhov's letters show him to be not only optimistic but at times light-hearted (pp. 122-37).

1702 Shestov, Leon. Penultimate Words and Other Essays. Boston: Luce, 1916. Chekhov is the poet of hopelessness. "He plagues, tortures, and worries himself in every way" (pp. 3-60).

1703 Shipler, David K. Russia: Broken Idols, Solemn Dreams. N.Y.: Times Books, 1983. Anatoly Efros discusses anti-Semitism as his production of The Three Sisters comes under attack at a meeting of the Soviet Writers' Union (pp. 335-6).

1704 Simmons, Ernest J. Introduction to Russian Realism. Bloomington: Indiana Univ Pr, 1965. To Chekhov, the unadorned style was a requisite, for he knew that the writer who strives for a "beautiful" style usually betrays both his life and his art (pp. 181-224).

1705 ------.An Outline of Modern Russian Literature. Ithaca: Cornell Univ Pr, 1943. Chekhov influenced Gorky, Kuprin, Bunin, Andreyev, and Konstantin Fedin (pp. 15-6, 18,19,21,45).

1706 Sixth International Congress of Slavists, 1968: American Contributions. Ed. by William E. Harkins. The Hague: Mouton, 1968. Rufus Mathewson, "Intimations of Immortality in Four Cexov Stories"; Hugh McLean, "Cexov's 'In the Ravine': Six Antipodes" (vol II, pp. 261-305).

1707 Sixth International Congress of Slavists, 1968: Dutch Contributions. Ibid., Seventh, 1973. The Hague: Mouton, 1968, 1973. Each issue has an article on Chekhov by H. Hamburger.

1708 Skinner, Richard Dana. Our Changing Theatre. N.Y.:Dial, 1931. The Sea Gull lacks only a note of catharsis and a deletion of some of its self-pity to be "as complete and engrossing a study of human conflict as you are apt to find in the near-classic theatre" (pp. 229-31).

1709 Slonim, Marc. From Chekhov to the Revolution: Russian Literature, 1900-1917. London: Oxford Univ Pr, 1962.

1710 ------. Modern Russian Literature from Chekhov to the Present. N.Y.:Oxford Univ Pr, 1953. From 1918-47 Chekhov's books published in the USSR passed the eighteen million mark. Russian writers influenced by Chekhov include Andreyev, Bunin, Fedin, Gorky, Korolenko, Kuprin, Zaitsev, and the Russian Symbolists. Abroad, his influence is seen upon such writers as Ernest Hemingway, Katherine Mansfield, Dorothy Parker, Katherine Ann Porter, Virginia Woolf, and writers in Germany and

Scandinavia (pp. 60-1,77-8,136,169-73,191,307-8,322).

1711 ------. An Outline of Russian Literature. N.Y.: New Amer Libr, 1958. While remaining a realist, Chekhov absorbed many devices of symbolism and poetic narration. His impact upon Russian literature has been enormous (pp. 125-6, 135, 149-50).

1712 ------. Russian Theater from the Empire to the Soviets. Cleveland: World Publ. Co., 1961. A discussion of how the Moscow Art Theatre interpreted Chekhov's plays (pp. 116-32).

1713 Slote, Bernice, ed. Myth and Symbol: Critical Approaches and Applications. Lincoln: Univ of Nebraska Pr, 1962. Thomas G. Winner, "Myth as a Device in the Works of Chekhov," tells of Chekhov's indebtedness to classical mythology (pp. 71-8).

1714 Snow, Valentine. Russian Writers. N.Y.: International Book Service, 1946. Chekhov's tales evoke mood and atmosphere in an impressionistic manner (p. 31).

1715 Sokel, Walter H., et al, eds. Probleme der Komparatistik und Interpretation. Bonn: Bouvier: 1978. Arvids Ziedonis, "Problems of Modernization in Blaumanis's Indrani and Chekhov's The Cherry Orchard"; Adolph Wegener, "Harold Pinter: Chekhov's Heir Apparent" (pp. 153-64, 296-315).

1716 Spector, Ivar. The Golden Age of Russian Literature. Rev.ed. Caldwell, ID: Caxton Pr, 1943. The modern English reaction against sentimentality made Chekhov's objective realism popular there. Chekhov had also used the merchant capitalist as a symbol of material progress in a way pleasing to Englishmen (pp. 208-10).

1717 Stanislavsky, Konstantin S. My Life in Art. Boston: Little,Brown, 1924. Tr. by J.J. Robbins. The famous director and co-founder of the Moscow Art Theatre recounts his experiences with Chekhov and his plays (chaps. 34, 35, 37, 43).

1718 Steinberg, Mollie B. The History of the Fourteenth Street Theatre. N.Y.: Dial, 1931. Describes Chekhov's plays performed by Eva Le Gallienne's Civic Repertory Theatre from 1926 to 1931 (p. 103).

1719 Steiner, George. The Death of Tragedy. N.Y.: Knopf, 1961. Chekhov explored the inner space between comedy and tragedy. Both Chekhov and Ibsen move from "the real of the letter to the more real of the spirit" (pp. 300-6).

1720 Stuart, Donald C. The Development of Dramatic Art. N.Y.: Appleton, 1928. Chekhov's plays arouse a mystical dreamlike emotion (pp. 606-9).

1721 Styan, J.L. Dark Comedy. 2nd ed. Cambridge: Cambridge Univ Pr, 1968. Chekhov was the first writer of dark comedy. He shows the tragedy underlying everyday life. Surface gaiety covers a deep Weltschmerz (pp. 74-112).

1722 ------. The Elements of Drama. Cambridge: Cambridge Univ Pr, 1960. Trivialities in Chekhov's plays are organic. The Three Sisters is a play about time's erosive influence (pp. 72-85, 206-12).

1723 Swinnerton, Frank. The Georgian Scene. N.Y.: Farrar & Rinehart, 1934. Following World War I, Chekhov was discovered and eulogized. His slavish admirers had two reactions: imitate him, or give up writing since one can never equal him. Katherine Mansfield's tales suffer from too great an imitation of Chekhov's (p. 251).

1724 ------. Swinnerton: An Autobiography. N.Y.: Doubleday Doran, 1936. Early performances of Chekhov's plays by the London Stage Society (pp. 127-33, 199-200).

1725 Teleshov, N.D. A Writer Remembers. London: Hutchinson, n.d. Especially as a young man, Chekhov had laughing eyes, full of life's merriment. As a doctor, he never refused treatment to anyone. He constantly helped young writers with their problems (chaps. 4, 12).

1726 Thompson, Alan R. The Anatomy of Drama. Berkeley: Univ of Calif Pr, 1946. Because he himself was humane and objective, Chekhov's characters show the tragedy of frustration beneath an unstated tyranny. His use of sound motifs gives to even trivial actions "a special lyricism and significance" (pp. 336-41).

1727 Tindall, William Y. Forces in Modern British Literature, 1885-1946. N.Y.: Knopf, 1947. Chekhov influenced Elizabeth Bowen, A.E. Coppard, James Joyce, Frank O'Connor, Sean O'Faolain, and Virginia Woolf (pp. 99, 101, 140, 295, 304, 313-4).

1728 Todd, William Mills III. Literature and Society in Imperial Russia, 1800-1914. Stanford: Stanford Univ Pr, 1978. A group of peasants, hearing Chekhov's "Peasant Women" read to them, used the story as a moral model: Mashenka is guilty! A group of workers said of the story "Peasants" that peasants should live better than that, and further that Chekhov should have shown the positive side of the peasants' lives (p. 142).

1729 Trautman, Joanne, ed. Healing Arts in Dialogue. Carbondale: Southern Illinois Univ Pr, 1981. "Dr. Chekhov's Prison" comments on Chekhov's trip to Sakhalin (pp. 125-37).

1730 Trilling, Lionel. The Experience of Literature. N.Y.: Holt, Rinehart & Winston, 1967. The Three Sisters shows how the influence of environment on character and fate has profoundly changed traditional morality and politics. The story "Enemies" indicates how Chekhov's innate modesty penetrates his subjects and style, making him most attractive to modern lovers of democracy (pp. 28-36, 96-101).

1731 Twentieth-Century Literary Criticism. Detroit: Gale Research Co., 1980. Vol 3. Ed. by Sharon K. Hall. Biography of Chekhov, bibliog, and articles by Maurice Baring, Eric Bentley, Penelope Curtis, Ruth Davies, Ashley Dukes, N. Bryllion Fagin, Francis Fergusson, Edward Garnett, John Gassner, William Gerhardi, Richard Gilman, Maxim Gorky, Ronald Hingley, David Magarshack, Thomas Mann, D.S. Mirsky, Howard Moss, J. M. Murry, Frank O'Connor, William Lyon Phelps, Harvey Pitcher, V.S. Pritchett, Lev Shestov, Nina Toumanova, Maurice Valency, Edmund Wilson, & Leonard Woolf (pp. 144-76).

1732 ------. 1983. Vol 10. Ed. by Dennis Poupard. Biography of Chekhov, bibliog, and articles by John Mason Brown, W.H. Bruford, Abraham Cahan, James T. Farrell, John Galsworthy, Joseph Wood Krutch, Sophie Lafitte, Donald Rayfield, Kenneth Rexroth, Virginia Llewellyn Smith, Konstantin Stanislavsky, Ieva Vitins, Anthony Winner, and Virginia Woolf (pp. 98-118).

1733 Tynan, Kenneth. Curtains. N.Y.: Atheneum, 1961. Periodical reviews of Chekhov productions from 1950 to 1960 (pp. 6-8, 433-9).

1734 Valency, Maurice. The Flower and the Castle. N. Y.: Grosset & Dunlap, 1966. Chekhov went beyond Ibsen's symbolism by being neither mysterious nor obvious (pp. 384-5).

1735 Volpe, Edmond L. & Marvin Magalaner. An Introduction to Literature: Drama. N.Y.: Random House, 1967. Biographical sketch of Chekhov, stating that his chief contribution is to reveal the subtle and complex emotions that people experience because they are isolated and living in a world they fear for they can neither understand nor control it (pp. 343-52).

1736 Voss, Arthur. The American Short Story: A Critical Survey. Norman: Univ of Oklahoma Pr, 1973. Although James T. Farrell lacks the artistry of Chekhov and James Joyce, in a few stories he does have their intensity, moral seriousness, and the ability powerfully to move the reader (pp. 267-8).

1737 Waliszewski, Kazimierz. A History Of Russian Literature. N.Y.: Appleton, 1900. Chekhov has humor, but his tales lack unity, realism, and catharsis (pp. 426-32).

1738 Wall, Vincent and James P. McCormick, eds. Seven Plays of the Modern Theater. N.Y.: American Book Co., 1950. Chekhov had boundless faith in man and his potential for progress. His characters are always defeated but they never lose faith in themselves. Chekhov finally showed that he could create serious drama based upon a large number of characters, rather than revolving around one person (pp. 91-8).

1739 Ward, Alfred C. Aspects of the Modern Short Story. London: Univ of London Pr, 1924. Although Chekhov's style is simple, its effect is profound--nothing less than a representation of life's complexity and profundity (pp. 268-90).

1740 The Warner Library. N.Y.: Knickerbocker Pr, 1917. Critical essay on Chekhov by Charles Johnston (vol 6, p. 3600.

1741 Watson, George J. Drama: An Introduction. N.Y.: St. Martins Pr, 1983. "Chekhov and the Drama of Social Change: The Cherry Orchard" (pp. 132-46).

1742 Weiss, Samuel A., ed. Drama in the Modern World: Plays and Essays. Boston: Heath, 1964. Chekhov spoke of building a sanatorium for sick village teachers. In his presence one felt that one must be simpler and better. The dreamy idealists in his plays express sentiments that he often stated as his own (Maxim Gorky, "Anton Chekhov" pp. 115-9).

1743 Welty, Eudora. The Eye of the Story. N.Y.:Random House, 1977. "Reality in Chekhov's Stories" (pp. 61-81). Discussion of "The Darling" (pp. 90-4).

1744 West, Ray B.,Jr. The Short Story in America, 1900-1950. Freeport, NY: Books for Libraries Pr, 1952. Caroline Gordon's acknowledged masters are Chekhov and Henry James (p. 77).

1745 Whitaker, Thomas R. Fields of Play in Modern Drama. Princeton: Princeton Univ Pr, 1977. Analysis of The Three Sisters (pp. 79-89).

1746 Whitman, Charles H., ed. Representative Modern Dramas. N.Y.: Macmillan, 1936. Chekhov breathed life not only into his characters but into inanimate objects also: a bookcase, a bedroom, the aroma of a house. Misery, he felt, was a transient condition, to be overcome by hard work and a faith in the future (pp. 195-8).

1747 Wiener, Leo. The Contemporary Drama of Russia. Boston: Little,Brown, 1923. Chekhov's plays were successful even before the Moscow Art Theatre staged them. In fact, it was Chekhov who saved The Cherry Orchard from misinterpretation by that theater (pp. 113-4, 123).

1748 ------, ed. Anthology of Russian Literature. N.Y.: Putnam, 1903. Chekhov has talent, but his characters are "fit subjects for psychiatrists" and his language "a series of semi-articulated hysterical ejaculations" (part 2, pp. 459-60).

1749 Wilde, Percival. The Craftsmanship of the One-Act Play. Boston: Little,Brown, 1923. Chekhov's one-act plays are vastly overrated, being merely jokebook humor that relies upon one final farcical scene (p. 203).

1750 Williams, Harold W. Russia of the Russians. Chekhov lifts decadence to the level of art by discerning beneath the monotony of everyday life the undertones of vibrating humanity (pp. 185-9).

1751 Williams, Raymond. Drama from Ibsen to Brecht. London: Chatto & Windus, 1968. There is no modern dramatist whose characters are so persistently determined to reveal themselves as Chekhov's (pp. 101-9).

1752 ------. Drama from Ibsen to Eliot. London: Oxford Univ Pr, 1953. Chekhov is the most characteristic of all naturalistic playwrights, with all their faults and virtues (pp. 126-37).

1753 ------. Drama in Performance. Rev. ed. N.Y.: Basic Books, 1968. The Sea Gull is discussed as theater, considering such things as stage directions, actors' movements, and stage pictures (pp. 107-33).

1754 Wilson, Edmund. The Bit Between My Teeth: A Literary Chronicle of 1950-1965. N.Y.: Noonday Pr, 1967. Like Chekhov, Angus Wilson shows the sad sardonic side of life, but he does not show Chekhov's faith in human dignity (p. 272).

1755 ------. O Canada. N.Y.: Noonday Pr, 1966. Chekhov is the source of Morley Callaghan's art: honesty, fidelity, no sensationalism, use a gentle ending (passim).

1756 ------. A Window on Russia. N.Y.: Farrar, Straus & Giroux, 1972. Chekhov's tales moved through satirical jokes to ironic anecdotes, and ended up as dense but concise studies of character and situation (pp.52-68).

1757 Wilson, Norman. European Drama. London: Nicholson & Watson, 1937. See pp. 193-6.

1758 Woolf, Virginia. The Common Reader. London: Hogarth Pr, 1925. Chekhov places his emphasis in such unexpected places that initially his tales seem to lack unity. Reading more closely, one discovers that Chekhov's emphasis is always upon "the soul's relation to health and goodness." The stories expose some affectation, some insincerity, or perhaps a false relationship. Someone has been perverted by the inhumanity of his situation. Once the reader experiences this combination of freedom and honesty, he can never again be satisfied with the trumped-up endings of popular fiction (pp. 216, 246-9).

1759 Yarmolinsky, Avrahm. Russian Literature. Chicago: Amer Libr Assn, 1931. Chekhov is an uncorruptible witness, whose seemingly casual tales reveal a deep insight into universal human nature (pp. 18-9).

1760 ------, ed. A Treasury of Great Russian Short Stories. N.Y.: Macmillan, 1944. Reading Chekhov's tales gives one a feeling for the opportunities, rather than the limitations, of his medium (intro).

1761 Young, Stark. Immortal Shadows. N.Y.: Scribner, 1948. For Shaw to think he wrote an English Cherry Orchard in Heartbreak House is ridiculous, for Chekhov sees his people as rooted in something, whereas Shaw sees his people in the light of their opinions (pp.200-10).

1762 ------. The Theater. N.Y.: Doran, 1927. Chekhov is a realist, but his plays, through suggestive use of what is not done, capture an "inner poetry or idea" not achieved by previous realists (pp. 161-2).

1763 Ziedonis, Arvids. A Study of Rudolfs Blaumanis. Hamburg: Buske, 1979. "Blaumanis's Indrani and The Cherry Orchard: A Comparison" (pp. 207-20).

Doctoral Dissertations (alphabetical by author)

1764 Berton, Luba H. Chekhov Unbound: An Exploration of Untranslatable Material. Univ of Michigan, 1975.

1765 Blair, Rhonda L. A Langerian Analysis of Chekhov's Major Plays. Univ of Kansas, 1982.

1766 Clyman, Toby W. Women in Chekhov's Prose Works. New York Univ, 1971.

1767 De Kir, Antoinette. Phenomenological Perspectives on Space in the Reading of Drama: An Analysis of "Thérèse Raquin", "Vor Sonnenaufgang", and "The Three Sisters". Univ of Toronto, 1981.

1768 Eisen, Donald G. The Art of Anton Chekhov: Principles of Technique in His Drama and Fiction. Univ of Pittsburgh, 1982. Contains a bibliog of works by and about Chekhov, a chronological index of his works, a Russian title index, and an index of variant translations of Russian titles.

1769 Eschliman, Herbert R. Chekhov in the English Short Story. Univ of Minnesota, 1960.

1770 Evans, Jack E. Structure and Style of Speech in the Drama of A.P. Cexov. Yale Univ, 1970.

1771 Filipp, Valerie. Modes of Address in Cexov's Plays. New York Univ, 1973.

1772 Forowa, Natalie I. Structural Irony in Chekhov's Stories. Univ of Pennsylvania, 1978.

1773 Frost, Edgar L. Concepts of Time in the Works of Anton Cexov. Univ of Illinois (Urbana), 1973.

1774 Frydman, Anne. A Study of the Endings of Anton Chekhov's Short Stories. Columbia Univ, 1978.

1775 Gamble, C.E. The English Chekhovians: The Influence of Anton Chekhov on the Short Story and Drama in England. Univ of London, 1979.

1776 Gotman, Sonia K. Cexov's Use of Irony in His Fiction. Ohio State Univ, 1971.
1777 Gottlieb, Lois J. Chekhov and Some Chekhovians in the English-Speaking Theater, 1910-1935. Univ of Michigan, 1969.
1778 Hellweg, John D. The Dimensions of Language, Character, Time and Space in Chekhov's Major Plays. Univ of California (Berkeley), 1975.
1779 Hubbs, Clayton A. Chekhovian Ritual in the Avant-Garde Theatre. Univ of Washington, 1971.
1780 Katsell, Jerome H. The Potential for Growth and Change: Chekhov's Mature Prose, 1888-1903. Univ of California (Los Angeles), 1972.
1781 Kobler, Mary T.S. Chekhov as Moralist: The Man with a Hammer. Univ of Texas (Austin), 1968.
1782 Kramer, Karl D. The Chameleon and the Dream: A Study of Anton Cexov's Shifting Perception of Reality in His Short Stories. Univ of Washington, 1964.
1783 Kurylo, Charanne C. Chekhov and Katherine Mansfield: A Study in Literary Influence. Univ of North Carolina (Chapel Hill), 1974.
1784 Lantz, Kenneth A. Aspects of Chekhov's Comedy: 1880-1887. Univ of Toronto, 1974.
1785 Lau, Joseph S. Ts'ao Yu, The Reluctant Disciple of Chekhov and O'Neill: A Study in Literary Influence.Indiana Univ, 1966.
1786 Lindsey, Byron T. Early Chekhov: Development of Character and Meaning in the Short Stories, 1880-1887. Cornell Univ, 1975.
1787 Majstorovic, Savka. The Motif of Loneliness in Selected Dramas by Gerhart Hauptmann and Anton Chekhov. Florida State Univ, 1980.
1788 Master, Carol T. The Development of the Chekhovian Scene: A Study in Dramatic Structure. Columbia Univ, 1982.
1789 Maxwell, David E. The Role of Setting in the Prose of A.P. Cexov: A Structural Approach. Brown Univ, 1974.
1790 Meister, Charles W. English and American Criticism of Chekhov. Univ of Chicago, 1948.
1791 Moravcevich, Nicholas. Chekhovian Dramatic Innovations. Univ of Wisconsin, 1964.
1792 Murdock, Michael J. The Humor of Anton Chekhov: A Tempering of Tears. A Study of the Elemental Nature of Humor in Chekhov's Major Plays. Univ of Wisconsin, 1971.
1793 Narin, Sandra G. The Use of Irony in Cexov's Stories. Univ of Pennsylvania, 1973.
1794 Polakiewicz, Leonard A. The Image of the Doctor in Cexov's Works. Univ of Wisconsin, 1978.

1795 Raviv, Zeev. The Productions of Chekhov's Plays on the American Professional Stage. Yale Univ, 1964.

1796 Rukalski, Zygmunt. Anton Chekhov and Guy de Maupassant: A Comparative Study. Cambridge Univ, 1958.

1797 Saal-Losq, Christine. Literary Allusion in Anton Chekhov's Short Stories, 1889-1904. Stanford Univ, 1978.

1798 Scielzo, Caroline Anne Gray. The Doctor in Chekhov's Works. New York Univ, 1976.

1799 Senderovich, Marena. The Implicit Semantic Unities in Chekhov's Work of 1886-89. (Russian text). New York Univ, 1981.

1800 Sklar, S. The Relationship between Social Context and Individual Character in the Naturalist Drama, with Special Reference to Chekhov, D.H. Lawrence, and David Storey. Univ of London, 1975.

1801 Slejskova, Nadezda. The Illusion of Off-Stage Life in Theatre and Its Application to Chekhov's Drama: An Analysis of "The Sea Gull". McGill Univ, 1981.

1802 Smith, Virginia Llewellyn. Women in Chekhov's Work and Life. Oxford Univ, 1970.

1803 Stowell, H. Peter. The Prismatic Sensibility: Henry James and Anton Cexov as Impressionists. Univ of Washington, 1972.

1804 Strongin, Carol D. The Anguished Laughter of Shakespeare, Chekhov, and Beckett: An Exploration of Their Tragicomic Drama. Brown Univ, 1975.

1805 Toumanova, Nina A. Anton Chekhov, The Voice of Twilight Russia. Columbia Univ, 1937.

1806 Tracy, Robert E. The Flight of a Seagull: Chekhov's Plays on the English Stage. Harvard Univ, 1960.

1807 True, Warren R. Chekhovian Dramaturgy in the Plays of Tennessee Williams, Harold Pinter, and Ed Bullins. Univ of Tennessee, 1976.

1808 Tulloch, John C. Anton Chekhov: A Case Study in the Sociology of Literature. Univ of Sussex, 1973.

1809 Urbanski, Henry. Chekhov as Viewed by His Russian Literary Contemporaries. New York Univ, 1973.

1810 Walters, Mary Anne. Anton Chekhov and American Theater in the Fifties: A Study in Influence. Michigan State Univ, 1975.

1811 Weingarten, Aaron. Chekhov and the American Director. City Univ of New York, 1972. Locates prompt scripts of 3 productions of The Cherry Orchard, 4 productions of The Sea Gull, and 3 productions of The Three Sisters.

1812 Williames, Lee J. Anton Chekhov: A Source for the Social Historian. State Univ of New York at Binghamton, 1981.

1813 Yoder, Hilda V. Dramatizations of Social Change: Herman Heijermans's Plays as Compared with Selected Dramas by Ibsen, Hauptmann, and Chekhov. Indiana Univ, 1974.

Theses

1814 Borny, Geoffrey. The Subjective and Objective Levels of Reality in Chekhov's "Ivanov" & "The Cherry Orchard":A Study in Dramatic Technique. Fourth year drama thesis, Univ of New South Wales, 1969.

1815 Christmas, P. G. The Reception and Influence of Chekhov's Fiction in England. M.A. thesis. Univ of Wales at Swansea, 1969.

1816 Garlinski, J.E.J. Chekhov in France, 1893-1939. M.Phil. thesis. Univ of London: School of Slavonic Studies, 1972.

1817 Gerhardi, William A. Anton Chehov: A Critical Study. B.Litt. thesis. Oxford Univ, 1923.

1818 Gill, L. F. Chekhov's Concept of Dramatic Time. M.Phil. thesis. Univ of London: School of Slavonic Studies, 1975.

1819 Gottlieb, Vera A.R. Chekhov: From Farce to Tragicomedy. M.Litt. thesis. Univ of Bristol, 1979.

1820 Greene, Karen S. The Search for Freedom in the Stories of Anton Chekhov. M.A.thesis. Univ of Louisville,1978.

1821 Koch, Vivienne. Chekhov in England. M.A. thesis. Columbia Univ, 1933.

1822 Kutscheroff, Alexander. Chekhov and His Place in World Literature. B.A. thesis. Wesleyan Univ, 1946.

1823 Lake, Linda K. "Uncle Vanya": An Emotional Approach. M.A. thesis. Univ of Nevada at Reno, 1981.

1824 Le Fleming, L. S. K. The Language of Chekhov's Later Stories. M. Litt. thesis. Cambridge Univ, 1968.

1825 Martin, D. W. Stylistic Devices and Narrative Technique in Chekhov's Short Stories, 1888-1903. B.Litt. thesis. Oxford Univ, 1976.

1826 Michl, Keith A. An Analysis of the Character Lopahin in "The Cherry Orchard". M.A. thesis. Calif State Univ at Long Beach, 1972.

1827 Thomas, Susan I. A Record of the Development and Execution of Settings, Costumes, and Make-up for a Production of "The Cherry Orchard". M.A. thesis. Calif State Univ at Long Beach, 1973.

Musical Compositions

1828 The Bear. Adapted from the libretto by Paul Dehn and William Walton. A musical composition based on Chekhov's play. London: Oxford Univ Pr, 1967.

1829 Elmslie, Kenneth. The Seagull. Melville, NY: Belwin-Mills, 1974. Elmslie tells of Thomas Pasatieri's opera based on Chekhov's play.

1830 Strano, Alfredo. Sulla via maestra. A musical composition based upon Chekhov's play On the High Road.

Pamphlets

1831 Elton, Oliver. Chekhov. The Taylorian Lecture. Oxford: Clarendon Pr, 1929. 24 pp. Chekhov is no pessimist,but a realist who refuses to provide unrealistically happy endings. A study of his early works shows that he is, from first to last, a humorist. Review: New Statesman 34 (16 Nov 1929) 204.

1832 Thoms, Herbert. Anton Chekhov--Physician and Literary Artist. New Haven: American Medical Assn, 1922. 8 pp.

Parodies

1833 Burnett, Beatrice, & Lilly Raywid & Isabel Pitt (81 Van Rensselaer Avenue, Stamford, CT 06904). Tchekoff and Double Tchekoff. Copyright 1931. Unpublished.

1834 Poppe, Harold. The Cheery Orchard: A Fantastic Travesty in One Act. N.Y.: French, 1935.

Plays about Chekhov

1835 Driver, John & Jeffrey Haddow. Chekhov in Yalta. An imaginary meeting of Chekhov and Stanislavsky.

1836 Gray, Richard & Mayo Loiseau. The World of Anton Chekhov. "A two-act dramatic entertainment from his life, his work, and his contemporaries."

1837 Malyugin, L. A. How Comical My Happiness. Tr. by Olga Franklin. "Portrays, on a somewhat superficial level, Chekhov's relationship to L.S. Mizinova" (p. 220 of Virginia Llewellyn Smith, Anton Chekhov and the Lady with the Dog; see #1436).

1838 Winer, Elihu. Chekhov on the Lawn. Chekhov discusses his works and reads excerpts from them to his friends in the Moscow Art Theatre.

Plays Based on Chekhov's Plays

1839 Hellman, Lillian. The Autumn Garden. Boston: Little, Brown, 1951. The Cherry Orchard adapted to an American setting in the South.

1840 Hoffman, William M. & Anthony Holland. The Cherry Orchard, Part II. N.Y.: 1983.

1841 Logan, Joshua. The Wisteria Trees: An American Play Based upon Anton Chekhov's "The Cherry Orchard". N.Y.: Random House, 1950.

Plays Made from Chekhov's Stories

1842 The Artist. One-act play from "An Artist's Story." In Miles Malleson, Young Heaven and Three Other Plays. London: Allen & Unwin, 1928, pp. 53-81.
1843 The Chekhov Sketchbook. "In a Music Shop," "The Vagabond," and "The Witch," dramatized by Joseph Buloff & Luba Kadison. New York: French, 1982.
1844 The Chorus Girl. Based on story of same name. By John A. Stone. In First Stage 1 (Dec 1961) 41-9.
1845 The Duel. Based on story of same name. By Jack Holton Dell. In Players 15 (Jun 1968) 27-43.
1846 A Happy Ending. Based on story of same name. By Evrom Allen Mintz. Boston: Baker's Plays, 1946.
1847 A Helpless Woman. Based on "The Darling." By Alek Zolin. In One-Act Play Magazine 2 (Jun-Jul 1938) 176-86.
1848 Ladies. Based on story of same name. By Mark Schweid. New York: French, 1937.
1849 Surgery. Based on story of same name. By Michael Visoroff. New York: 1924.

Poems about Chekhov

1850 "Chekhov: A Poem." By Howard Moss. New York: Albondocani Pr, 1972. 12 pp.
1851 "Chekhov on the West Heath." By Denise Levertov. Andes, NY: Woolmer-Brotherson, 1977. 14 pp. Printed for Cornell Univ Library Associates.

Radio Scripts

1852 The Boor; The Proposal. In Melvin R. White, Radio and Assembly Plays: A Collection of Five Adaptations from Literature. Minneapolis: Northwestern Pr, 1941.
1853 The Cherry Orchard. In Reid Erekson and Elmer Ziebarth, Six Classic Plays for Radio. Minneapolis: Burgess Pub. Co., 1939.
1854 The Cherry Orchard; The Proposal. Radioplay, P.O. Box 368, Hollywood, CA 90052.

Story about Chekhov

1855 James McConkey, "In Praise of Chekhov," Hudson R 20 (Autumn 1967) 417-28.

Part III

Productions of Anton Chekhov's Works

American Stage Productions (with reviews)

(American productions are in New York City, unless otherwise stated. See pp. 5-6 for list of abbreviations).

The Anniversary

1856 25 May 1955 O.B. Greenwich Mews Theatre Jack Sydow, Dir. Review: N.Y.Times, 26 May, p. 34.

1857 Apr 1961 O.B. Key Theatre Amnon Kabatchnik, Dir. Julius West, Tr. Reviews: Nation (N.Y.) 192 (13 May) 419; N.Y.Times, 21 Apr, p. 26.

1858 1972 season O.O.B. Amer. Center for Stanislavsky Art Sonia Moore, Dir.

1859 1 Mar 1974 O.O.B. West Side Community Repertory Theater Andres Castro, Dir.

1860 Mar 1977 O.O.B. Drama Committee Repertory Theater Arthur Reel, Dir.

1861 15 Apr 1977 O.O.B. Amer. Center for Stanislavsky Art Sonia Moore, Dir.

The Bear

1862 28 Mar 1914 Berkeley Theatre Socialist Press Club Review: N.Y.Times, 29 Mar, 4:6.

1863 24 May 1915 Bandbox Theatre Washington Square Players Roy Temple House, Tr. Review: N.Y.Times, 25 May, p.15.

1864 30 Aug 1916 Comedy Theatre Washington Square Players Roy Temple House, Tr. Reviews: Nation (N.Y.) 103 (7 Sep) 225; N.Y.Times, 31 Aug, p. 7.

1865 1919 season Stuyvesant Players.

1866 1927 season Washington Heights YMHA-YWHA.

1867 5 Feb 1948 (14) City Center N.Y.C. Theatre Company Richard Barr & Jose Ferrer, Dirs. Reviews: N.Y.Times, 6 Feb, p. 29; New Yorker 23 (14 Feb) 44.

1868 24 Mar 1976 O.O.B.

1869 1980 season National Theatre of the Deaf Shanny Mow, Dir.

1870 A Night in the Ukraine. Adapted from The Bear by Dick Vosburgh; ran with A Day in Hollywood, also by Vosburgh. 1 May 1980 (36) John Golden Theatre Alexander

H. Cohen & Hildy Parks, Producers. Moved to Royale Theatre on 17 Jun 1980 (588). Review: N.Y. Theatre Critics' Reviews, 1980, p. 256.

The Boor

1871 1972 season O.O.B. Amer. Center for Stanislavsky Art Sonia Moore, Dir.

1872 16 Jan 1975 O.O.B.

1873 14 Oct 1975 O.O.B.

1874 15 Apr 1977 O.O.B. Amer. Stanislavsky Theater Sonia Moore, Dir.

1875 24 Feb 1978 O.O.B. Amer. Stanislavsky Theater Sonia Moore, Dir.

1876 10 Jul 1979 (18) O.O.B. Quaigh Theatre Adapted by Louise Henry Will Lieberson, Dir.

1877 26 Feb 1980 O.O.B. Quaigh Theatre Adapted by Louise Henry Will Lieberson, Dir.

The Cherry Orchard

1878 22 Jan 1923 (16) 59th St. Theatre Moscow Art Theatre Performed in Russian Reviews: New Republic 34 (28 Jan) 19; N.Y.Clipper 70 (31 Jan) 14; N.Y.Times, 23 Jan, p. 18 & 28 Jan, 7:1 & 4 Feb, 7:1; N.Y.Tribune, 23 Jan, p. 8; N.Y.World, 23 Jan; North American R 217 (Mar) 343-52. Robert Allerton Parker in Independent 110 (3 Feb) 97-8 said that in this play, a new art of dramatic counterpoint had been created. Edmund Wilson, Jr., in Dial 74 (Mar) 319 discovered a rare set of esthetic values:"the beauty and poignancy of an atmosphere are put before us with the highest art."

1879 8 May 1924 (2) Imperial Theatre Moscow Art Theatre Performed in Russian.

1880 5 Mar 1928 (5) Bijou Theatre James B. Fagin, Dir. George Calderon, Tr. Reviews: N.Y.Times, 4 Mar, 9:2 & 6 Mar, p. 20 & 11 Mar, 8:1; Theatre Arts 12 (May)316.

1881 15 Oct 1928 (63) 14th St. Theatre Civic Repertory Theatre Eva Le Gallienne, Dir. Constance Garnett, Tr. Reviews: Literary Digest 99 (8 Dec) 27; Modern Q 5 (Spring 1929) 267; Theatre Arts Monthly 12 (Dec) 858-70; Vogue 72 (8 Dec) 98. Brooks Atkinson in N.Y. Times, 16 Oct, p.28 said that Chekhov delved into the unconscious, mingling relevancies and irrelevancies into a "luminous pattern of beguiling life." Joseph Wood Krutch in Nation (N.Y.) 127 (31 Oct) 461 admired Chekhov's ability to create a unity out of satire and sentiment. Richard Watts,Jr., in N.Y.Tribune, 16 Oct, p. 26 found the production "so replete with pathos of unintentionally lovable people that its sad gentle beauty seems inescapable." Euphemia Wyatt in Catholic World 129 (Apr 1929) 78-80 said that Alla Nazimova captured each slight deflection in intention in Mme. Ranevskaya, a figure of "graceful futility, selfish tenderness, and unreasonable charm."

1882 7 Nov 1928 Yiddish Art Theatre Leo Bulgakov, Dir. Review: N.Y.Times, 8 Nov, p. 26.

1883 23 Sep 1929 (14) 14th St. Theatre Civic Repertory Theatre Eva Le Gallienne, Dir. Constance Garnett, Tr. Review: Hound & Horn 3 (Apr-Jun 1930) 416.

1884 4 May 1931 (2) 14th St. Theatre Civic Repertory Theatre Eva Le Gallienne, Dir. Constance Garnett, Tr.

1885 6 Mar 1933 (30) New Amsterdam Theatre Eva Le Gallienne, Dir. Constance Garnett, Tr. Reviews: New Outlook 161 (Apr) 47; N.Y.Herald-Tribune, 7 Mar, p. 10; N.Y.Times, 7 Mar, p. 20. John Mason Brown in N.Y.Eve Post, 18 Mar, said that because the play refused to "iron out" the complexities of its characters, actors found new depths of meaning in roles they had performed for twenty years. Richard Dana Skinner in Commonweal 17 (19 Apr) 693 credited Eva Le Gallienne and Alla Nazimova with having achieved "a complete mastery of subtle, unspoken feeling."

1886 25 Jan 1944 (96) National Theatre Eva Le Gallienne, Margaret Webster, & Carly Wharton, Dirs. Irina Skariatina, Tr. Reviews: America 70 (12 Feb) 529; Catholic World 158 (Mar) 584-5; Commonweal 39 (11 Feb) 420; Life 16 (28 Feb) 101-2; N.Y.Theatre Critics' Reviews, 1944, p. 276; N.Y.Times, 26 Jan, p. 22 & 6 Feb, 2:1; Scholastic 44 (10 Apr) 20; Theatre Arts 28 (Apr) 197-208; Time 43 (7 Feb) 94; Variety 153 (12 Jan) 58 & 153 (2 Feb) 44. Howard Barnes in N.Y.Herald-Tribune 26 Jan, p. 10 found the play "an illumination of human experience" that was "universal and abiding," a profound commentary on life in a world at war. Margaret Marshall in Nation (N.Y.) 158 (5 Feb) 167 felt that this production so exaggerated the humor as to violate the texture and the tone of the play. Stark Young judged the translation to be far above the usual acting version, albeit occasionally lacking in fluency.

1887 1 Jan 1945 (8) Continuation of #1886 at N.Y. City Center Reviews: American Mercury 60 (Mar) 318; N.Y. Times, 2 Jan, p. 16.

1888 18 Oct 1955 (104) O.B. Fourth St. Theatre David Ross, Dir. Stark Young, Tr. Reviews: America 94 (5 Nov)

167; Commonweal 63 (2 Dec) 223-5; Nation (N.Y.) 181 (5 Nov) 406; New Republic 133 (21 Nov) 30; Saturday R (N.Y.) 38 (19 Nov) 37. Brooks Atkinson in N.Y.Times, 19 Oct, p. 38 said that this production triumphed over the awkwardness of its physical setting, and that no one was better fit to direct Chekhov than David Ross.

1889 3 Jun 1960 O.B. Workshop production of Acts I & IV Institute for Advanced Studies in the Theatre Arts Yuri Zavadski, Dir. Eva Le Gallienne, Tr. Reviews: N.Y.Times, 16 Apr, p. 10; 20 Apr, p. 41; 4 Jun, p.17.

1890 14 Nov 1962 (61) O.B. Theater Four David Ross, Dir. Reviews: America 108 (19 Jan 1963) 121-2; N.Y.Times, 15 Nov, p. 46; New Yorker 38 (24 Nov) 118. Leonard Harris in N.Y.World-Telegram & Sun, 15 Nov, found good acting and directing and a "charming new theater." Walter Kerr in N.Y.Herald-Tribune, 15 Nov, said that the production came apart at the seams, perhaps because the actors and director took too much for granted. Michael Smith in Village Voice, 22 Nov, found the theater itself hopeless, with bad sight lines and no sensible division between actors and audience.

1891 1964 National Repertory Theatre Eva Le Gallienne, Dir. Review: N.Y.Sun, 26 Jan.

1892 9 Feb 1965 (11) City Center Moscow Art Theatre Victor Stanitsyn, Dir. Performed in Russian Reviews: New Republic 152 (27 Feb) 26-8; N.Y.Times, 31 Jan, 2:1 & 10 Feb, p. 46 & 12 Feb, p. 15; New Yorker 41 (20 Feb) 54; Newsweek 65 (22 Feb) 93-4. Howard Taubman in N.Y.Times, 21 Feb, 2:1 saw the value of a permanent repertory theater. Even the tramp in this play gives an outstanding performance, because he has a secure career and can thus focus on serving the playwright's intent.

1893 19 Mar 1968 (38) Lyceum Theatre Assn of Producing Artists--Phoenix Theatre T. Edward Hambleton & Eva Le Gallienne, Dirs. Eva Le Gallienne, Tr. Reviews: America 118 (20 Apr) 551; N.Y.Post, 20 Mar; N.Y.Theatre Critics' Reviews, 1968, pp. 307, 318; N.Y.Times, 7 Apr, 2:3 & 14 Apr, 2:3; New Yorker 44 (30 Mar) 104. Clive Barnes in N.Y.Times, 20 Mar, p. 41 said that "although Eva Le Gallienne has done more than anyone for Chekhov in America, this production does not have the air of life about it." Martin Gottfried in Women's Wear Daily, 20 Mar found the effort dull and boring, with "not the slightest sense of ensemble work."

1894 9 Apr 1970 (5) American National Theater & Academy John Fernald, Dir. J.P. Davis, Tr. Played without scenery because of stagehand strike. Reviews: Critical Digest 22 (6 Apr) 1 & 22 (13 Apr) 1; N.Y.Theatre Critics' Reviews, 1970, p. 257; N.Y.Times, 7 May, p. 63.

1895 1970 season O.O.B. Amer. Center for Stanislavsky Theater Art Sonia Moore, Dir. Irene & Sonia Moore, Trs.

1896 7 Dec 1972 (86) O.B. Anspacher Theater N.Y. Shakespeare Festival Public Theater Michael Schultz, Dir. Avrahm Yarmolinsky, Tr. All-black cast. Reviews: America 128 (3 Feb) 103; Nation (N.Y.) 216 (29 Jan) 157-8; N.Y.Theatre Critics' Reviews, 1973, p. 318; N.Y.Times, 12 Jan, p. 21 & 21 Jan, 2:1 & 4 Feb, 2:1; New Yorker 48 (20 Jan) 59; Newsweek 81 (22 Jan) 65-6; Time 101 (29 Jan) 56.

1897 1972 season O.O.B. Amer. Center for Stanislavsky Theater Art Sonia Moore, Dir.

1898 Feb 1975 O.O.B. Amer. Center for Stanislavsky Theater Art Sonia Moore, Dir. Irene & Sonia Moore, Trs. Review: Plays & Players 22 (Aug 1975) 40-1.

1899 1 Nov 1975 O.O.B.

1900 22 Jan 1976 O.O.B.

1901 24 Apr 1976 (56) O.B. Roundabout Stage One Roundabout Theater Company Robert Mandel, Dir. Reviews: Critical Digest 28 (19 Apr) 2; N.Y.Times, 27 Apr, p. 30.

1902 25 Jun 1976 O.O.B. West Side Community Repertory Theater Andres Castro, Dir.

1903 17 Feb 1977 (62) Vivian Beaumont Theater N.Y. Shakespeare Festival Andrei Serban, Dir. Jean-Claude van Itallie, Tr. Elizabeth Swados, incidental music. Reviews: America 136 (19 Mar) 241; Critical Digest 28 (7 Mar) 2; Dance Magazine 51 (May) 37; Educational Theatre J 29 (May) 252; Nation (N.Y.) 224 (12 Mar) 313-4; New Republic 176 (26 Mar) 28; N.Y.Theatre Critics' Reviews, 1977, p. 336; N.Y.Times, 13 Feb, 2:1 & 18 Feb, 2:3 & 10 Mar, p. 46 & 13 Mar, 2:4; New Yorker 53 (28 Feb) 54; Plays & Players 24 (May) 34-5 & 24 (Jun) 37; Yale Theatre 8 (Spring) 136-41. Richard Eder in N.Y.Times Magazine, 13 Feb, p. 42 found that Serban, with links to Antonin Artaud, Peter Brook, and Jerzy Grotowski, gave "physical expression to primal forces, the archetypes beneath the characters' motivations." Walter Kerr in N.Y.Times, 27 Feb, 2:1 found it to be a "daring, alternately vulgar and delicate, perverse, funny, deeply original and visually stunning event." "The comedy," he said, "ranges from the hilariously plausible to the frantically forced." Jack Kroll in Newsweek 89 (28 Feb) 78 said that "The Cherry Orchard is arguably the greatest play of the twentieth century," and that "a rare sense of adventure hangs over this production, an air of freshness and rediscovery." C.P. in Time, 28 Feb, p. 56 felt that Serban "emblazons even quite ordinary moments with extraordinary stage effects. The results are bold, sometimes beautiful, but only partly successful." Lally Weymouth in N.Y.Times, 6 Mar, 2:5 remarked that John Simon had called the production "a total betrayal of Chekhov's simplicity" and that Brendan Gill said that Serban is "on occasion gratuitously vulgar," but that Irene Worth, who played Mme. Ranevskaya, believed that Serban had brought out both the play's farce and its political protest.

1904 28 Jun 1977 (48) Re-opening of #1903. Reviews: Hudson R 30 (Summer) 267-9; N.Y.Times, 1 Jul, 2:3.

1905 17 Jan 1982 (39) O.B. Classic Stage Company Rene Buch, Dir. Alex Szogyi, Tr.

1906 2 Oct 1983 (closed) O.B. Alvina Krause Theater Meat and Potatoes Company Neal Weaver, Dir.

1907 20 May 1984 (closed) O.O.B. New Media Repertory Company Mary Hayden, Dir.

Ivanov

1908 26 Nov 1923 (8) 59th Street Theatre Moscow Art Theatre Performed in Russian Reviews: N.Y.Times, 27 Nov, p. 23; N.Y.Tribune, 27 Nov, p. 13; N.Y.World, 28 Nov, p. 12; North American R 219 (1924) 874-82; Theatre Arts Monthly 7 (1924) 215-28.

1909 7 Oct 1958 O.B. Renata Theatre William Ball, Dir. Elisaveta Fen, Tr. Reviews: Commonweal 69 (6 Feb 1959) 496-7; Hudson R 12 (Spring 1959) 94-6; N.Y.Herald-Tribune, 8 Oct; N.Y.Times, 19 Oct, 2:1; New Yorker 34 (18 Oct) 58; Saturday R (N.Y.) 41 (25 Oct) 26; Village Voice, 15 Oct. Brooks Atkinson in N.Y.Times, 8 Oct, p. 42 found the performance "sensitive and sure." Elisaveta Fen in N.Y.Times, 5 Oct, 2:3 said that "like Ivanov, Chekhov must have experienced the disgust of having to struggle against so much inertia and downright dishonesty in his environment." John McClain in N.Y.Journal-American, 8 Oct found it to be a first-class production, with brilliant sets, expert direction, and impressive acting.

1910 3 May 1966 (47) Shubert Theatre Alexander H. Cohen presentation of H.M. Tennent Ltd. production. John Gielgud, Dir. & Adapter Ariadne Nicolaeff, Tr. Reviews: America 114 (4 Jun) 812-3; Life 60 (27 May) 16; Nation (N.Y.) 202 (30 May) 661-2; N.Y.Times,

3 May, 2:1 & 4 May, p. 50 & 15 May, 2:1; New Yorker 42 (14 May) 114; Newsweek 67 (16 May) 98; Saturday R (N.Y.) 49 (7 May) p. 10 & 49 (21 May) p. 47; Time 87 (13 May) 75. John Gielgud in N.Y.Times, 1 May, 2:1 tells of how difficult the lead role is: Ivanov has the self-destructive potential of Hamlet but without Hamlet's motivation for revenge. Although Ivanov is a neurotic failure, he knows it, and he is too honest to face the petty world about him. Wilfred Sheed in Commonweal 84 (27 May) 283 said that "the melancholy fascination which neurasthenia and paralysis of the will used to hold for Russian writers is difficult for Americans to share or cope with."

1911 14 Aug 1975 O.O.B. Alex Szogyi, Tr.

1912 24 Apr 1976 O.O.B. Impossible Ragtime Theater Ted Story, Dir.

1913 2 Jun 1977 O.O.B. Jewish Repertory Theater Don Marlette, Dir. Alex Szogyi, Tr.

On the Harmfulness of Tobacco

1914 5 Feb 1948 (14) City Center N.Y. City Theatre Company Richard Barr and Jose Ferrer, Dirs. Reviews: N.Y. Times, 6 Feb, p. 29; New Yorker 23 (14 Feb) 44.

1915 25 Apr 1956 O.B. Downtown Theatre Engrav Players Anthony Carbone, Dir. Review: N.Y.Times, 26 Apr,p. 38.

1916 15 Apr 1959 (37) Playhouse Theatre Theatre Guild and Dore Schary Hume Cronyn, Dir. Reviews: N.Y.Times, 16 Apr, p. 28 & 26 Apr, 2:1.

1917 5 Mar 1968 (6) O.O.B. East 74th St. Theater Yon Enterprises Charles Fischer, Dir. & Tr. Review: N.Y. Times, 6 Mar, p. 34.

1918 5 Mar 1969 (6) Longacre Theatre National Theater of the Deaf Alvin Epstein, Dir. Bernard Bragg, Adapter. Review: N.Y.Times, 9 Mar, p. 76.

1919 16 Jan 1975 O.O.B.

1920 16 Mar 1977 O.O.B.

On the High Road

1921 14 Jan 1929 (18) 14th Street Theatre Civic Repertory Theatre Eva Le Gallienne, Dir. Constance Garnett,Tr. Reviews: Nation (N.Y.) 128 (30 Jan) 142; N.Y.Times, 15 Jan, p. 22.

1922 20 Apr 1961 O.B. Key Theatre Amnon Kabatchnik, Dir. Julius West, Tr. Reviews: Nation (N.Y.) 192 (13 May) 419; N.Y.Times, 21 Apr, p. 26.

Platonov

(for variant titles, see below)

1923 14 May 1940 Closed 23 May 1940 Called Fireworks on the James Provincetown Playhouse (N.Y.C.) Donald Wetmore, Dir. Elizabeth McCormick, Adapter. Review: N.Y.Times, 15 May, p. 30.

1924 22 Apr 1954 Called Don Juan in the Russian Manner Wigs and Cues of Barnard College A.J. Sweet, Dir. Basil Ashmore, Adapter. Review: N.Y.Times, 23 Apr, p. 23.

1925 5 May 1960 (203) (O.B.) Called A Country Scandal Greenwich Mews Theatre Amnon Kabatchnik, Dir. Alex Szogyi, Tr. Reviews: America 103 (11 Jun) 362; Nation (N.Y.) 190 (21 May) 459-60; N.Y.Times, 6 May, p. 21 & 15 May, 2:1; New Yorker 36 (14 May) 94; Saturday R (N.Y.) 43 (28 May) 26.

1926 Apr 1975 O.O.B. Called Platonov Riverside Church Theater Mark Ross, Dir.

1927 25 Sep 1975 (28) O.B. Called A Country Scandal Alex Szogyi, Tr. Review: N.Y.Times, 8 Oct, p. 24.

1928 24 Mar 1976 O.O.B. Called Platonov.

The Proposal

1929 1916 Neighborhood Playhouse Review: Nation (N.Y.) 102 (4 May) 483.

1930 18 May 1939 O.B. Theresa L. Kaufmann Auditorium Guild Center Players (blind actors).

1931 27 Jun 1966 O.O.B. Theater in the Street In L.S. Lavandero's Spanish translation. Review: N.Y.Times, 28 Jun, p. 51.

1932 1972 season O.O.B. Amer. Center for Stanislavsky Theater Art Sonia Moore, Dir.

1933 May 1975 O.O.B. Comedy Stage Company Tim Ward, Dir.

1934 24 Mar 1976 O.O.B.

1935 Feb 1977 O.O.B. The Family Marvin Felix Camillo,Dir.

1936 15 Apr 1977 O.O.B. Amer. Center for Stanislavsky Theater Art Sonia Moore, Dir.

1937 17 Dec 1980 O.O.B. The Family Marvin Felix Camillo, Dir. & Adapter.

1938 26 May 1984 (closed) O.O.B. C.U.A.N.D.O. Marvin Felix Camillo, Dir. & Adapter. (Set in the Caribbean).

1939 6 Feb 1985 Closed 24 Feb 1985 American Stanislavsky Theater.

The Sea Gull

1940 22 Dec 1905 Orlenev's Russian Lyceum Paul Orlenev, Dir. Performed in Russian Reviews: Cosmopolitan 40 (Apr 1906) 616-7; Current Literature 40 (Apr 1906) 407-8.

1941 22 May 1916 (9) Bandbox Theatre Washington Square Players Marian Fell, Tr. Reviews: N.Y.Herald, 23 May, p. 9; N.Y.Times, 23 May, p. 9; N.Y.Tribune, 24 May, p. 11; N.Y.World, 23 May, p. 9; Theatre 24 (Jul) 10-1. The reviewer in Nation (N.Y.) 102 (1 Jun) 603 said it was absurd for an American even to try "to take seriously the neurasthenic maunderings which in this play are paraded in the guise of dramatic complications." Philip Littell in New Republic 7 (17 Jun) 175 was impressed by "the liberty which Chekhov gives the characters to be themselves." He predicted that playgoers would henceforth be dissatisfied with the "unlifelike relevance and orderliness" of the usual American play.

1942 9 Apr 1929 (31) Comedy Theatre Leo Bulgakov, Dir. Reviews: Catholic World 129 (Apr) 79-80; Commonweal 10 (8 May) 21; Nation (N.Y.) 128 (22 May) 626-7; Theatre Arts 13 (Jun) 401-2. Brooks Atkinson in N.Y. Times, 10 Apr, p. 32 said that the director employed proper pacing and lucid groupings in a play with a universal plot. Howard Barnes in N.Y.Tribune, 10 Apr, p. 24 was "profoundly moved" by "one of the season's finest plays."

1943 16 Sep 1929 (63) 14th Street Theatre Civic Repertory Theatre Eva Le Gallienne, Dir. Constance Garnett,Tr. Reviews: Arts & Decoration 32 (Nov) 67; Catholic World 130 (Dec) 330-1; Nation (N.Y.) 129 (2 Oct) 366-7; New Yorker 5 (28 Sep) 41; Outlook & Independent 153 (25 Dec) 672. The reviewer in America 42 (26 Oct) 68 said that the play taught that "if one is not wretched, one must be a fool." Brooks Atkinson in N.Y.Times, 17 Sep, p. 34 found the play "an exquisite study in monotone, the quintessence of human life." The critic in Commonweal 10 (2 Oct) 564 objected to the play's "declining spiritual tempo." Stark Young in New Republic 60 (9 Oct) 205 said that American dramatists had much to learn from Chekhov: "more delicacy of perception, more deeply interwoven themes, more subtlety of feeling, more poignancy, sincerity and truth of intention."

1944 25 Feb 1930 (5) Waldorf Theatre Leo Bulgakov, Dir. Reviews: N.Y.Herald-Tribune, 26 Feb, p. 16; N.Y.Times, 23 Feb, 3:7 & 26 Feb, p. 22. Stewart Beach in Theatre

51 (Apr) 74 admired the play's construction: "The tragedy is in the words, the gestures, the groupings, the subtle climaxes of hopelessness that Chekhov builds up, the ghastly tragedy that grows inevitably out of little things."

1945 1937 season Brattleboro Theatre Brooklyn.

1946 28 Mar 1938 (41) Shubert Theatre Theater Guild Stark Young, Tr. Reviews: Brooklyn Daily Eagle, 20 Mar; Catholic World 147 (May) 214-5; Commonweal 27 (15 Apr) 692; New Republic 94 (13 Apr) 305; N.Y.Herald-Tribune, 27 Mar, 6:2 & 29 Mar, p. 10; N.Y.Times, 17 Mar, p. 16 & 29 Mar, p. 19 & 3 Apr, 11:1; Stage 15 (May) 10-1; Theatre Arts Monthly 22 (May) 326-8; Variety 130 (30 Mar) 56. John Mason Brown in N.Y.Evening Post, 29 Mar felt that Lynn Fontanne overplayed Arkadina, refusing "to let us discover her faults for ourselves." Joseph Wood Krutch in Nation 146 (9 Apr) 422-3 believed that Alfred Lunt and Lynn Fontanne had properly subordinated themselves to the overall effect. George Jean Nathan in Newsweek 11 (11 Apr) 22 objected to the Lunts using surface acting idiosyncracies applicable to a Ferenc Molnar play in a dramatic vehicle of far greater depth. The reviewer in Time 31 (11 Apr) 36-8 admired Chekhov's unobtrusive technique of revealing character growth: "It is in delimiting his characters without disfiguring them, in acknowledging their souls but questioning their perspective that Chekhov gives to The Sea Gull an ember-like glow."

1947 11 May 1954 (40) O.B. Phoenix Theatre Norris Houghton, Dir. Adapted by Montgomery Clift, Kevin McCarthy, and Mina Rostova. Reviews: America 91 (29 May) 257; Catholic World 179 (Jul) 307; Commonweal 60 (18 Jun) 269; Nation (N.Y.) 178 (29 May) 469-70; N.Y.Theatre Critics' Reviews, 1954, p. 327; N.Y.Times, 9 May, 2:2 & 12 May, p. 38 & 7 Jul, p. 22; New Yorker 30 (22 May) 70; Saturday R (N.Y.) 37 (29 May) 22-3; Theatre Arts 38 (Aug) 33; Time 63 (24 May) 71. Brooks Atkinson in N.Y.Times, 23 May, 2:1 said that "in every period Chekhov seems to be the writer with the most profound insight. He is for all times and all places because he goes to the roots of life." John Beaufort in Christian Sci Monitor, 15 May found the production good in humor and in the tragic aspects of misdirected love, but lacking sub-surface tension and ensemble acting. George Freedley in Morning Telegraph, 11 May hailed the all-star cast reminiscent of the Lunt-Fontanne production in 1938. Richard Watts, Jr., in N.Y. Post, 11 May granted the talented cast, but found the production colorless and lacking orchestration.

1948 22 Oct 1956 O.B. Fourth Street Theatre David Ross, Dir. Constance Garnett, Tr. Reviews: America 96 (8 Dec) 310; Catholic World 184 (Dec) 227; Nation (N.Y.) 183 (10 Nov) 415. Brooks Atkinson in N.Y.Times, 23 Oct, p. 38 found good technical effects but felt that poor casting and the ineffective translation made the performance a failure. Walter Kerr in N.Y.Herald-Tribune, 23 Oct said that the production "flares and flickers as fitfully as the candles on the tables."

1949 21 Mar 1962 (11) Folksbiene Playhouse Assn of Producing Artists Ellis Rabb, Dir. Alex Szogyi, Tr. Reviews: Commonweal 76 (20 Apr) 87; New Republic 146 (14 May) 37; N.Y.Times, 22 Mar, p. 42; New Yorker 38 (7 Apr) 115-6. Howard Taubman in N.Y.Times, 1 Apr, 2:1 said that this company, playing in modern dress, transforms Chekhov's picture of decaying Czarist Russia into "what looks like a troubled house party of middle-class Americans. But by an obstinate paradox, the more Russian Chekhov's characters remain, the more readily other people can see themselves mirrored in them."

1950 5 Apr 1964 (16) National Repertory Theatre Eva Le Gallienne, Dir. & Tr. Reviews: N.Y.Theatre Critics' Reviews, 1964, p. 298; Variety, 8 Apr. John McClain in N.Y.Journal-American, 6 Apr called this "the best production of Chekhov's introspective excursion that we are apt to see in our time." Howard Taubman in N.Y.Times, 6 Apr, p. 36 said that "Chekhov's rueful mood is summoned and sustained."

1951 7 Nov 1973 Philip Nolan Theater Ensemble Theater Co. Stark Young, Tr. Review: N.Y.Times, 8 Nov, p. 61.

1952 18 Dec 1973 (105) O.B. Roundabout Theater Company Gene Feist, Dir. & Adapter. Reviews: Critical Digest 25 (11 Feb 1974) 2; N.Y.Times, 24 Jan 1974, p. 47 & 3 Feb 1974, 2:5.

1953 5 Dec 1974 (11) O.O.B. The Cubiculo Phillip Meister, Dir.

1954 8 Jan 1975 (42) O.B. Public Theater The Manhattan Project (N.Y. Shakespeare Festival) Andre Gregory,Dir. 3 playing areas designed by Ming Cho Lee; audience moves for each act. Reviews: Critical Digest 26 (20 Jan) 2; Drama R 19 (Mar) 112-3; N.Y.Times, 5 Jan, 2:5 & 9 Jan, p. 49; New Yorker 50 (20 Jan) 62.

1955 21 Jan 1975 (24) O.B. Manhattan Theatre Club Joseph Chaikin, Dir. Jean-Claude van Itallie, Tr. Reviews: Critical Digest 26 (17 Feb) 2; N.Y.Times, 31 Jan, p. 22.

1956 9 Sep 1976 O.O.B. Drama Committee Repertory Theater Arthur Reel, Dir.

1957 16 Sep 1976 O.O.B. National Arts Theater Robert Sterling, Dir.

1958 9 Feb 1977 O.O.B. N.Y. Theater Ensemble Ann Ciccolla, Dir.

1959 21 Feb 1977 Universalist Church Eugenie Leontovich, Dir. & Tr. Review: N.Y.Times, 22 Feb, p. 36.

1960 26 Apr 1979 (16) O.B. Meat and Potatoes Company Neal Weaver, Dir.

1961 8 Feb 1980 (12) O.B. Separate Theater Company James Harter, Dir.

1962 25 Apr 1980 (18) O.O.B. Impossible Ragtime Theatre Ted Story, Dir. Robert W. Corrigan, Tr.

1963 11 Nov 1980 (40) O.B. Public Theatre N.Y. Shakespeare Festival Andre Serban, Dir. Jean-Claude van Itallie, Tr. Elizabeth Swados, incidental music. Reviews: Hudson R 34 (Spring 1981) 99-104; Nation (N.Y.) 231 (29 Nov) 589; New Republic 183 (6 Dec) 28-9; N.Y.Theatre Critics' Reviews, 1980, p. 102; N.Y.Times, 24 Nov, 13:55-7; New Yorker 56 (24 Nov) 135; Newsweek 96 (24 Nov) 131; Time 116 (24 Nov) 64. Walter Kerr in N.Y.Times, 23 Nov, 2:1 chastised Serban for allowing "his players to lapse back into the slow and moody languors of stock Chekhov." Why did he give up his earlier vision that "farce and heartbreak can be the closest of friends?"

1964 20 Nov 1983 American Place Theater Circle Repertory Company Elinor Renfield, Dir. Jean-Claude van Itallie, Tr. Review: Edith Oliver in New Yorker, 5 Dec, p. 183 felt that set designer John Lee Beatty was the star of this production for his "enchanting scenery and leafy circular scrim." Judd Hirsch is convincing as the successful writer Trigorin, but "Richard Thomas's muted Treplev is without any fire or desperation."

1965 31 May 1984 (closed) O.O.B. Theater Studio Ann Raychel, Dir.

Swan Song

1966 1940 season O.B. Davenport Free Theatre.

1967 1943 season O.B. Davenport Free Theatre.

1968 15 Oct 1951 O.O.B. Club Baron Committee for the Negro in the Arts. Review: N.Y.Times, 16 Oct, p. 35.

1969 1 Mar 1974 O.O.B. West Side Community Repertory Theater Andres Castro, Dir.

1970 16 Jan 1975 O.O.B.

Tatyana Repina

1971 31 Mar 1978 (12) O.O.B. Judson Poets' Theater Arne Zaslove, Dir. John Racin, Tr.

The Three Sisters

1972 29 Jan 1923 (8) 59th St. Theatre Moscow Art Theatre Performed in Russian Reviews: Independent 110 (17 Feb) 140-1; New Republic 34 (28 Feb) 19-20; N.Y.Herald, 31 Jan, p. 10; N.Y.Times, 31 Jan, p. 14 & 4 Feb, 7:1; N.Y.World, 30 Jan. John Corbin in N.Y.Times, 30 Jan, p. 12 called it static and unconvincing drama which left the audience cold "and perhaps inclined to resentment." Percy Hammond in N.Y.Tribune, 30 Jan, p. 6 noted that Chekhov's sympathy, even when coupled with irony, illuminated the general gloom. The critic in N.Y.Times, 4 Jun, p. 13, describing a later production that year, said that "one of the most remarkable demonstrations in the history of the American theatre was staged by the capacity audience." After twelve curtain calls, Stanislavsky spoke to the audience in French and Russian, after which the applause lasted nearly half an hour.

1973 26 Oct 1926 (38) 14th St. Theatre Civic Repertory Theatre Eva Le Gallienne, Dir. Constance Garnett,Tr. Reviews: Drama Calendar 9 (1 Nov) 3-4; N.Y.Herald-Tribune, 27 Oct, p. 21; N.Y.Times, 27 Oct, p. 24 & 7 Nov, 8:1; Theatre Arts Monthly 11 (Jan 1927) 9-22; Vogue 69 (1 Jan 1927) 80. Walter Pritchard Eaton in McNaught's Monthly 6 (Dec) 187 called it a masterpiece of realism, and said that to call it dull betrayed a dramatic palate made abnormal by sensationalism. Arthur Hornblow in Theatre 45 (Jan 1927) 18 said that the "poetic melancholy and rowdy gaiety" of the tone of Russian provincial society had been richly evoked. Joseph Wood Krutch in Nation (N.Y.) 123 (10 Nov) 488 found that a "dozen delicately delineated characters" had been brought alive. Gilbert Seldes in Dial 82 (Jan 1927) 79 praised the purposeful illogic of the plot, noting that the play uncovered intense passions and a surprising amount of action.

1974 1927 season (13) 14th St. Theatre Civic Repertory Theatre Eva Le Gallienne, Dir. Constance Garnett, Tr.

1975 8 Jan 1930 (3) American Laboratory Theatre Reviews: N.Y.Herald-Tribune, 9 Jan, p. 20; N.Y.Times, 9 Jan, p. 22; Theatre Arts Monthly 14 (Mar) 194; Time 15 (20 Jan) 34.

1976 10 Nov 1930 (8) 14th St. Theatre Civic Repertory Theatre Eva Le Gallienne, Dir. Constance Garnett,Tr.

1977 14 Oct 1939 (9) Longacre Theatre Surry Theatre Players Samuel Rosen, Dir. Bernard G. Guerney, Tr. Reviews: Commonweal 31 (27 Oct) 14; New Republic 100 (1 Nov) 368-9; N.Y.Herald-Tribune, 16 Oct, p. 11; N.Y.Times,

16 Oct, p. 23; Theatre Arts 23 (Dec) 651-64; John Mason Brown in N.Y.Post, 16 Oct had a "feeling of outrage" at the desecration of the text of a play which he felt resembled a musical score with exquisite intonation. The reviewer in Variety 136 (18 Oct) 50 said that the high ceiling over the set inappropriately suggested ampleness of space when the characters suffered from spiritual confinement.

1978 21 Dec 1942 (123) Ethel Barrymore Theatre Guthrie McClintic, Dir. Alexander Koiransky & Guthrie McClintic, Trs. Reviews: America 68 (9 Jan 1943) 388; American Mercury 56 (Mar 1943) 361; Catholic World 156 (Feb 1943) 597-8; Christian Sci Monitor, 22 Dec; Current History n.s. 3 (Feb 1943) 548; Life 14 (4 Jan 1943) 33-5; New Republic 107 (28 Dec) 857; N.Y.Daily Mirror, 22 Dec; N.Y.Eve Post, 22 Dec; N.Y.Herald-Tribune, 22 Dec, p. 31; N.Y.Theatre Critics' Reviews, 1942, p. 135; N.Y.Times, 13 Dec, 7:32 & 14 Dec, p. 18 & 22 Dec, p. 31 & 27 Dec, 8:1; N.Y.World-Telegram, 22 Dec; New Yorker 18 (2 Jan 1943) 32; Newsweek 21 (4 Jan 1943) 64; Partisan R 10 (Mar-Apr 1943) 184-6; Theatre Arts 27 (Jan 1943) 46 & 27 (Feb 1943) 73-6 & 28 (Oct 1943) 603-6; Time, vol. 40, pp. 45-9; Variety 149 (23 Dec) 50. Joseph Wood Krutch in Nation (N.Y.) 156 (2 Jan 1943) 31-2 lamented the absence of strong characters in the play and the lack of faith in human nature on Chekhov's part. Burns Mantle in N.Y.Daily News, 22 Dec said, "I find myself of a mind to raise the money and send the Prozorov girls to Moscow with single-trip tickets." George Jean Nathan in American Mercury 56 (Jun 1943) 749 observed that the play was among the leading money-earners of the season, and that, far from being gloomy, Chekhov "was a pretty hand at lively farce and satire." James N. Vaughan in Commonweal 37 (15 Jan 1943) 326 said that the Prozorov sisters were appropriate in a world that was spiritually lonely, and that frustrated as they are, they at least suffer with dignity.

1979 1946 season Equity-Library Theatre.

1980 25 Feb 1955 (102) O.B. Fourth St. Theatre David Ross, Dir. Stark Young, Tr. Reviews: Commonweal 62 (6 May) 127; Nation (N.Y.) 180 (2 Apr) 293-4; New Republic 132 (21 Mar) p. 22 & 133 (21 Nov) p. 30; N.Y. Times, 26 Feb, p. 13 & 20 Mar, 2:1. Judith Crist in N.Y.Herald-Tribune, 28 Feb said that the excellent cast "made it not only bearable but brought many moments of tragic intensity and intended moments of comedy." George Freedley in Morning Telegraph, 30 Mar praised the artistic adviser James Light for his work on the sets. Maurice Zolotow in Theatre Arts 39 (May) 87-8 named it the best ensemble performance of Chekhov that he had seen. He said it had "a sense of the grotesque that is the essence of Chekhov's comedy."

1981 21 Sep 1959 (257) O.B. Fourth St. Theatre David Ross, Dir. Stark Young, Tr. Reviews: America 102 (10 Oct) 55; Nation (N.Y.) 189 (10 Oct) 218-9; N.Y.Times, 21 Aug, p. 23 & 22 Sep, p. 46 & 2 May 1960, p. 36; New Yorker 35 (3 Oct) 96-8. Brooks Atkinson in N.Y. Times, 4 Oct, 2:1 said that "to see The Three Sisters is to be moved by the purity of Chekhov's mind and soul." Unfortunately, he added, this production lacked humor, and thus Chekhov's points were stated too sharply.

1982 22 Jun 1964 (119) Morosco Theatre Actors Studio Theater Lee Strasberg, Dir. Randall Jarrell, Tr. Reviews: America 111 (11 Jul) 54; Nation (N.Y.) 199 (27 Jul) 37-9; New Republic, 25 Jul, 33-5; N.Y.Daily News, 23 Jun; N.Y.Post, 23 Jun; N.Y.Theatre Critics' Reviews, 1964, p. 238; N.Y.Times, 21 Jun, 2:1 & 23 Jun, p. 24 & 28 Jul, p. 26; N.Y.World-Telegram & Sun, 23 Jun; New Yorker 40 (4 Jul) 56; Newsweek 64 (6 Jul) 45; Saturday R (N.Y.) 47 (18 Jul) 25; Time 84 (3 Jul) 72. Judith Crist in N.Y.Herald-Tribune, 23 Jun felt that Kim Stanley was marvelous as Masha, but that the variety of acting styles and the diversity of moods vitiated the cumulative impact of the play. Howard Taubman in N.Y.Times, 5 Jul, 2:1 stated that at the end of the play the sisters are not self-pitying victims of forces beyond their control but a "chorus affirming the promise of the future and 'the regenerative powers of work'."

1983 11 Feb 1965 (8) City Center Moscow Art Theatre Vladimir Nemirovich-Danchenko, N.N. Litovtseva, & Iosef Raevsky, Dirs. Performed in Russian Reviews: Harper's 231 (Sep) 32; New Republic 152 (27 Feb) 26-8; N.Y.Times, 31 Jan, 2:1 & 12 Feb, pp. 12, 15; New Yorker 41 (27 Feb) 96; Newsweek 65 (22 Feb) 94. Howard Taubman in N.Y.Times, 21 Feb, 2:1 said that the 3 sisters are "individualized yet indivisible," and that the Moscow Art Theatre's "radiant art argues the case for creative repertory theater with irresistible eloquence."

1984 9 Oct 1969 (11) American National Theatre Assn Amer. Conservatory Theater William Ball, Dir. Reviews: Nation (N.Y.) 209 (3 Nov) 486; N.Y.Magazine, 3 Nov, p. 64; N.Y.Post, 13 Oct, p. 77; N.Y.Theatre Critics' Reviews, 1969, p. 338; N.Y.Times, 10 Oct, p. 38 & 13 Oct & 19 Oct, 2:3; New Yorker 45 (18 Oct) 149; Women's Wear Daily, 10 Oct. Stanley Kauffmann in New

Republic 161 (1 Nov) 33 said that it is easy to make this or any Chekhov play look good: "The moody lighting, the Victorian clutter, the picturesque groupings, all are accessible even to a modest directing talent."

1985 1970 season (20) American National Theatre Assn Invitational Series. Reviews: New Republic 162 (21 Mar) 31; Time 95 (23 Feb) 68.

1986 19 Dec 1973 (7) Billy Rose Theater N.Y. City Center Acting Company Boris Tumarin, Dir. Tyrone Guthrie & Leonid Kipnis, Trs. Reviews: Critical Digest 25 (31 Dec) 2; N.Y.Theatre Critics' Reviews, 1973, p. 134; N.Y.Times, 30 Dec, p. 55; New Yorker 49 (31 Dec) 42.

1987 4 Nov 1975 (8) Juilliard Drama School Acting Company Tyrone Guthrie, Tr. Reviews: Critical Digest 27 (17 Nov) 4; Modern Drama 18 (Dec) 365-9; N.Y.Theatre Critics' Reviews, 1975, p. 157; N.Y.Times, 5 Nov, p. 36.

1988 3 May 1977 (24) O.B. Brooklyn Academy of Music Frank Dunlop, Dir. Stark Young, Tr. Reviews: Nation (N.Y.) 224 (21 May) 634-6; N.Y.Theatre Critics' Reviews, 1977, p. 221; N.Y.Times, 5 May, 2:22 & 15 May, 2:3; New Yorker 53 (16 May) 74; Saturday R (N.Y.) 4 (9 Jul) 50-1. Anna Quindlen in N.Y.Times, 1 May, 2:1 quotes Tovah Feldshuh (who plays Irina): "The play is really about the struggle against banality and toward endurance." Frank Dunlop, the director, calls Chekhov's technique pointillism;it uses delicate strokes, like impressionistic painting.

1989 1 Feb 1979 (24) O.O.B. Lion Theatre Company Gene Nye, Dir.

1990 Oct 1980 O.O.B. Squat Theater.

1991 30 Nov 1982 O.B. Manhattan Theater Club Lynne Meadow, Dir. Jean-Claude van Itallie, Tr.

A Tragedian in Spite of Himself
(also called A Summer in the Country)

1992 5 Feb 1948 (14) City Center N.Y.C. Theatre Company Richard Barr and Jose Ferrer, Dirs. Reviews: N.Y. Times, 6 Feb, p. 29; New Yorker 23 (14 Feb) 44.

1993 1 Mar 1974 O.O.B. Called A Summer in the Country West Side Community Repertory Theater Andres Castro, Dir.

1994 16 Jan 1975 O.O.B. Called A Summer in the Country.

Uncle Vanya

1995 28 Jan 1924 (8) 59th St. Theatre Moscow Art Theatre Performed in Russian Reviews: N.Y.Times, 27 Jan, 7:2 & 29 Jan, p. 16; N.Y.World, 29 Jan, p. 13. The critic in N.Y.Tribune, 29 Jan, p. 8 stated that the play had a gripping interest because of the characters' foibles, vanities, and unrequited loves.

1996 24 May 1929 (2) Morosco Theatre Irma Kraft, Dir. Jennie Covan, Tr. Reviews: N.Y.Times, 25 May, p. 17; N.Y.World, 25 May, p. 13.

1997 15 Apr 1930 (71) Cort Theatre Jed Harris, Dir. Rose Caylor, Tr. Reviews: Catholic World 131 (Jun) 338-9; Christian Century 11 (30 Apr) 742-3; Life,9 May,p.16; New Freeman 1 (26 Apr)157; N.Y.American, 16 Apr; N.Y. Eve Post, 16 Apr & 21 May; N.Y.Herald-Tribune,18 Apr; N.Y.Times, 16 Apr, p. 26 & 20 Apr, 8:1 & 4 May, 9:1; N.Y.World, 16 Apr, p. 15 & 20 Apr, metro section, p. 3; Outlook & Independent 154 (30 Apr) 711; Scribner's 87 (Sep) 328; Theatre 51 (Jun) 42; Theatre Arts Monthly 14 (Jun) 454-62; Vogue 75 (Jun) 68-9. Joseph Wood Krutch in Nation 130 (7 May) 554-6 found the play to be primarily a character study, in which sentimentalism and cynicism were discarded in favor of complete understanding. Richard Dana Skinner in Commonweal 11 (30 Apr) 742-3 finally found the catharsis, "the great upward sweep," that he had long hoped to find in Chekhov's drama. The reviewer in Time 15 (28 Apr) 68 said that this play was a lesson to dramatists that a series of seductions were not necessary to portray "a subtle, intense, ably handled series of human emotions." To Stark Young in New Republic 62 (30 Apr) 299-300 the meditations and subjective passages in the play sounded like a prose Shakespeare.

1998 22 Sep 1930 (16) Re-opening of #1997 at Booth Theatre. Review: N.Y.Times, 23 Sept, p. 30.

1999 17 Nov 1930 (16) Re-opening of #1997 at Biltmore Theatre. Review: N.Y.Times, 18 Nov, p. 28.

2000 13 May 1946 (8) Century Theatre Old Vic Company Tyrone Guthrie, Dir. Constance Garnett, Tr. Reviews: Catholic World 163 (Jul) 357-8; Commonweal 44 (31 May) 166; Forum 106 (Jul) 79-80; New Republic 114 (3 Jun) 805; N.Y.Theatre Critics' Reviews, 1946, p. 389; N.Y.Times, 12 May, 2:1 & 14 May, p. 18 & 19 May, 2:1; Newsweek 27 (27 May) 84; Time 47 (27 May) 66. John Mason Brown in Saturday R of Lit 29 (1 Jun) 32-4 said that even though the production was inferior to that of Jed Harris in 1930, the play remained a profound study of human inner probing. Wolcott Gibbs in New Yorker 22 (25 May) 44-6 demurred, calling the play "a deliberate and wicked parody of all Russian drama." Joseph Wood Krutch in Nation 162 (1 Jun) 671 found the play to be richer than he had previously assumed. He was fascinated by the "pastel, elegiac" restraint of the playwright's mind.

2001 31 Jan 1956 O.B. Fourth St. Theatre David Ross, Dir. Stark Young, Tr. Reviews: America 94 (10 Mar) 646; Catholic World 183 (20 Apr) 65; Nation (N.Y.) 182 (18 Feb) 147; N.Y.Times, 1 Feb, p. 25 & 12 Feb, 6:29 & 4 Mar, 2:1 & 24 Jun, 6:34; Saturday R (N.Y.) 39 (18 Feb) 24; Time 67 (13 Feb) 48; Variety, 8 Feb. Brooks Atkinson in N.Y.Times, 12 Feb, 2:1 stated that the principal characters are transformed by their experiences. Chekhov's world, he said, "quivers with hope and longing. Personalities clash; destinies are settled; lives are destroyed." Richard Hayes in Commonweal 64(20 Apr) 75-6 praised the translations of Stark Young as "creative and reconstitutive acts of the highest fidelity and love." Walter Kerr in N.Y. Herald-Tribune, 1 Feb thanked David Ross for having captured Chekhov's "wild strain of fatuous anguish and comic despair." Stark Young in N.Y.Times, 29 Jan, 2:3 explained how to translate Chekhov. His supposed gloominess, said Young, is actually patient good temper and kindly wit. He uses repetitions knowingly: "the sequence of the speeches is part of the whole idea of dramatic movement."

2002 12 Feb 1960 O.B. Master Institute Theatre New Russian Theatre (Russian emigres) Barbara Bulgakov, Dir. Performed in Russian Reviews: N.Y.Times, 13 Feb, p. 13 & 14 Feb, p. 19.

2003 1970 season (15) O.B. C S C Repertory (Greenwich Village) Christopher Martin, Dir. Constance Garnett, Tr.

2004 24 Jan 1971 (54) O.B. Roundabout Repertory Company Gene Feist, Dir. & Adapter. Reviews: Critical Digest 22 (1 Feb) 2; N.Y.Times, 25 Jan, p. 23 & 21 Feb, 2:29 & 10 Mar, p. 33 & 27 Mar, p. 16; Time 97 (22 Feb) 52.

2005 4 Jun 1973 (64) Joseph E. Levine Theater Circle in the Square Mike Nichols, Dir. Mike Nichols & Albert Todd, Trs. Reviews: Critical Digest 25 (18 Jun) 2; Nation (N.Y.) 216 (25 Jun) 827-8; National R 25 (6 Jul) 742; New Republic 168 (30 Jun) 24; N.Y.Theatre Critics' Reviews, 1973, p. 260; N.Y.Times, 3 Jun, 2:1 & 5 Jun, p. 35 & 10 Jun, 2:1 & 18 Jun, p. 36; New Yorker 49 (9 Jun) 88; Newsweek 81 (18 Jun) 112; Time 101 (18 Jun) 70.

2006 14 Mar 1974 O.B. Terry Schreiber Studio Lee Wallace, Dir.

2007 13 Feb 1975 (16) O.B. Counterpoint Theatre Company Gonzalo Madurga, Dir.

2008 15 Jan 1976 O.O.B.

2009 15 Apr 1977 (11) O.O.B. Provincetown Playhouse (N.Y.C.) Actors' Alliance, Inc. Bruce Jordan, Dir. Jack Poggi, Tr.

2010 30 Apr 1977 O.O.B. Soho Repertory Theatre Marlene Swartz, Dir. & Adapter.

2011 12 Oct 1979 (12) O.B. Separate Theatre Company Anne Lucas, Dir.

2012 1982 season Public Theater N.Y. Shakespeare Festival Peter Von Berg, Dir. Ann Dunnigan, Tr.

2013 11 Sep 1983 (closed 2 Oct 1983) O.B. La Mama Annex Andrei Serban, Dir. Jean-Claude van Itallie, Tr. Reviews: N.Y.Theatre Critics' Reviews, 1983, p. 157. Benedict Nightingale in N.Y.Times, 18 Sep, 2:1 said that when Vanya's gun misses fire, tragicomedy was restored to the modern theater. But in this production Serban seems to have lost his nerve. The set itself is a gorgeous folly: gigantic, with countless walkways leading nowhere. Edith Oliver in New Yorker, 26 Sep, pp. 126-7 calls the production eccentric. The play, she feels, hinges on Astrov, and fortunately F. Murray Abraham does a good job with the role.

2014 8 Feb 1985 Closed 3 Mar 1985. O.B. New Media Repertory.

The Wedding (also called The Marriage)

2015 1936 season Called The Marriage. New Theatre School Studio.

2016 5 Feb 1948 (14) City Center N.Y.C. Theatre Company Richard Barr and Jose Ferrer, Dirs. Reviews: N.Y. Times, 6 Feb, p. 29; New Yorker 23 (14 Feb) 44.

2017 1961 O.B. Key Theatre Amnon Kabatchnik, Dir. Julius West, Tr. Reviews: N.Y.Times, 21 Apr, p. 26; New Yorker, 6 May, p. 123.

The Wood Demon

2018 1966 season (9) O.B. Master Theater Equity Theatre William Woodman, Dir. Alex Szogyi, Tr.

2019 29 Jan 1974 (10) O.B. Brooklyn Academy of Music Actors Theatre (British company) David Giles, Dir. Ronald Hingley, Tr. Reviews: America 130 (23 Feb) 133; Critical Digest 25 (11 Feb) 2; Drama 113 (Summer) 53-4; Nation (N.Y.) 218 (16 Feb) 222; N.Y. Theatre Critics' Reviews, 1974, p. 370; N.Y.Times, 8 Sep 1973, p. 20 & 27 Jan, 2:3 & 30 Jan, p. 23 & 10 Feb, 2:1; New Yorker 49 (11 Feb) 71; Time 103 (18 Feb) 95.

2020 1 Apr 1978 O.O.B. Assn of Theater Artists Roderick Nash, Dir.

Productions--U.S. Regional

The Anniversary (see The Jubilee)

The Bear (see also The Boor and The Brute)

2021 8 Feb 1915 Boston: Modern Drama Players at Toy Theatre. Review: Boston Transcript, 9 Feb.
2022 1916 season Galesburg, IL: Prairie Playhouse.
2023 7 Jan 1917 (5) Chicago: Washington Square Players at Playhouse Theater Roy Temple House, Tr.
2024 1917 Philadelphia: Little Theatre.
2025 1918 season Kansas City, MO: Comedy Club.
2026 1919 season Hollywood, CA: Community Theatre.
2027 1919 season Newark, NJ: Little Theatre Guild.
2028 1920 season Adrian, MI: Adrian College.
2029 1922 season Lawrence, KA: Univ of Kansas Players.
2030 1922 season Saratoga Springs, NY: Skidmore College.
2031 1924 season Orono, ME: Univ of Maine.
2032 1925 season Fort Humphreys, VA: Little Theatre.
2033 1925 season Topeka, KA: Little Theatre.
2034 1926 season West Liberty, WV: Hilltop Players.
2035 1928 season Sacramento, CA: Community Players.
2036 1928 season Washington, DC: Arts Club.
2037 1928 season Washington, DC: Columbia Players.
2038 1929 season Norman, OK: Univ of Oklahoma Playhouse.
2039 1929 season Williamstown, MA: Williams College.
2040 1930 season Chapel Hill, NC: Carolina Playmakers.
2041 1930 season Talladega, AL: Talladega College.
2042 1931 season Seattle: Univ of Washington.
2043 1932 season Seattle: Univ of Washington.
2044 1934 season Ashland, WI: Northland College.
2045 1935 season Auburn, AL: Alabama Polytechnic Institute.
2046 1936 season Chapel Hill, NC: Carolina Playmakers.
2047 1940 season Spokane, WA: Whetworth College.
2048 21 Jun 1973 (39) Abingdon, VA: Barter Theater. Dorothy Marie, Dir.
2049 22 Mar 1979 (17) Milwaukee: Milwaukee Repertory Theatre Jack McLaughlin-Gray, Dir. Earle Egerton, Tr.
2050 17 Jun 1984 A Night in the Ukraine (adapted from The Bear). Matunuck, RI: Theater-By-The-Sea.

The Boor

2051 9 Oct 1973 (12) Louisville, KY: Actors Theater. Jon Jory, Dir. Gary Barker, Tr.
2052 7 Aug 1980 (6) Lakewood, OH: Great Lakes Shakespeare Festival. Edward Stern, Dir.
2053 26 Jun 1984 (2) Alfred, NY: Alfred Univ Summer Theater.

The Brute

2054 9 Dec 1977 (20) Montclair, NJ: The Whole Theater Company. Arnold Mittelman, Dir. Eric Bentley, Tr.
2055 9 Nov 1978 (28) Los Gatos, CA: California Actors' Theater. Israel Hicks, Dir.

The Cherry Orchard

2056 9 Apr 1923 (6) Chicago: Moscow Art Theatre at Great Northern Theatre. Performed in Russian. Reviews: Chicago Daily News, 11 Apr, p. 20; Chicago Tribune, 11 Apr, p. 21.
2057 18 Apr 1924 (3) Chicago: Moscow Art Theatre at Great Northern Theatre.
2058 1931 season Iowa City: Univ of Iowa.
2059 1933 season Fargo, ND: Little Country Theatre.
2060 1935 season Grand Forks, ND: Univ of North Dakota.
2061 1935 season Pasadena, CA: Community Playhouse.
2062 1939 season Evanston, IL: Northwestern Univ.
2063 1940 season New Haven, CT: Yale Univ.
2064 1941 season Atlanta: Atlanta Univ.
2065 1943 season Austin: Univ of Texas.
2066 2 Oct 1944 (26) Chicago: Blackstone Theatre. Eva Le Gallienne, Margaret Webster, and Carly Wharton, Dirs. Irina Skariatina, Tr. Reviews: Chicago Daily News, 2 Oct, p. 22; Chicago Tribune, 4 Oct, p. 18.
2067 1945 season Denton, TX: State College for Women.
2068 12 Jan 1960 Washington, DC: Arena Theatre. Alan Schneider, Dir. Reviews: Washington Evening Star, 13 Jan, p. C18; Washington Post, 14 Jan, p. D8.
2069 1963 Minneapolis: Minnesota Theatre Company. Tyrone Guthrie, Dir. Review: America 108 (19 Jan) 121-2.
2070 24 Feb 1965 (16) Seattle: Seattle Repertory Theater. Thomas Hill, Dir.
2071 15 Jun 1965 (48) Minneapolis: Minnesota Theatre Co. at Guthrie Theater. Tyrone Guthrie, Dir. Tyrone Guthrie and Leonid Kipnis, Trs. Reviews: Nation (N.Y.) 201 (16 Aug) 87-8; N.Y.Times, 2 Aug, p. 17.
2072 19 Jan 1966 (11) Seattle: Seattle Repertory Theater. Stuart Vaughan, Dir.
2073 1 Mar 1967 (15) Stanford, CA: Stanford Repertory Theater. Mel Shapiro, Dir.
2074 3 Mar 1967 (10) Morristown, NJ: Morris Theater. Michael Del Medico, Dir.
2075 23 Mar 1967 (16) Atlanta: Pocket Theater. Richard C. Munroe, Dir. Stark Young, Tr.
2076 5 Apr 1971 (12) Chicago: Goodman Memorial Theater. Tyrone Guthrie and Leonid Kipnis, Trs.

2077 11 Jan 1974 (23) West Springfield, MA: Stage/West Theater. John Ulmer, Dir.
2078 19 Mar 1974 (27) San Francisco: American Conservatory Theater. William Ball, Dir. William Ball and Dennis Powers, Trs.
2079 4 Oct 1974 (44) Chicago: Goodman Memorial Theater. Brian Murray, Dir. Tyrone Guthrie & Leonid Kipnis,Trs.
2080 13 Dec 1974 (44) Hartford, CT: Hartford Stage Company. Paul Weidner, Dir. Review: N.Y.Times, 26 Dec, p. 56.
2081 1976 season Austin, TX: Center Stage Theatre.
2082 Mar 1978 Albuquerque: Univ of New Mexico. Review: Albuquerque J, 5 Mar.
2083 27 Jul 1979 (17) Sarasota, FL: Asolo State Theater. Mark Epstein, Dir.
2084 31 Jan 1980 (38) Houston: Alley Theatre. Louis Criss, Dir. Tyrone Guthrie and Leonid Kipnis, Trs.
2085 19 Feb 1980 (32) Cincinnati: Cincinnati Playhouse. John Going, Dir. World premiere of new translation by Michael Henry Heim.
2086 29 Sep 1981 (32) Berkeley, CA: Berkeley Repertory Theater. James Moll, Dir.
2087 12 May 1983 (47) New Haven, CT: Long Wharf Theater. Arvin Brown, Dir. Jean-Claude van Itallie, Tr.

Ivanov

2088 6 Apr 1924 (5) Chicago: Moscow Art Theatre at Great Northern Theatre. Performed in Russian. Reviews: Chicago Daily News, 7 Apr, p. 20; Chicago Tribune, 7 Apr, p. 21.
2089 19 Nov 1976 (31) New Haven, CT: Yale Repertory Theatre. Ron Daniels, Dir. Kitty Hunter Blair and Jeremy Brooks, Trs.

The Jubilee

2090 1923 season Chicago: Coach House Players.

On the Harmfulness of Tobacco

2091 1976 season San Francisco: Amer. Conservatory Theater.

Platonov (also called A Country Scandal)

2092 1 Apr 1964 (23) Called A Country Scandal. Boston: Theatre Company. Frank Cassidy, Dir.

The Proposal

2093 1916 season Rochester, NY: Prince Street Players.
2094 1920 season Indianapolis: Little Theatre Society.
2095 1926 season Chicago: Chicago Art Theatre.
2096 1927 season Camp Hill, AL: Southern Industrial Institute Players.
2097 1927 season Evansville, IN: Evansville Coll. Thespians
2098 1928 Poughkeepsie, NY: Vassar College. Reviews: Theatre 47 (May) 46-8; Theatre Arts Monthly 12 (Jan) 70.
2099 1928 season Chicago: YMCA Little Theatre.
2100 1928 season Cranford, NJ: Dramatic Club.
2101 1930 season Ada, OK: East Central State Teachers Coll.
2102 1930 season Anniston, AL: Little Theatre.
2103 1930 season Mt. Vernon, NY: Community Players.
2104 1930 season Redlands, CA: Univ of Redlands.
2105 1931 season Columbus, OH: Ohio State Univ Strollers.
2106 1933 season Chapel Hill, NC: Carolina Playmakers.
2107 1934 season Richmond, VA: Univ of Richmond.
2108 1936 season Seattle: Univ of Washington.
2109 1939 season Lorain, OH: Institute of Arts & Sciences.
2110 1940 season Hanover, NH: Dartmouth Univ.
2111 1943 season Richmond, VA: College of William and Mary.
2112 1961 Houston: Alley Theatre. Nina Vance & John Wylie, Dirs. Review: N.Y.Times, 11 May, p. 43.
2113 27 Feb 1965 (10) Princeton, NJ: McCarter Theater. Arthur Lithgow, Dir.
2114 21 Jun 1973 Abingdon, VA: Barter Theater. Dorothy Marie, Dir.
2115 Summer 1975 Beverly, MA: Theatre Venture '75. Jack Edleman, Dir.
2116 9 Nov 1978 (28) Los Gatos, CA: California Actors' Theater. Israel Hicks, Dir. Theodore Hoffman, Tr.
2117 18 May 1979 (12) Abingdon, VA: Barter Theater. Owen Phillips, Dir.

The Sea Gull

2118 1929 season Hamilton, NY: Little Theatre.
2119 1930 season Chicago: Goodman Memorial Theatre.
2120 1930 season Fairmont, WV: State College Masquers.
2121 1930 season Nashville, TN: Little Theatre.
2122 1940 season Los Angeles: Occidental College.
2123 1944 season Chicago: Goodman Memorial Theatre.
2124 1949 Los Angeles: UCLA Circle Players. Kenneth Macgowan, Dir. Review: N.Y.Times, 23 Apr, p. 10.
2125 10 Jan 1964 (40) Los Angeles: Theatre Group. John Houseman, Dir.
2126 1966 season San Francisco: American Conservatory Theater. Edward Payson Call, Dir.

2127 22 Feb 1967 (47) Houston: Alley Theatre. Nina Vance, Dir. & Adapter.

2128 11 Oct 1968 (44) Hartford, CT: Hartford Stage Company. Paul Weidner, Dir. Eva Le Gallienne, Tr.

2129 1968 season Oklahoma City, OK: Mummers Theater. Mack Scism, Dir. Anya Lachman and Mack Scism, Trs.

2130 12 Jan 1971 (21) Dallas: Dallas Theater Center. Paul Baker, Dir. David Magarshack, Tr.

2131 28 Nov 1971 (24) Baltimore: Center Stage. Robert Lewis, Dir. Stark Young, Tr.

2132 4 Oct 1973 (10) Princeton, NJ: McCarter Theater. Louis Criss, Dir. Jean-Claude van Itallie, Tr. Review: N.Y. Times, 8 Oct, p. 41.

2133 1 Mar 1974 (33) New Haven, CT: Long Wharf Theater. Arvin Brown, Dir. Stark Young, Tr.

2134 1974 Williamstown, MA: Williamstown Theater Festival. N. Psacharopoulos, Dir. Review: N.Y.Times, 8 Jul,p.43.

2135 21 Feb 1975 Athens, OH: Ohio Univ. Rex McGraw, Dir. Review: Educational Theatre J 27 (Oct) 412-3.

2136 10 Oct 1976 (8) University Park, PA: Penn. State Univ.

2137 15 Jan 1977 (24) Syracuse, NY: Syracuse Stage. Arthur Storch, Dir. Review: N.Y.Times, 21 Jan, 3:8.

2138 11 Nov 1977 Chicago: Goodman Memorial Theatre. Gregory Mosher, Dir. Jean-Claude van Itallie, Tr.

2139 17 Jan 1978 (35) San Diego: Old Globe Theater. Craig Noel, Dir.

2140 17 Feb 1978 Indianapolis: Indiana Repertory Theatre. Edward Stern Dir. Jean-Claude van Itallie, Tr.

2141 27 Jul 1978 Kansas City, MO: Missouri Repertory Theatre. Boris Tumarin, Dir. Jean-Claude van Itallie, Tr.

2142 16 Feb 1979 (28) New Haven, CT: Yale Repertory Theatre. Robert Brustein, Dir. Jean-Claude van Itallie, Tr.

2143 8 Nov 1979 (54) Pittsburgh, PA: Pittsburgh Public Theater. John Going, Dir. Michael Henry Heim, Tr.

2144 1979 season Dallas: Theatre Three.

2145 4 Mar 1980 (19) Tucson: Arizona Theatre Company. Mark Lamos, Dir. Ann Jellicoe & Ariadne Nicolaeff, Trs.

2146 29 Oct 1982 (30) St. Paul: Actors Theater. Michael A. Miner, Dir.

2147 1984 Minneapolis: Guthrie Theater. Lucian Pintilie, Dir. Review: Performing Arts J 8 (1984) 83-6.

Swan Song

2148 1917 Chicago: Chicago Theatre Society production at Fine Arts Theatre. Review: Drama, May 1917, p. 232.

2149 1917 season Fargo, ND: Little Country Theatre.

2150 1917 season Philadelphia: Plays and Players' Club.

2151 1918 season Boston: Modern Drama Players.

2152 1919 season Ypsilanti, MI: Ypsilanti Players.
2153 1928 season Hartford, CT: Drama Society.
2154 17 Mar 1972 (25) New Haven, CT: Long Wharf Theater. Arvin Brown, Dir. Morris Carnovsky, Tr. Review: N.Y. Times, 26 Mar, p. 61.
2155 12 Dec 1974 (27) Louisville, KY: Actors' Theater. Jon Jory, Dir.
2156 9 Nov 1978 (28) Los Gatos, CA: California Actors' Theater. Israel Hicks, Dir. Theodore Hoffman, Tr.

The Three Sisters

2157 16 Apr 1923 (5) Chicago: Moscow Art Theatre at Great Northern Theatre. Performed in Russian. Reviews: Chicago Daily News, 17 Apr, p. 28; Chicago Tribune, 18 Apr, p. 21; N.Y.Times, 14 Mar, p. 14.
2158 1928 season Pasadena, CA: Community Playhouse.
2159 1932 season Chicago: Goodman Memorial Theatre.
2160 1939 season Boston: Erskine School.
2161 1940 season Chicago: Goodman Memorial Theatre.
2162 1940 season Evanston, IL: Northwestern Univ.
2163 1942 season Asheville, NC: Black Mountain College.
2164 17 May 1943 (32) Chicago: Erlanger Theatre. Guthrie McClintic, Dir. Reviews: Chicago Daily News, 18 May, p. 14; Chicago Sun, 18 May, p. 15; Chicago Tribune, 18 May, p. 14.
2165 1945 season Seattle: Univ of Washington.
2166 1960 Los Angeles: Theatre Group.
2167 1961 season San Francisco: Actors' Workshop. Robert Symonds, Dir.
2168 7 Jun 1963 (25) Dallas: Theater Center. Paul Baker, Dir. Stark Young, Tr.
2169 18 Jun 1963 Minneapolis: Minnesota Repertory Theater at Guthrie Theatre. Tyrone Guthrie, Dir. Tyrone Guthrie & Leonid Kipnis, Trs. Reviews: N.Y.Times, 20 Jun, p. 30 & 22 Jul, p. 19; Saturday R (N.Y.) 46 (24 Aug) 34; Theatre Arts 47 (Aug) 13.
2170 29 Nov 1963 (20) Chicago: Goodman Memorial Theatre. Eugenie Leontovich, Dir. Tyrone Guthrie and Leonid Kipnis, Trs.
2171 26 Feb 1964 (41) Houston: Alley Theatre. Nina Vance, Dir. & Adapter.
2172 10 Feb 1966 (33) Washington, DC: Arena Stage. Zelda Fichandler, Dir. Stark Young, Tr.
2173 4 Nov 1966 (31) New Haven, CT: Long Wharf Theater. Arvin Brown, Dir. Tyrone Guthrie & Leonid Kipnis, Trs.
2174 16 Dec 1966 (34) Hartford, CT: Hartford Stage Company. Jacques Cartier, Dir.
2175 1966 season Rochester, MI: John Fernald Company. John Fernald, Dir. J.P. Davis, Tr.

2176 10 Mar 1967 (23) Pittsburgh, PA: Pittsburgh Playhouse. Thomas Hill, Dir. Tyrone Guthrie & Leonid Kipnis, Trs.

2177 26 Apr 1967 (14) Providence, RI: Trinity Square Playhouse. Adrian Hall, Dir. Robert Corrigan, Tr.

2178 3 Mar 1968 (14) New Haven, CT: Yale School of Drama. Larry Arrick,Dir. Tyrone Guthrie & Leonid Kipnis, Trs. Review: N.Y.Times, 18 Mar, p. 56.

2179 31 Jan 1969 (36) Milwaukee: Milwaukee Repertory Theater. Boris Tumarin, Dir.Tyrone Guthrie & Leonid Kipnis, Trs.

2180 31 Jan 1969 (8) Princeton, NJ: McCarter Theater. Tom Brennan, Dir.

2181 19 Feb 1969 San Francisco: American Conservatory Theater. William Ball, Dir. Reviews: San Francisco Chronicle, 14 Feb, p. 48 & 20 Feb, p. 47; Sat R of Lit 52 (5 Jul) 20.

2182 1969 Stratford, CT: American Shakespeare Festival Theater. Michael Kahn, Dir. Reviews: America 121 (6 Sep) N.Y.Times, 4 Aug, p. 29 & 10 Aug, 2:3.

2183 1969 Los Angeles: Center Theater Group. Harold Clurman, Dir. Review: N.Y.Times, 31 Aug, 2:4.

2184 1970 Los Angeles: National Theatre of Britain at Music Center. Laurence Olivier, Dir. Moura Budberg, Tr. Reviews: New Republic, 162 (21 Mar) 31; N.Y.Times, 12 Feb, p.30 & 22 Feb, 2:1; Time 95 (23 Feb) 68.

2185 11 Mar 1974 (7) Waltham, MA: Guest production by N.Y. City Center Acting Company at Spingold Theater.

2186 17 Oct 1975 Georgetown, TX: Southwestern Univ.

2187 23 Feb 1976 Los Angeles: Mark Taper Forum. Edward Parone, Dir. Michael Heim, Tr. Review: Educational Theatre J 28 (Dec) 556-7.

2188 11 Jan 1977 (33) Dallas: Dallas Theater Center. Ken Latimer, Dir. Robert Corrigan, Tr.

2189 11 Feb 1978 (22) West Springfield, MA: Stage West. Rae Allen, Dir.

2190 15 Mar 1978 (18) Stamford, CT: Hartman Theater Company. Wendy Chapin, Dir.

2191 2 Feb 1979 (35) St. Louis: Loretto-Hilton Repertory Theatre. Geoffrey Sherman, Dir.

2192 31 Mar 1981 (25) San Francisco: American Conservatory Theatre. Tom Moore & Larry Russell, Dirs.

2193 9 Jul 1981 (16) Kansas City, MO: Missouri Repertory Theater. Cedric Messina, Dir. Elisaveta Fen, Tr.

2194 27 Oct 1981 (13) San Francisco: American Conservatory Theatre. Tom Moore, Dir.

2195 1 Dec 1982 (21) Cambridge, MA: American Repertory Theater. Andrei Serban, Dir. Jean-Claude van Itallie, Tr. Review: Theatre J 35 (May 1983) 243-4.

2196 4 Mar 1983 (16) Princeton, NJ: McCarter Theater. Nagle Jackson, Dir. Randall Jarrell, Tr.
2197 1983 Boston: American Repertory Theatre. Andrei Serban, Dir. Review: Performing Arts J, vol 7, pp. 71-3.
2198 19 Jul 1984 Bloomsburg, PA:Bloomsburg Theater Ensemble.

Uncle Vanya

2199 18 Apr 1922 St. Louis: Artist' Guild. Gregory Zilboorg, Dir.
2200 10 Apr 1924 (4) Chicago: Moscow Art Theatre at Great Northern Theatre. Performed in Russian. Reviews: Chicago Daily News, 12 Apr, p. 14; Chicago Tribune, 11 Apr, p. 21.
2201 1927 season Denver: Studio Playhouse.
2202 1928 season Philadelphia: Duse Art Theatre.
2203 20 Oct 1930 (12) Chicago: Harris Theatre. Jed Harris, Dir. Rose Caylor, Tr. Reviews: Chicago Daily News, 21 Oct, p. 15; Chicago Tribune, 21 Oct, p. 29.
2204 1930 season San Francisco: Travers Players.
2205 1933 season Ann Arbor, MI: Univ of Michigan.
2206 1933 season Bennington, VT: Theatre Guild.
2207 1934 season Ithaca, NY: Cornell Univ.
2208 1935 season Seattle: Univ of Washington.
2209 1936 season Los Angeles: Musart Theatre.
2210 28 Mar 1962 (31) Boston: Charles Playhouse. Michael Murray, Dir.
2211 17 Apr 1962 (28) Washington, DC: Arena Theatre. Alan Schneider, Dir. Stark Young, Tr. Reviews: Washington Evening Star, 18 Apr, p. B10; Washington Post, 19 Apr, p. C21.
2212 1 Jan 1965 (39) San Francisco: Actors' Workshop. Herbert Blau, Dir.
2213 6 Jan 1965 (24) Providence, RI: Trinity Square Playhouse. George Keathley, Dir. Robert W. Corrigan, Tr.
2214 16 Jan 1965 (22) Milwaukee: Milwaukee Repertory Theatre. Adrian Hall, Dir. Robert W. Corrigan, Tr.
2215 16 Nov 1965 (40) Philadelphia: Theater of the Living Arts. Andre Gregory, Dir. Alex Szogyi, Tr.
2216 24 Nov 1965 (6) Cleveland: Cleveland Playhouse at the Drury Theater. Robert Snook, Dir.
2217 1965 season Pittsburgh, PA: American Conservatory Theatre. William Ball, Dir.
2218 11 Mar 1966 (25) New Haven, CT: Long Wharf Theater. Jon Jory, Dir. Robert Snook, Adapter.
2219 27 Feb 1969 (20) Louisville, KY: Actors Theater. Richard Block, Dir.
2220 20 Aug 1969 Los Angeles: Center Theater Group at Mark Taper Forum. Harold Clurman, Dir. Reviews: Los Angeles Times, 22 Aug, p. 15; Nation (N.Y.) 209 (22 Sep) 293;

N.Y.Times, 31 Aug, 2:4; Saturday R (N.Y.) 52 (15 Nov) 20; Variety, 27 Aug, p. 76.

2221 4 Jul 1972 (23) Ashland, OR: Oregon Shakespearean Festival. Larry Oliver, Dir. & Adapter.

2222 30 Nov 1973 (26) Baltimore: Center Stage. Jacques Cartier, Dir.

2223 28 Mar 1975 Berkeley, CA: Berkeley Repertory Theater. Douglas Johnson, Dir. & Tr.

2224 1975 season Minneapolis: Univ of Minnesota.

2225 24 Aug 1976 (21) Washington, DC: Wolf Trap Farm Park. John Going, Dir.

2226 Oct 1976 Pittsburgh, PA: Public Theater. Ben Shaktman, Dir. World premiere translation by Michael Henry Heim. Review: Educational Theatre J 29 (Oct 1977) 419-20.

2227 7 Dec 1977 (9) Waltham, MA: Brandeis Univ. Vivian Matalon, Dir.

2228 8 Feb 1978 (30) Seattle: Repertory Theater. Duncan Ross, Dir.

2229 1 Mar 1978 (23) Philadelphia: Drama Guild. Douglas Seale, Dir.

2230 14 Dec 1978 (13) Washington, DC: Royal Alexandra Theater Company at John F. Kennedy Center. Nat Brenner & Roderick Cook, Dirs. Frederick Monnoyer, Tr. Reviews: Macleans 91 (9 Oct) 70; Theater 10 (Spring 1979) 134.

2231 25 Jan 1979 (45) Portsmouth, NH: Theatre-By-The-Sea. Jon Kimbell, Dir. John Murrell, Tr.

2232 31 Jul 1979 (24) Lake Forest, IL: Academy Festival Theater. George Keathley, Dir.

2233 9 Oct 1981 (21) New Haven, CT: Yale Repertory Theater. Lloyd Richards, Dir. Constance Garnett, Tr.

2234 12 Jan 1983 (12) Phoenix: Phoenix College Theater.

2235 18 Jan 1983 (28) San Francisco: American Conservatory Theater. Eugene Barcone, Helen Burns, & Michael Langham, Dirs. Pam Gems, Tr.

2236 25 Feb 1983 (45) Milwaukee: Repertory Theater. Richard Cottrell, Dir.

2237 5 Mar 1983 (28) Tucson: Arizona Theater Company. Gary Gisselman, Dir.

2238 24 Jul 1984 Williamstown, MA: Theater Festival.

The Wedding

2239 17 Mar 1972 (25) New Haven, CT: Long Wharf Theater. Morris Carnofsky, Dir. & Adapter. Review: N.Y.Times, 26 Mar, p. 61.

American Films of Chekhov's Works

2240 The Beneficiary. Based on a Chekhov story. National Film School, 1979. B/W; sound; 47 min; 16 mm.

2241 The Bet. Based on a Chekhov story. Pyramid Films & Video. Ron Waller photography. B/W; sound; 23 min; 16 mm. Color is used at significant points.

2242 B/W films based on Chekhov stories available from MacMillan Films (34 MacQueston Parkway South, Mt. Vernon, NY 10550): The Boarding House (27 min); Desire to Sleep (14 min); The Fugitive (15 min); Revenge (26 min); Rothschild's Fiddle (23 min); Volodya (25 min).

2243 The Cherry Orchard, Part I. Chekhov: Innovator of Modern Drama. Encyclopedia Britannica Educational Corporation, 1967. Color or B/W; sound; 21 min; 16 mm. Director Norris Houghton uses scenes from the play to explain Chekhov's technique.

2244 The Cherry Orchard, Part II. Comedy or Tragedy? Encyclopedia Britannica Educational Corporation, 1967. Color; sound; 21 min; 16 mm. Norris Houghton shows how Chekhov dramatized inner action, and what is meant by the subtext of Chekhov's plays.

2245 The Swan Song. Carousel Films, 1973. Color; sound; 25 min; 16 mm.

2246 The Three Sisters. American Film Theatre. Laurence Olivier, Dir. Olivier plays Dr. Chebutykin.

2247 Uncle Vanya. Marionet Parsonnet, Producer. John Goetz, Dir. Stark Young, Tr. Franchot Tone plays Vanya.

American TV Productions of Chekhov's Works

2248 The Cherry Orchard. Stark Young, Tr. Play of the Week Production, 28 Dec 1959--3 Jan 1960.

2249 The Sea Gull. PBS, 29 Jan 1975. Part of WNET's "Theater in America" Series. Staged by Williamstown Festival Theater. Nikos Psacharopoulos, Dir. Review: TV Guide, 25 Jan 1975, pp. 19-20.

British Stage Productions (with reviews)

(British productions are in London, unless otherwise noted.)

The Anniversary (also called The Jubilee)

2250 2 Dec 1931 (3) Called The Jubilee Kingsway Theatre Moscow Art Theatre Performed in Russian Review: Era, 9 Dec 1931, p. 10.

2251 1960 Twentieth Century Theatre, Westbourne Grove Council of Five Review: Times (London), 4 Apr, p.6e.

The Bear

2252 14 May 1911 Kingsway Theatre Curtain raiser to a film.

2253 25 Jan 1920 St. Martin's Theatre Pioneer Players Reviews: Pall Mall Gazette, 26 Jan, p. 3. M. Lykiardopoulos in New Statesman 14 (31 Jan) 496 felt that the play had been played too rapidly to bring out its clever dialgue. The reviewer in Times (London), 26 Jan, p. 10b considered the play to be thin and crude.

2254 24 May 1926 Everyman Theatre Everyman Players Reviews: Outlook (London), vol. 57, p. 393. Francis Birrell in Nation & Athenaeum 39 (5 Jun) 248 called it "a perfect divertissement in which the absurdity never palls for an instant." The critic in Times (London), 26 May, p. 12c found "no variety or enthusiasm" in the play.

2255 1948 Arts Theatre.

2256 1960 Hovendon Theatre Club Review: Times (London), 6 Jul, p. 4d.

The Cherry Orchard

2257 28 May 1911 Aldwych Theatre Incorporated Stage Society Constance Garnett, Tr. Reviews: Academy & Literature 80 (3 Jun) 684; Daily Telegraph, 30 May, p. 14; Morning Post, 30 May, p. 6; Nation (London), 3 Jun, pp. 359-60; Sunday Times, 4 Jun, p. 6. Arnold Bennett under the pseudonym "Jacob Tonson" in New Age n.s. 9 (8 Jun) 132 commended the play for its "positively daring" naturalism. John Palmer in Saturday R (London) 111 (3 Jun) 677-8 found the play a true work of art, in which each seeming irrelevancy contributed to a mysteriously cumulative effect. The reviewer in Times (London), 30 May, p. 13d called it "something queer, outlandish, even silly."

2258 25 May 1925 Lyric Theatre, Hammersmith Oxford Players James B. Fagan, Dir. George Calderon, Tr. Reviews: Adelphi 3 (Jul) 129-30; Bookman (London), vol. 58,pp. 231-2; Contemporary R, vol. 129, pp. 756-62; Daily News, 26 May, p. 8; Illustrated London News 76 (6 Jun) 1136; Illustrated Sporting & Dramatic News, 6 Jun, p. 632; Nation & Athenaeum 37 (30 May) 267-8; Spectator, 134 (6 Jun) 924-5; Star, 26 May, p. 6; Sunday Times, 31 May, p. 4; Times (London), 26 May, p. 14c. Ivor Brown in Saturday R (London) 139 (30 May) 583 said that the play exhibited a rhythmical texture in which pettiness itself became "exquisitely poignant." Desmond MacCarthy in New Statesman 25 (13 Jun) 253-4 found the play "swarming with life," but felt that the strong comic element had been lost.

2259 28 Sept 1926 Barnes Theatre Theodore Komisarjevsky, Dir. Constance Garnett, Tr. Reviews: N.Y.Times,

17 Oct, 8:2; Times (London), 26 May, p. 12c. Desmond MacCarthy in New Statesman 27 (2 Oct) 706 accused the director of overstressing the ludicrous to the detriment of the play's pathos. The reviewer in Nation & Athenaeum 40 (9 Oct) 21 complained of "the general lifelessness of the actors."

2260 11 Apr 1928 Garrick Theatre Moscow Art Theatre (Groupe de Prague) Performed in Russian Reviews: Manchester Guardian, 12 Apr, p. 10; New Statesman 31 (28 Apr) 81-2; N.Y.Times, 6 May, 9:2; Saturday R (London) 145 (21 Apr) 491-2; Sunday Times, 15 Apr, p. 6; Times (London), 12 Apr, p. 10b.

2261 21 Dec 1931 (7) Kingsway Theatre Moscow Art Theatre Performed in Russian.

2262 9 Oct 1933 Old Vic Theatre Old Vic Company Tyrone Guthrie, Dir. Hubert M. Butler, Tr. Reviews: Daily Telegraph, 10 Oct, p. 10; Era, 11 Oct, p. 8; London Observer, 15 Oct; Spectator 151 (20 Oct) 522; Theatre Arts Monthly 17 (Dec) 922-8; Times (London), 10 Oct, p. 12c. Desmond MacCarthy in New Statesman & Nation n.s. 6 (21 Oct) 481-2 called the play the most complete expression of the universal egotism and isolation that governs human affairs. The critic in Time & Tide 14 (21 Oct) 1267 said that Chekhov was the closest approach to "the Shakespearean insight into the mind of humanity," for "the least of his creatures share some thought, some habit, common to humanity."

2263 28 Aug 1941 New Theatre Old Vic Company Tyrone Guthrie, Dir. Constance Garnett, Tr. Reviews: Daily Telegraph, 28 Aug; London Observer, 31 Aug; N.Y.Times, 7 Sep, 9:2; Theatre Arts 26 (Apr 1942) 241; Theatre World, vol. 35, p. 44; Times (London), 29 Aug, p. 6c. Alan Dent in Time & Tide 22 (6 Sep) 752-3 regretted that by ignoring stage directions the cast had marred the beauty of "one of the subtlest plays ever written." Graham Greene in Spectator 167 (5 Sep) 235 said that the director had avoided an excess of nostalgia, a threat to anyone who ignored "the savage critical core" of the play.

2264 1948 St. James's Theatre Liverpool Repertory Company John Fernald, Dir.

2265 25 Nov 1948 New Theatre Old Vic Company Hugh Hunt, Dir. Reviews: Spectator 181 (3 Dec) 729; Times (London), 26 Nov, p. 2d.

2266 21 May 1954 Lyric Theatre, Hammersmith John Gielgud, Dir. & Adapter. Review: Times (London), 22 May, p. 8f.

2267 1957 Guildhall School students John Holgate, Dir. Review: Times (London), 20 Nov, p. 3c.

2268 15 May 1958 Sadler's Wells Moscow Art Theatre Victor Stanitsyn, Dir. Performed in Russian Reviews: Nation (N.Y.) 186 (7 Jun) 522-3; New Statesman 55 (24 May) 662-4; N.Y.Times, 16 May, p. 22; Times (London), 15 May, p. 5c & 16 May, p. 3c.

2269 1959 Vanbrugh Theatre Royal Academy of Dramatic Arts Review: Times (London), 13 Nov, p. 15c.

2270 14 Dec 1961 Aldwych Theatre Royal Shakespeare Company Michel Saint-Denis, Dir. John Gielgud, Adapter. Reviews: N.Y.Times, 15 Dec, p. 49; Times (London), 30 Oct, p. 14g & 16 Nov, p. 15b & 15 Dec, p. 16b.

2271 May 1964 Aldwych Theatre Moscow Art Theatre Reviews: Drama n.s. 74 (Autumn) 19; N.Y.Times, 18 Jun, p. 29; Times (London), 30 May, p. 5a.

2272 1967 Prospect Productions Richard Cottrell, Dir. Review: Drama no. 87 (Winter) 22-4.

2273 1968 Moscow Art Theatre.

2274 1973 (5) Old Vic Company Ronald Hingley, Tr. Review: N.Y.Times, 19 Jun, p. 32.

2275 12 Jan 1978 Riverside Studios, Hammersmith Peter Gill, Dir. & Tr. Reviews: Drama 128 (Spring) 38-40; Plays & Players 25 (Mar) 24-5.

2276 14 Feb 1978 Oliver Theatre National Theatre Company Peter Hall, Dir. Michael Frayn, Tr. Reviews: Drama 128 (Spring) 34-5,38-40; Plays & Players 25 (Apr) 26.

2277 9 Aug 1982 Round House Oxford Playhouse Company Mike Alfreds, Dir. Mike Alfreds & Lilia Sokolov, Trs. Reviews: London Theatre Record 2 (15 Jul-11 Aug) 435-7; Plays & Players no. 349 (Oct) 35.

2278 18 Oct 1983 Theatre Royal, Haymarket Triumph Apollo Productions Lindsay Anderson, Dir. Reviews: London Theatre Record 3 (8 Oct-21 Oct) 898-902; N.Y.Times, 6 Nov, 2:5 & 18 Dec, 2:17; Plays & Players no. 363 (Dec) 23-4.

Ivanov

2279 6 Dec 1925 Duke of York's Theatre Incorporated Stage Society Theodore Komisarjevsky, Dir. Marian Fell,Tr. Reviews: Contemporary R 129 (1926) 759-60; Daily News, 8 Dec, p. 9; Morning Post, 8 Dec, p. 9; Outlook (London), vol. 56, p. 405; Stage, 10 Dec, p. 31. Ivor Brown in Saturday R (London) 140 (24 Oct) 472-3 named it a composition in the unheroic, amusing for its many idiosyncratic secondary characters. Desmond MacCarthy in New Statesman 26 (19 Dec) 301 said that he could feel Ivanov's inner tension and refinement. The critic in Times (London), 8 Dec, p. 14b said that the hero, being irresponsible, was no fit protagonist.

2280 1950 Arts Theatre John Fernald, Dir. J.P. Davis, Tr. Reviews: New Republic 123 (3 Jul) 21; Times (London), 21 Apr, p. 3f.

2281 Nov 1961 Vanbrugh Theatre John Fernald, Dir. Review: Times (London), 24 Nov, p. 15g.

2282 1965 Vanbrugh Theatre John Fernald, Dir. Review: Times (London), 12 May, p. 15a.

2283 1965 John Gielgud, Dir. & Adapter of translation by Ariadne Nicolaeff. Reviews: Drama n.s. 79 (Winter) 21-2; Salmagundi 2 (Spring 1967) 88-93.

2284 1976 Aldwych Theatre Royal Shakespeare Company David Jones, Dir. Reviews: Critical Digest 28 (20 Sep) 4; Drama no. 123 (Winter) 36-7; N.Y.Times, 18 Sep, p. 25 & 25 Nov, p. 38; Plays & Players 24 (Nov) 26-7; Times Literary Supplement, 24 Sep, p.1208a. Benedict Nightingale in N.Y.Times, 26 Sep, 2:5 called the play "a clinical study of spiritual menopause, assembled with sympathy and insight." This production, he felt, avoided the monotony of despair in a brisk effort to be "painfully funny."

2285 14 Aug 1978 Old Vic Theatre Prospect Theatre Company Toby Robertson, Dir. Ariadne Nicolaeff, Tr. Reviews: Drama no.130 (Autumn) 57; Plays & Players 26 (Oct)20.

On the Harmfulness of Tobacco

2286 1951 New Lindsey Theatre Review: Times (London), 29 Nov, p. 6e.

2287 1970 season (6) Stanley Lebor as monologist.

On the High Road

2288 1972 season (14).

2289 25 Jan 1982 Old Half Moon Theatre Yorick Players Michael Batz, Dir. & Tr. Review: London Theatre Record 2 (1 Jan-27 Jan) 29-30.

Platonov (also called Wild Honey)

2290 1957 Reviews (plans & production): Times (London), 25 Apr 1956, p. 3d & 1 May 1956, p. 3d & 3 Dec 1956, p. 5c & 8 Jan, p. 3a.

2291 13 Oct 1960 Royal Court Theatre English Stage Company John Blatchley & George Devine, Dirs. Dmitri Makaroff, Tr. Review: Times (London), 14 Oct, p. 18a.

2292 19 Jul 1984 Michael Frayn's adaptation called Wild Honey. Lyttelton Theatre National Theatre Company Christopher Morahan, Dir. Reviews: N.Y.Times, 5 Aug, 2:7; Plays & Players no. 372 (Sep) 28.

The Proposal

2293 3 Dec 1918 St. James's Theatre Julius West, Tr.

2294 2 Dec 1931 Kingsway Theatre Moscow Art Theatre Performed in Russian Review: Era, 9 Dec, p. 10.

2295 10 Feb 1949 New Theatre Old Vic Company Laurence Olivier, Dir.

2296 Apr 1960 Twentieth Century Theatre, Westbourne Grove Council of Five Review: Times (London), 4 Apr, p. 6e.

2297 Jul 1960 Hovendon Theatre Club Review: Times (London), 6 Jul, p. 4d.

2298 28 Jul 1960 Lyric Theatre, Hammersmith Caravel Productions Leila Blake, Dir. Elisaveta Fen, Tr. Reviews (plans & production): Times (London), 8 Jun, p. 16d & 29 Jul, p. 13d.

2299 1972 season (10).

The Sea Gull

2300 31 Mar 1912 Little Theatre Adelphi Play Society George Calderon, Tr. Reviews: Daily Telegraph, 1 Apr, p. 13; New Age, n.s. vol 10, p. 619; N.Y.Times, 21 Apr, 7:9; Times (London), 1 Apr, p. 12d. The reviewer in Academy 82 (13 Apr) 471 said that good acting was wasted on a play that was structurally weak,that lacked living characters, and that portrayed social conditions strange to England. John Palmer in Saturday R(London) 114 (13 Apr) 453-4 regretted that the actors had not achieved ensemble acting, and had thus upset the rhythm of the play.

2301 1 Jun 1919 Haymarket Theatre London Art Theatre Mme. Donnet, Dir. Marian Fell, Tr. Reviews: Athenaeum, 13 Jun, pp. 469-70; New Statesman, vol 13, pp. 238-9; Sunday Times, 8 Jun, p. 4. Gilbert Cannan in Nation (London) 25 (7 Jun) 293 said that the speeches and actions of the characters went "down to the center of their being, releasing and revealing their passions." The reviewer in Daily News, 3 Jun, p. 3 judged that drama cannot be made out of such negative natures.

2302 19 Oct 1925 Little Theatre Philip Ridgeway, Dir. Constance Garnett, Tr. Reviews: English R 41 (Dec) 879; Nation & Athenaeum 38 (31 Oct) 180; Saturday R (London) 140 (24 Oct) 472-3; Spectator 135 (31 Oct) 753; Stage, 22 Oct, p. 18; Times (London), 20 Oct, p. 12b. Desmond MacCarthy in New Statesman 26 (14 Nov) 143 admired the use of the leitmotif device, and the compassionate spirit which provided artistic unity. J.C. Squire in London Mercury 13 (Dec) 200-1 found little of interest in character or dialogue in the play.

2303 16 Jan 1929 Arts Theatre Arts Theatre Club Philip Ridgeway, Dir. Constance Garnett, Tr. Reviews: Daily Telegraph, 17 Jan, p. 7; Era, 23 Jan, p. 1; London Observer, 20 Jan, p. 13; Times (London), 17 Jan, p. 10c. The reviewer in Nation & Athenaeum 44 (26 Jan) 584 panned the play as shallow and monotonous but still concluded: "Of course, a bad play by Tchehov is better than a good play by almost anyone else." The critic in New Statesman 32 (26 Jan) 497 believed that Chekhov's characters were far more real than Shaw's, showing "all the mercurial alternations of mood which real men and women know."

2304 1929 season St. Pancras People's Theatre.

2305 20 May 1936 New Theatre Theodore Komisarjevsky, Dir. Constance Garnett, Tr. Reviews: Evening News, 21 May, p. 7; Evening Standard, 21 May, p. 9; Life & Letters Today 15 (Autumn) 162-3; London Mercury 34 (Jul) 249; London Observer, 24 May; New Statesman & Nation, n.s. vol. 11, pp. 858-60; N.Y.Times, 21 May, p. 19 & 4 Jun, 9:1 & 21 Jun, 9:1 & 30 Aug, 9:1; Theatre Arts Monthly 20 (Sep) 665-70 & 20 (Oct) 770; Times (London), 21 May, p. 14b. P.T. in New English Weekly 9 (18 Jun) 194-5 lamented the slow staging, saying that the play demanded rapid movement in order to heighten the bitterness of the climax. Derek Verschoyle in Spectator 156 (29 May) 978 said that because it offered "superb material for acting," it was one of the "most delightful and satisfying" plays of all time.

2306 1948 Tennent Productions.

2307 16 Nov 1949 Lyric Theatre, Hammersmith & St. James's Theatre Company of Four Review: Times (London), 17 Nov, p. 7d.

2308 1953 Arts Theatre J. P. Davis, Tr. Review: Times (London), 24 Apr, p. 3e.

2309 2 Aug 1956 Saville Theatre Michael MacOwan, Dir. David Magarshack, Tr. Reviews (plans & production): Theatre Arts 41 (May 1957) 26; Times (London), 18 Jun, p. 5b & 3 Aug, p. 5g.

2310 1960 Unity Theatre Ann Dyson, Dir. David Magarshack, Tr. Review: Times (London), 18 Jun, p. 12e.

2311 1 Sep 1960 Old Vic Theatre Old Vic Company John Fernald, Dir. J.P. Davis, Tr. Review: Times (London), 2 Sep, p. 13e.

2312 1962 Hampstead Theatre Club Theatre West Company James Roose-Evans, Dir. Review: Times (London), 18 Dec, p. 5b.

2313 1964 Queen's Theatre English Stage Company Tony Richardson, Dir. Review: Drama n.s. no. 73 (Summer) 20; London Magazine 4 (May) 63-7; Reporter 30 (4 Jun) 34-5; Times (London) 12 Feb, p. 13f & 13 Mar, p. 10a.

2314 1970 season (12) Moscow Art Theatre.

2315 31 Jan 1974 (24) Greenwich Theater Jonathan Miller, Dir. Elisaveta Fen, Tr. Reviews: Educational Theatre J 26 (Oct) 406-7; Plays & Players 21 (Mar) 36-9.

2316 28 Oct 1975 Lyric Theatre Lindsay Anderson, Dir. Lindsay Anderson & Galina von Meck, Trs. Reviews: Critical Digest 27 (17 Nov) 4; Drama no. 119 (Winter) 50-1; N.Y.Times, 23 Nov, 2:7; Plays & Players 23 (Jan 1976) 30-1.

2317 1976 Duke of York's Theatre Triumph Theatre Ltd. Mark Woolgar, Dir. & Tr. Reviews: Drama no. 122, pp. 53-5; N.Y.Times, 18 Sep, p. 25; Plays & Players 24 (Oct) 26-7.

2318 8 Apr 1981 Royal Court Theatre English Stage Company Max Stafford-Clark, Dir. Thomas Kilroy, Tr. Reviews: Drama no. 141 (Autumn) 28: London Theatre Record 1 (26 Mar-8 Apr) 162-4.

2319 13 Oct 1981 Almeida, Islington Shared Experience Mike Alfreds, Dir. Mike Alfreds & Lilia Sokolov, Trs. Reviews: Drama no. 143 (Spring 1982) 47: London Theatre Record 1 (8 Oct-21 Oct) 542-3.

2320 1984 Greenwich Theatre Philip Prowse, Dir. Review: Plays & Players no. 370 (Jul) 24.

Swan Song

2321 1970 season (6) Stanley Lebor as monologist.

The Three Sisters

2322 8 Mar 1920 Royal Court Theatre Art Theatre Company Constance Garnett, Tr. Reviews: Athenaeum, 19 Mar, p. 378; London Mercury 1 (Apr) 755-6; Morning Post, 9 Mar, p. 5; Nation (London), vol 26, p. 806; New Statesman, vol 14, pp. 676-7. The reviewer in Times (London) 9 Mar, p. 14b said that the spectator could not fail to enjoy Chekhov's masterful arrangement of significant touches into "music with a dying fall of haunting beauty." Ralph Wright in Everyman 15 (20 Mar) 513-4 said that the play evinced irony minus scorn, and that at least seven characters of equal importance were developed unobtrusively yet convincingly.

2323 16 Feb 1926 Barnes Theatre Theodore Komisarjevsky, Dir. Constance Garnett & Theodore Komisarjevsky, Trs. Reviews: Contemporary R, vol 129, pp. 756-62; Daily News, 17 Feb, p. 5; English R, vol 42, pp. 563-5; Illustrated London News, 27 Feb, p. 366; Nation &

Athenaeum 38 (27 Feb) 745; Outlook (London), vol 57, p. 150; Saturday R (London) 141 (27 Feb) 257-88; Spectator 136 (27 Feb) 363-4; Star, 17 Feb, p. 3; Times (London), 17 Feb, p. 12c. Desmond MacCarthy in New Statesman 26 (6 Mar) 646 found a musical structure achieved through harmonious interweaving of the themes of individual despair and hope for mankind. Milton Waldman in London Mercury 13 (Apr) 648-9 admired how Chekhov could reveal a whole lifetime in a single gesture.

2324 25 Oct 1926 Barnes Theatre Theodore Komisarjevsky, Dir. Theodore Komisarjevsky & Constance Garnett, Trs. Reviews: Adelphi 4 (Dec) 379-82; Nation & Athenaeum 40 (30 Oct) 146.

2325 23 Oct 1929 Fortune Theatre Theodore Komisarjevsky & Philip Ridgeway, Dirs. Theodore Komisarjevsky & Constance Garnett, Trs. Reviews: Daily News, 24 Oct, p. 10; Graphic 126 (9 Nov) 275; Illustrated Sporting & Dramatic News, 2 Nov, p. 294; Nation & Athenaeum, vol 46, p. 171; New Statesman 34 (30 Nov) 263-4; Observer (London), 27 Oct, p. 15; Saturday R (London) 148 (2 Nov) 508; Times (London), 24 Oct, p. 14c.

2326 12 Nov 1935 Old Vic Theatre Old Vic Company Constance Garnett, Tr. Reviews: Manchester Guardian, 13 Nov, p. 6; Observer (London), 17 Nov, p. 17; Times (London), 13 Nov, p. 10b & 17 Nov, p. 6. Michael Sayers in New English Weekly 8 (21 Nov) 113-4 said this play was "nothing but action," being essentially a spectacle in which everything related to the "purely theatrical revelation of character." Derek Verschoyle in Spectator 155 (15 Nov) 814 missed the elements of gaiety and hopefulness in this production.

2327 28 Jan 1938 Queen's Theatre Michel Saint-Denis, Dir. Constance Garnett, Tr. Reviews: Daily Express, 29 Jan, p. 15; Illustrated London News 102 (12 Feb) 242; London Observer, 30 Jan; New English Weekly 12 (10 Feb) 354-5; New Statesman & Nation, n.s. vol 15, pp. 205-7; N.Y.Times, 13 Feb, 10:3; News Chronicle, 1 Feb, p. 9; Spectator 160 (4 Feb) 179; Stage, 3 Feb, p. 10; Theatre World, vol 29, pp. 117-27. Henry Adler in London Mercury 39 (Nov) 47-55 praised the director's "subtle French psychological intuition" which enabled him to grasp subtle fluctuations in the mind and mood of the characters. Ashley Dukes in Theatre Arts Monthly 22 (Jun) 407 marvelled at the "lifelikeness" of Chekhov's drama. P.F.G. in Time & Tide 29 (5 Feb) 186 felt that Chekhov better than other dramatists captured the full emotional significance of the ironic timing in which comedy interrupted serious human crises.

2328 3 May 1951 Aldwych Theatre Peter Ashmore, Dir. Peter Ashmore and Mary Britnieva, Adapters.
2329 16 May 1958 Sadler's Wells Moscow Art Theatre Yosif M. Rayevski, Dir. Reviews: Nation (N.Y.) 186 (7 Jun) 522-3; New Statesman 55 (24 May) 662-4; Times (London), 17 May, p. 3a.
2330 1959 London Academy of Music & Dramatic Art (2 acts only) Review: Times (London), 14 Jul, p. 8c.
2331 1963 Old Vic Company Fulton Mackay, Dir. Review: Times (London), 20 May, p. 6a.
2332 1964 Oxford Playhouse Company Frank Hauser, Dir. Ariadne Nicolaeff, Tr. Review: Times (London), 28 Apr, p. 15d.
2333 13 May 1965 World Theater Actors Studio (U.S.) Lee Strasberg, Dir.
2334 1967 Old Vic Theatre National Theatre Company Laurence Olivier, Dir.
2335 1967 Royal Court Theatre English Stage Company William Gaskill, Dir. Edward Bond, Tr. Review: Drama no. 85 (Summer) 19-20.
2336 1968 Moscow Art Theatre.
2337 1972 season (25) Elisaveta Fen, Tr.
2338 23 Jun 1976 Cambridge Theatre (London) Triumph Theatre Ltd. Jonathan Miller, Dir. Elisaveta Fen, Tr. Reviews: Contemporary R 229 (Aug) 91-2; Critical Digest 28 (19 Jul) 4; Drama 122 (Autumn) 55; Evening Standard, 23 Jun; Guardian, 24 Jun; J of Canadian Studies 11 (Nov) 46-8; N.Y.Times, 18 Sep, p. 25; Plays & Players 23 (Aug) 20-1; Sunday Telegraph, 27 Jun; Times (London), 24 Jun.
2339 2 Apr 1980 The Warehouse Royal Shakespeare Company Trevor Nunn, Dir. Richard Cottrell, Tr. Review: Plays & Players 27 (May) 26-7.

A Tragedian in Spite of Himself

2340 1973 season (12).

Uncle Vanya

2341 11 May 1914 Aldwych Theatre Incorporated Stage Society Rochelle S. Townsend, Tr. Reviews: Athenaeum, 16 May, p. 700; Daily Chronicle, 12 May, p. 4; Daily News & Leader, 12 May, p. 3; Daily Telegraph, 12 May, p. 6; Nation (London) 15 (16 May) 265-6; Times (London), 12 May, p. 11d. This, said Desmond MacCarthy in New Statesman 3 (16 May) 180-1, is true tragedy, with the "flatness and poignancy of life itself. Desolation is a delicate thing." But Egan Mew in Academy 86 (23 May) 662-3 demurred: "We are not ready for such cold realism, such repetitions, such slow and elusive action, such vague pictures of the characters."

2342 27 Nov 1921 Court Theatre Incorporated Stage Society Theodore Komisarjevsky, Dir. Constance Garnett, Tr. Reviews: Bookman (London) 61 (Dec) 169-70; Nation & Athenaeum 30 (3 Dec) 390-2; New Statesman, vol 18, pp. 254-5; Referee, 4 Dec, p. 7; Saturday R (London) 132 (10 Dec) 658-9; Sunday Times, 4 Dec, p. 6; Times (London), 29 Nov, p. 8d. The reviewer in Spectator 127 (3 Dec) 743-4 promised rich rewards to the careful playgoer who noted the sub-pattern carried out by small stage actions. W.J.Turner in London Mercury 5 (Jan 1922) 311 said that no one since Shakespeare had probed so deeply into the depths of personality.

2343 16 Jan 1926 Barnes Theatre Theodore Komisarjevsky and Philip Ridgeway, Dirs. Theodore Komisarjevsky & Constance Garnett, Trs. Reviews: Daily Herald, 18 Feb, p. 4; Daily Telegraph, 18 Jan, p. 13; English R 42 (Apr) 563-5; Morning Post, 18 Jan, p. 7; Nation & Athenaeum 38 (23 Jan) 583-4; New Statesman, vol 26, pp. 645-6; Outlook (London), vol 57, p. 150; Times (London), 18 Jan, p. 12c. John Shand in Adelphi 3 (Mar) 691-3 described the performance as "a cathedral experience," with the characters uttering "the unexpressed feelings in a myriad of hearts." The reviewer in Spectator 136 (23 Jan) 124-5 commended Chekhov for his artful use of soliloquy and for his recognition that people know only themselves.

2344 30 Apr 1928 Garrick Theatre Moscow Art Theatre (Groupe de Prague) Performed in Russian Reviews: Daily Telegraph, 1 May, p. 8; Observer (London), 6 May, p. 15; Times (London), 29 May, p. 10. The critic in Times (London) 1 May, p. 14c called the play "profound and moving," filled with the tenderness, compassion, and unerring insight that only Chekhov could give in the theater.

2345 5 Feb 1937 Westminster Theatre Anmer Hall, Dir. Constance Garnett, Tr. Reviews: New English Weekly 10 (18 Feb) 375; New Statesman & Nation n.s. 13 (13 Feb) 241-2; Observer (London), 7 Feb, p. 15; Times (London), 6 Feb, p. 10d. P.F.G. in Time & Tide 18 (13 Feb) 192 praised the dialogue for its "divine inconsequence" and "ruthless self-analysis." Derek Verschoyle in Spectator 158 (12 Feb) 267 said the play's effect stemmed from the "passions of the characters, broken idealisms, pointless self-reproaches, and still more pointless hopes."

2346 2 Sep 1943 Westminster Theatre Norman Marshall, Dir. Constance Garnett, Tr. Reviews: London News Chronicle, 3 Sep, p. 3; Manchester Guardian, 4 Sep, p. 7; Spectator 171 (10 Sep) 239; Time & Tide 24 (11 Sep) 742. Ashley Dukes in Theatre Arts 27 (Dec) 721-2 said that Chekhov, "the dramatist to end dramatists," had shelved the "well-made" play for all time. Desmond MacCarthy in New Statesman & Nation 26 (11 Sep) 167-8 stated that Chekhov created characters whose frankness constantly evokes more sympathy than contempt.

2347 16 Jan 1945 New Theatre Old Vic Company Constance Garnett, Tr. Reviews: Evening Standard, 29 Jan; London News Chronicle, 17 Jan, p. 3; New English Weekly 26 (15 Feb) 139; New Statesman & Nation n.s. 29 (27 Jan) 55-6; N.Y.Times, 25 Mar, 2:2; Observer (London), 21 Jan, p. 2; Sunday Graphic, 21 Jan, p.12; Tatler & Bystander, vol. 175, pp. 272-3; Theatre World, vol. 41, p. 7; Times (London), 17 Jan, p. 6. Philip Page in Sphere 180 (27 Jan) 122 found the play tedious. James Redfern in Spectator 174 (26 Jan) 79 said that Chekhov was the first dramatist to present "the ordinary human being in all his full sensibility and as Western civilization and Christianity have hammered him into shape."

2348 1952 Arts Theatre Review: Times (London), 28 Mar,p.8.

2349 20 May 1958 Sadler's Wells Moscow Art Theatre M.M. Kedrov, Dir. Performed in Russian Reviews: New Statesman 55 (24 May) 662-4; Times (London), 21 May, p. 3a.

2350 1963 Old Vic Theatre National Theatre Company Laurence Olivier, Dir. Reviews: Listener 70 (5 Dec) 913; New Statesman 66 (25 Oct) 582; Reporter 30 (4 Jun 1964) 34-5; Times (London), 20 Nov, p. 5a.

2351 1970 Royal Court Theatre English Stage Company Anthony Page, Dir. Christopher Hampton, Tr. Review: N.Y.Times, 15 Mar, 2:7.

2352 1980 Hampstead Theatre Nancy Meckler, Dir. Pam Gems, Tr. Review: Plays & Players 27 (Feb) 29.

2353 6 Feb 1981 Orange Tree, Richmond Sam Walters, Dir. Elisaveta Fen, Tr. Review: London Theatre Record 1 (29 Jan-11 Feb) 62.

2354 18 May 1982 Lyttelton Theatre National Theatre Company Michael Bogdanov, Dir. Pam Gems, Tr. Reviews: London Theatre Record 2 (6 May-19 May) 258-62; Plays & Players no. 346 (Jul) 24-5; Theatre J 35 (Mar 1983) 118-9.

2355 5 Aug 1982 Theatre Royal, Haymarket Triumph Apollo Productions Christopher Fettes, Dir. John Murrell, Tr. Reviews: London Theatre Record 2 (15 Jul-11 Aug) 426-30; Plays & Players no. 349 (Oct) 26-7.

The Wedding (also called The Marriage)

2356 1917 Grafton Gallery Nigel Playfair, Dir. Review: Star, 15 May.

2357 25 Jan 1920 St. Martin's Theatre Pioneer Players Reviews: Pall Mall Gazette, 26 Jan, p. 3; Times (London), 26 Jan, p.10b. M. Lykiardopoulos in New Statesman 14 (31 Jan) 496 said that the production showed that an English cast could concentrate to achieve the "concert pitch" necessary to stage Chekhov's plays.

2358 5 Dec 1931 (3) Called The Marriage Kingsway Theatre Moscow Art Theatre Performed in Russian.

2359 13 Mar 1951 Old Vic Theatre Old Vic Company George Devine, Dir. Constance Garnett, Tr.

2360 1959 Tower Theatre Adrian Rendle, Dir. Eric Bentley, Tr. Review: Times (London), 23 May, p. 5g.

The Wood Demon

2361 1974 (13) The Actors Company Review: Drama no. 113 (Summer) 53-4.

Productions--U.K. Regional

2362 1911 to 1929 6 Chekhov plays Newcastle: People's Theatre. Source: Observer (London) 20 Oct 1929, p. 13.

The Boor

2363 1918 season Birmingham Repertory Theatre.

The Cherry Orchard

2364 7 Feb 1938 Cambridge: Cambridge Univ Mummers. Review: Times (London), 8 Feb, p. 12c.

2365 1966 Chichester: Chichester Festival Theatre. Lindsay Anderson, Dir. Review: Times (London), 20 Jul, p. 6a.

2366 1980 Manchester: Royal Exchange Theatre. Casper Wrede, Dir. Michael Frayn, Tr. Reviews: Drama 135 (Jan) 59; Plays & Players 27 (Jan) 28.

2367 5 Sep 1983 Edinburgh: Triumph Apollo Productions at Royal Lyceum. Lindsay Anderson, Dir. Review: London Theatre Record 3 (27 Aug-9 Sep) 754.

Ivanov

2368 Nov 1962 Cambridge: Cambridge Univ A.D.C. Theatre. Review: Times, 30 Nov, p. 15a.

Platonov

2369 1959 Called Don Juan. Nottingham: Nottingham Playhouse. Val May, Dir. Basil Ashmore, Tr. Review: Times (London), 7 Apr, p. 14c.

The Proposal

2370 18 Mar 1916 Birmingham Repertory Theatre.
2371 21 Oct 1916 Birmingham Repertory Theatre.
2372 Mar 1953 Stratford: Theatre Workshop at Theatre Royal. Review: Times (London), 31 Mar, p. 9c.
2373 Jul 1964 Canterbury Cathedral: King's School Players. Review: Times (London), 23 Jul, p. 5b.

The Sea Gull

2374 2 Nov 1909 Glasgow: Royalty Theater. George Calderon, Dir. & Tr. Reviews: Glasgow Evening Times, 3 Nov; Glasgow Herald, 3 Nov, p. 9.
2375 Aug 1960 Edinburgh: Old Vic Company. John Fernald,Dir. Reviews: N.Y.Times, 24 Aug, p. 33; Times (London), 23 Aug, p. 11a.
2376 1964 Pitlochry: Festival Theatre. Jack Witikka, Dir. Review: Times (London), 17 Aug, p. 12e.
2377 1973 Chichester: Chichester Festival. Jonathan Miller, Dir.
2378 1976 Derby: Triumph Theatre Productions at Derby Playhouse. Mark Woolgar, Dir. & Tr.
2379 30 Aug 1978 Bristol: Old Vic Company at Theatre Royal. Richard Cottrell, Dir. & Tr. Review: Plays & Players 26 (Nov) 18.
2380 10 Nov 1978 Glasgow: Citizens Theatre. Robert MacDonald, Tr. Philip Prowse, Adapter. Review: Plays & Players, 26 (Jan) 21.
2381 5 Feb 1980 Brighton: Gardner Center. Patrick Lau, Dir. Vilma Hollingbery & Patrick Lau, Trs. Reviews: Drama no. 136 (Apr) 51-2; Plays & Players 27 (Mar) 28.

Swan Song

2382 1915 season Dublin: Little Theatre.

The Three Sisters

2383 May 1940 Dublin: Gate Theatre.
2384 4 Nov 1966 (11) Canonbury: Tavistock Repertory Company at Tower Theatre. Tyrone Guthrie & Leonid Kipnis, Trs. Reviews: Times (London), 25 Oct, p. 16c & 5 Nov,p.13.
2385 1976 Guilford: Triumph Theatre at Yvonne Arnaud Theatre. Jonathan Miller, Dir. Elisaveta Fen, Tr.
2386 1978 Edinburgh: Edinburgh Festival. Trevor Nunn, Dir. Review: Plays & Players 26 (Nov) 33.
2387 1980 Stratford-upon-Avon: Royal Shakespeare Company at The Other Place. Trevor Nunn, Dir. Richard Cottrell, Tr. Review: Drama no. 135 (Jan) 56-7.

Uncle Vanya

2388 1915 season Dublin: Little Theatre.
2389 1927 Birmingham Repertory Theatre.
2390 1948 Liverpool: Playhouse. John Fernald, Dir.
2391 1953 Cambridge: Cambridge Univ A.D.C. Review: Times (London), 20 Jan, p. 3f.
2392 1962 Chichester: Chichester Festival. Laurence Olivier, Dir. Reviews: N.Y.Times, 17 Jul, p. 18; Times (London), 17 Jul, p. 13a & 1 Aug, p. 12b.
2393 1963 Chichester: Chichester Festival. Laurence Olivier, Dir. Reviews: N.Y.Times, 2 Jul, p. 16; Newsweek 62 (5 Aug) 45; Times (London), 2 Jul, p. 13c.
2394 1975 Stratford-upon-Avon: Royal Shakespeare Company at The Other Place. Nicol Williamson, Dir. Mike Nichols & Albert Todd, Dirs. Reviews: Drama no. 116 (Spring) 58-61; Plays & Players 22 (Mar) 34.
2395 1976 Birmingham Repertory Theatre. John Dave, Dir. Review: Drama no. 121 (Summer) 66.
2396 17 Feb 1977 Manchester: Royal Exchange Theatre. Michael Elliott, Dir. Ariadne Nicolaeff, Tr. Reviews: Daily Telegraph, 26 Feb, p. 10 & 28 Feb, p. 9; Plays & Players 24 (Apr) 28-9.
2397 31 Oct 1979 Liverpool: Playhouse. David William, Dir. Ronald Hingley,Tr. Review: Plays & Players 27 (Jan)31.

The Wood Demon

2398 1938 Shere, Surry: The Otherwise Club of Cambridge Univ. Review: N.Y.Times, 7 Aug, 9:1.
2399 1961 Edinburgh: Birmingham Crescent Theatre at Pollock Hall. Morris Fishman, Dir. & Tr. Review: Times (London), 28 Aug, p. 5a.

British Films of Chekhov's Works

2400 The Marriage. Isadore Annensky, Dir. Review: New Statesman & Nation n.s. 30 (22 Dec 1945) 424.
2401 Summer Storm. 1944. Based on Chekhov's novel The Shooting Party. Douglas Sirk, Dir. Michael O'Hara, Adapter. Reviews: Nation (N.Y.) 159 (22 Jul) 107-8; New Statesman & Nation n.s. 28 (9 Dec) 388; Newsweek 24 (17 Jul) 87; Spectator 173 (8 Dec) 527; Time 44 (24 Jul) 87.
2402 The Birth of Modern Theater: Chekhov's "Uncle Vanya" in Perspective. Films for the Humanities, 1975. B/W; sound; 46 min; 16 mm. Analyzes Chekhov's technique through stop-motion photography. Act III. Laurence Olivier, Dir. Starring Olivier, Rosemary Harris, Joan Plowright, and Michael Redgrave.

2403 Uncle Vanya. Distributor: Harris/Films Hire. Stuart Burge, Dir. B/W; sound; 117 min. Recording of Laurence Olivier's production at the Chichester Festival Theatre in 1963.

British Radio Programs of Chekhov's Works

2404 The Cherry Orchard. 1937. Miss Burnham, Dir. Review: Listener 17 (14 Apr) 693.
2405 The Cherry Orchard. 1960. BBC. R. D. Smith, Dir. Manya Harari, Tr. Review: Times (London), 19 Jan, p. 13a.
2406 Ivanov. 1941. Review: Listener 26 (16 Oct) 544.
2407 Ivanov. 1958. BBC. Review: Times (London), 17 Apr,p.3.
2408 On the High Road. 1953. Review: Times (London), 21 Aug, p. 5e.
2409 The Sea Gull. 1942. Miss Burnham, Dir. Review: Listener 28 (12 Nov) 636.
2410 The Sea Gull. 1945. Review: Listener 34 (1 Nov) 504.
2411 The Three Sisters. 1941. Miss Burnham, Dir. Review: Listener 26 (27 Nov) 736.
2412 The Three Sisters. 1946. Miss Burnham, Dir. Review: Listener 35 (13 Jun) 792.

British TV Productions of Chekhov's Works

2413 The Baby. 1954. Review: Times (London), 8 Jul, p. 5f.
2414 The Cherry Orchard. 1958. BBC. Harold Clayton, Dir. Review: Times (London), 6 Jan, p. 3c.
2415 The Cherry Orchard. 1971. Review: Times (London), 20 Dec, p. 9a.
2416 Extracts from Chekhov's plays. 1973. Review: Times (London), 15 Jan, p. 8g.
2417 Ivanov. 1961. Henry Kaplan, Dir. Review: Times (London), 2 Aug, p. 5a.
2418 The Sea Gull. 1966. BBC.
2419 The Three Sisters. 1963. Review: Times (London), 4 Sep, p. 13d.
2420 The Three Sisters. 1983. Royal Shakespeare Company.
2421 Uncle Vanya. 1957. BBC. Michael Elliott, Dir. Review: Times (London), 21 Jan, p. 9g.

Canadian Stage Productions

The Cherry Orchard

2422 26 Jul 1965 (15) Stratford, Ontario: Shakespearian Festival Theater. John Hirsch, Dir. Tyrone Guthrie & Leonid Kipnis, Trs. Reviews: N.Y.Times, 2 Aug, p. 17; Times (London) 18 Oct, p. 8c.

2423 22 Nov 1974 (27) Winnipeg: Manitoba Theater Center. Edward Gilbert, Dir.

2424 1980 Niagara, Ontario: Niagara-on-the-Lake Shaw Festival. Radu Penciulescu,Dir. Review: Time 115 (9 Jun)65.

The Proposal

2425 29 Mar 1983 (12) Halifax, Nova Scotia: Neptune Theater. David Schurmann, Dir.

The Sea Gull

2426 24 Jul 1968 Stratford, Ontario: Stratford Festival. Jean Gascon, Dir. Review: N.Y.Times, 25 Jul, p. 27.

2427 4 Jun 1977 (31) Toronto: Tarragon Theater. Bill Glassco, Dir.

2428 2 Mar 1979 (21) Halifax, Nova Scotia: Neptune Theater. David French, Tr.

2429 15 Feb 1980 (18) Winnipeg: Manitoba Theater Center. Arif Hasnain, Dir. & Tr.

2430 8 Aug 1980 (17) Stratford, Ontario: Stratford Festival. Urjo Kareda & Robin Phillips, Dirs. John Murrell, Tr. Reviews: J of Canadian Studies 15 (Winter) 117-9; N.Y.Times, 7 Sep, 2:3.

The Three Sisters

2431 1 Sep 1976 (14) Stratford,Ontario: Stratford Festival. John Hirsch, Dir. Review: J of Canadian Studies 11 (Nov) 46-8.

Uncle Vanya

2432 3 Feb 1971 (33) Montreal: Centaur Theater Company. Jean-Pierre Ronford, Dir.

2433 7 Jun 1978 (30) Stratford, Ontario: Stratford Festival. Urjo Kareda & Robin Phillips, Dirs. John Murrell, Tr. Reviews: J of Canadian Studies 13 (Winter) 115-6; Theatre J 31 (Mar 1979) 119-20; Time 111 (26 Jun) 79.

Records and Cassettes

Records

2434 The Cherry Orchard. 1966. Caedmon; Theatre Recording Society 314. 33 1/3, stereo. Tyrone Guthrie, Dir. Tyrone Guthrie & Leonid Kipnis, Trs. Starring Hume Cronyn and Jessica Tandy.

2435 Ivanov. 1966. RCA Victor VDS 109. 33 1/3, stereo. John Gielgud, Adapter. Ariadne Nicolaeff, Tr.

2436 Michael Redgrave Reads Anton Chekhov. 1962. Spoken Arts SA-828. 33 1/3. 3 stories.

2437 The Sea Gull. 1954. Magic-tone CTG 4012. 33 1/3. Claire Ligget Kaye, Adapter. Alexander Kirkland Acting Group, dir. by Alexander Kirkland.

2438 The Three Sisters. Caedmon, TC 1221. Stereo. By Siobhan McKenna and others.

2439 The Three Sisters. 1968. Caedmon, TRS 325. 33 1/3, stereo. Constance Garnett, Tr.

2440 Uncle Vanya. 1964. Caedmon, TRS S-303. 33 1/3, stereo. Constance Garnett, Tr. From TV production by Stuart Burge.

2441 Uncle Vanya. Library Editions, LLP 4003. 33 1/3. Elayne Carroll & Robert M. Culp, Dirs. & Adapters. A Classic Theatre Guild production.

Video Cassettes

2442 The Bet. Pyramid Film & Video, #01330. Color; 24 min; Beta, VHS, & 3/4" U-matic formats.

2443 The Boor. Dallas County Community College, #42498. Color; 29 min. 3/4" U-matic. Analysis interspersed with acting scenes.

2444 The Boor. Maryland Center for Public Broadcasting, #50364. Color; 30 min. Beta, VHS, 3/4" U-matic & other formats.

2445 Chekhov's Stories. 3 vols. 1984. Mastervision. 3 cassettes of 50 min each. John Gielgud, Narrator. Review: N.Y.Times, 22 Jan 1984, 2:24.

2446 The Cherry Orchard, I. Britannica Films, #13984. Color; 22 min. Beta, VHS, & 3/4" U-matic. Norris Houghton uses excerpts from the play to explain its technique.

2447 The Cherry Orchard, II. Britannica Films, #13985. Color; 22 min. Beta, VHS, & 3/4" U-matic. Norris Houghton quotes Chekhov on whether the play is comedy or tragedy.

2448 Swan Song. Carousel Films, #19066. Color; 25 min. 3/4" U-matic. With Michael Dunn and Richard Kiley.

2449 The Three Sisters. BBC Films, #00819. Color; 60 min. Beta, VHS, 3/4" U-matic & other formats. Jose Ferrer gives character sketches of each sister, based on excerpts from Acts III & IV.

2450 The Three Sisters. Magnetic Video, #51466. Color; 165 min. Beta & VHS. Video Playhouse Series. Laurence Olivier, Dir. Screen version of entire play.

2451 Uncle Vanya. Films for the Humanities, #12796. B/W; 47 min. 3/4" U-matic. Stop-action photography analyzes roles played by Laurence Olivier and Michael Redgrave.

Russian Films

2452 Ignatyeva, N. "Chekhov Films," Soviet Literature no. 1 (Jan 1980) 164-70.

2453 Rokotov, Timofei. "Chekhov's Story on the Soviet Screen: The Film The Man in a Case," International Literature (Moscow) no. 8-9 (1939) 62-5.

Stories Dramatized--Productions

2454 After the Theatre. At Barbizon Plaza, N.Y.C. Performed by Chekhov's nephew, Michael Chekhov. With Happy Ending, I Forgot, The Story of Miss N.N., & The Witch. Review: N.Y.Times, 28 Sep 1942, p. 13.

2455 The Artist. 9 Feb 1919 King's Hall, London Pioneer Players Miles Malleson, Adapter. Reviews: New Statesman 12 (15 Feb) 422-3; Times (London), 10 Feb, p.11c.

2456 The Artist. 13 Jun 1927 Playgoer's Theatre, Kensington, London People's Players Miles Malleson, Adapter.

2457 Beware of the Dog. 1967 St. Martin's Theatre, London Adapted from Chekhov's stories & sketches by Gabriel Arout. Tr. from French by Yvonne Mitchell. Noel Willman, Dir. Review: Drama no. 86 (Autumn) 24.

2458 A Casual Affair. 14 Jun 1982 South Street Theater Company O.O.B. (N.Y.C.) Adapted, directed, & performed by Michael Fischetti & Jean Sullivan.

2459 The Chameleon. 1968 Theater in the Street, N.Y.C. Tr. into Spanish by Ernesto Gonzalez. Review: N.Y.Times, 2 Aug, p. 24.

2460 The Chekhov Sketchbook. Consists of In a Music Shop, The Vagabond, & The Witch. 9 Nov 1980 (106) Harold Clurman Theatre O.B. (N.Y.C.) Tony Giordano, Dir. Joseph Buloff & Luba Kadison, Trs.

2461 The Duel. 1968 Duke of York's Theater, London Jack Holton Dell, Adapter. Reviews: N.Y.Times, 18 Apr, p. 56; Times (London), 15 Apr, p. 5 & 17 Apr, p. 14c.

2462 The Duel. Seattle: Seattle Repertory Theater Robert Egan, Dir. David Gild, Adapter.

2463 Forgotten. 2 Dec 1931 (3) Kingsway Theatre, London Moscow Art Theatre Performed in Russian Review: Era, 9 Dec, p. 10.

2464 The Good Doctor. Neil Simon's dramatization of 12 Chekhov stories. 27 Nov 1973 (208) Eugene O'Neill Theater N.Y.C. A.J. Antoon, Dir. Reviews: Critical Digest 25 (17 Dec) 4; N.Y.Times, 28 Nov, p. 36 & 9 Dec, 2:3 & 10 Jul 1974, p. 44.

2465 The Good Doctor. 23 Nov 1979 (24) Richmond: Virginia Museum Theater Gordon Heath, Dir.

2466 The Good Doctor. 27 Nov 1979 (21) San Diego: Old Globe Theater Craig Noel, Dir.

2467 The Good Doctor. 22 Jun 1984 Camden, ME: Camden Shakespeare Company (in repertory).
2468 The Good Doctor. 27 Jun 1984 Abingdon, VA: Barter Theater (closed 15 Jul).
2469 Happy Ending. See #2454.
2470 I Forgot. 16 Feb 1935 (53) Majestic Theatre, N.Y.C. & (28) Public Theatre, N.Y.C. Moscow Art Players Review: N.Y.Times, 12 Mar, p. 24. See also #2454.
2471 In a Music Shop. See #2460.
2472 Masha. 1974 season Stage Directors & Choreographers Workshop O.O.B. (N.Y.C.) Tim Kelly, Adapter.
2473 A Moscow Hamlet. 14 Jun 1982 South Street Theater Company O.O.B. (N.Y.C.) Adapted, directed, & performed by Michael Fischetti & Jean Sullivan.
2474 The Music Shop. 15 Feb 1962 (94) Gramercy Arts Theatre, N.Y.C. Stanley Waren, Dir. Luba Kadison & Helen Waren, Adapters. With The Vagrant and The Witch.
2475 My Life. 1966 London Review: Times (London), 31 Oct, p. 6g.
2476 Physician. 2 Dec 1931 (3) Kingsway Theatre, London Moscow Art Theatre Performed in Russian Review: Era, 9 Dec, p. 10.
2477 The Story of Miss N.N.. See #2454.
2478 Surgery. 1927 Vaudeville Theatre, London Chauve-Souris Company Nikita Balieff, Dir. Review: Nation & Athenaeum 41 (7 May) 149.
2479 The Vagabond. See #2460.
2480 The Vagrant. See #2474.
2481 Ward Six. 8 Sep 1977 Drama Committee Repertory Theater O.O.B. (N.Y.C.) Arthur Reel, Dir. & Adapter.
2482 The Witch. See #2454, 2460, & 2474.

Part IV

Productions of Works about Anton Chekhov

Films

2483 A.P. Chekhov. 1980. Distributor: Educational & Television Films, Hire. 30 min. Biography of Chekhov.

2484 Anton Chekhov: A Writer's Life. 1974. Informational Materials. B/W; sound; 37 min; 16 mm. Biography of Chekhov. Includes scenes from plays performed by Moscow Art Theatre and Mosfilm Studios.

2485 Review of film biography Tchekhov: Times (London), 8 Mar 1955, p. 4f.

Plays

2486 Anton Chekhov's Garden Party. 22 Nov 1972 (22) Roundabout Theater Company, N.Y.C. Elihu Winer, Author. Chekhov reads from his works to friends at the Moscow Art Theatre.

2487 Chekhov. 1984 Cottesloe Theatre, London Devised & performed by Michael Pennington. Review: Plays & Players no. 371 (Aug) 29.

2488 A Chekhov Christmas. 1977 season Montclair, NJ: The Whole Theatre Company.

2489 Chekhov in Yalta. 24 May 1981 (35) Los Angeles: Mark Taper Forum Ellis Rabb & Gordon Davidson, Dirs. Written by John Driver & Jeffrey Haddow. An imaginary meeting between Chekhov & Stanislavsky.

2490 Chekhov in Yalta. 9 Apr 1982 (32) Cleveland: Cleveland Play House Kenneth Albers, Dir.

2491 Chekhov in Yalta. 20 Oct 1982 (32) Atlanta: Alliance Theater Company Fred Chappell, Dir.

2492 Chekhov in Yalta. 2 Nov 1982 (32) Berkeley, CA: Berkeley Repertory Theater Albert Takazaukas, Dir.

2493 Chekhov on the Lawn. 22 Sep 1981 (64) Theater East, N.Y.C. Written & directed by Elihu Winer. Performed by William Shust. Chekhov reads from his works to friends at the Moscow Art Theatre.

2494 Evenings with Chekhov. 1961 (61) O.B.

2495 Talking Things Over With Chekhov. Fall 1984 O.B. (N.Y.C.) Ensemble Studio Theater John Ford Noonan, Author.

2496 Voices in the Dark. Closed 28 Oct 1984 Clyde Vinson Studio O.O.B. (N.Y.C.) Lakota Theater Alan Becker, Author. A play about Chekhov, drawing from his letters and plays.

Radio Program

2497 Louis MacNeice presented a biography of Chekhov on the 40th anniversary of his death. London. Review: Listener 32 (20 Jul 1944) 80.

Sound Cassettes

2498 Chekhov: Humanity's Advocate. Lecture by Ernest J. Simmons. 46 min. N.Y.: J. Norton, Publishers, 1974. Originally issued by McGraw-Hill Company in 1968.

2499 The Cherry Orchard. Lecture by Howard Stein. 32 min. DeLand, FL: Everett/Edwards, 1976.

2500 The Sea Gull. Lecture by Howard Stein. 34 min. DeLand, FL: Everett/Edwards, 1976.

2501 The Three Sisters. Lecture by Howard Stein. 29 min. DeLand, FL: Everett/Edwards, 1976.

2502 Uncle Vanya. Lecture by Nonna D. Wellek. 42 min. DeLand, FL: Everett/Edwards, 1976.

Television Programs

2503 From Chekhov With Love. Mar 1967. London. Play based on Chekhov's letters. Jonathan Miller, Dir. John Gielgud, Narrator.

2504 Jun 1968. London. Program on Chekhov. Review: Times (London), 17 Jun, p. 6c.

Video Cassette

2505 Anton Chekhov: A Writer's Life. Mosfilm #15201 (Films for the Humanities). B/W; 47 min; 3/4" U-matic. Biography of Chekhov. Includes scenes from his plays performed by the Moscow Art Theatre and Mosfilm Studios.

Index

Numbers refer to entry numbers.